IN STALIN'S SHADOW

THE CAREER OF "SERGO" ORDZHONIKIDZE

Oleg V. Khlevniuk

Edited with an Introduction by Donald J. Raleigh
with the assistance of Kathy S. Transchel

Translated by David J. Nordlander

M.E. Sharpe
Armonk, New York
London, England

First published in Russian in 1993 by "Rossiia molodaia" under the title
Stalin i Ordzhonikidze: Konflikty v Politbiuro v 30-e gody.
© 1993 by O. V. Khlevniuk.

Library of Congress Cataloging-in-Publication Data

Khlevniuk, O. V. (Oleg Vital'evich)
[Stalin i Ordzhonikidze. English]
In Stalin's shadow : the career of "Sergo" Ordzhonikidze / by
Oleg V. Khlevniuk : edited by Donald J. Raleigh : with
the assistance of Kathy S. Transchel : translated by David J. Nordlander.
p.   cm. — (The new Russian history)
Includes bibliographical references and index.
ISBN 1-56324-562-0.   —   ISBN 1-56324-563-9 (pbk.)
1. Soviet Union—History—1925–1953.   2. Stalin, Joseph, 1879–1953.
3. Ordzhonikidze, Sergo, 1886–1937.   I. Raleigh, Donald J.
II. Transchel, Kathy S.   III. Title.   IV. Series.
DK267.K437813   1995
947.084—dc20   95-5694
CIP

Printed in the United States of America

The paper used in this publication meets the minimum requirements of
American National Standard for Information Sciences—
Permanence of Paper for Printed Library Materials,
ANSI Z 39.48-1984.

BM (c)   10   9   8   7   6   5   4   3   2   1
BM (p)   10   9   8   7   6   5   4   3   2   1

Contents

Editor's Introduction

Until recently, historical studies on the dark years of Iosif Vissari-onovich Stalin were hindered by the Kremlin's cloak of secretiveness. The inaccessibility of essential documents compelled investigators to snatch at whatever bits of information became available, including rumors and various other suspect sources, in constructing their narratives. The lack of hard data, however, did not prevent some historians from pleading their cases with passion and conviction. Not surprisingly, the intrusion of the authors' personal biases into their works has been characteristic of much of the writing on the Stalin period.

The opening in the post-Soviet era of some—but not all—of the archives needed for a full-scale reassessment of the Stalin years has led to a historiographical revolution of sorts, as has the fact that Russian historians have been freed from the constraints of Soviet dogma and rhetoric. Excited by the prospect of reinterpreting a pivotal era in their country's history, they have begun to contribute fresh analyses of the 1930s and 1940s. But despite serendipitous discoveries, it appears that the archives might not hold answers to all the burning questions. The imperfect record on some critical issues can nonetheless be put to good use by careful historians extending the parameters of debate, raising new questions, and throwing light on the most obscure chapters of Soviet history. A case in point is Oleg Khlevniuk's absorbing study of Grigorii K. (Sergo) Ordzhonikidze, *In Stalin's Shadow.*

Ordzhonikidze? Although not well known in this country outside academic circles, the name Ordzhonikidze is more than familiar to

Russian readers, thanks to a minor personality cult Soviet officialdom constructed around him. Schools and institutes, streets and highways, towns and farms carried and still carry his name. His ashes remain buried in the Kremlin walls, among the pantheon of fallen revolutionary heroes. Despite the efforts of Soviet historiography to present an "official" interpretation of his career, however, Ordzhonikidze has been the subject of sustained speculation and hearsay ever since his death in rather mysterious circumstances in 1937, a year in which so many other Old Bolsheviks perished at the hands of the secret police.

As one of Stalin's closest associates and most powerful and influential economic managers, Ordzhonikidze, a fellow Georgian, played no small role in Kremlin politics during the years leading up to his death. While keeping Ordzhonikidze as his focal point, Khlevniuk examines the career of Sergo to probe larger questions of Soviet political history. Was Stalin powerful enough to have the Politburo do his bidding, or did top party leaders play a significant role in decision making? Was there opposition to the "party line" within the organization's general membership or the inner sanctums of the Kremlin and, if so, did it ever emerge as a viable alternative to Stalinism? Were there conflicts between Stalin and his closest comrades? If so, how far did they go to oppose him?

Drawing on newly opened files in both the former Communist Party and Soviet government archives, the author builds on the two extant points of view found in the scholarly literature about Ordzhonikidze's role in Kremlin intrigues. Some authors, basing their arguments on memoirs and personal accounts, argue that Ordzhonikidze prepared to challenge Stalin openly and consequently paid with his life. A counter viewpoint is that no one among his contemporaries considered Ordzhonikidze a serious opponent of Stalin's policies, especially that of state terror, and that Sergo took his own life. Weighing both perspectives, Khlevniuk offers an alternative explanation that is more subtle and nuanced. And more convincing.

Khlevniuk's Ordzhonikidze is a tragic figure. A "soft Stalinist" deeply troubled by unfounded accusations of industrial sabotage and no longer able to comprehend and accommodate that which was going on around him, Sergo became defensive and confused. The ensuing crisis consumed him—and resulted in his murder. Or was it suicide? Khlevniuk interrogates the available sources and offers an answer to this recurrent question. What is so attractive about his compelling argument is that it helps explain how the Stalinist system worked.

Khlevniuk's study can be recommended to readers for several other reasons. His is not only the first published study of the Politburo in the 1930s based on recently declassified materials, but it is also one of the few works available that delves into the vital interlude between Sergei Kirov's murder in 1934, often viewed as the opening salvo of the Stalinist terror, and Ordzhonikidze's demise in 1937. Deftly weaving a tale of suspense and intrigue, Khlevniuk frequently lets the documents speak for themselves. Whenever the sources are silent or difficult to decode, he offers plausible versions of what might have been. Unlike many of his contemporaries who in the current scholarly atmosphere in Russia highlight the moral turpitude and historical guilt of Soviet leaders, Khlevniuk adopts a detached tone in passing judgment on his protagonists.

It is my pleasure to invite readers to enjoy this, the second volume in a series of historical works in translation, *The New Russian History*, whose purpose is to make available to English readers the finest works of the most eminent historians of Russia today. Born in 1959, Oleg Khlevniuk defended his candidate degree in history at the Institute of History of the then-Soviet Academy of Sciences in 1987. His dissertation and early publications treat of Soviet urbanization and the formation of a working class in the 1930s. During the Mikhail Sergeevich Gorbachev years, Khlevniuk joined the editorial collective of the journal *Kommunist* (Communist), an official organ of the Communist Party. He also gained access to the Communist Party archive in Moscow. Using materials from it and related repositories, he published a second book in Moscow in 1992 entitled *1937–i: Stalin, NKVD i Sovetskoe obshchestvo* (The Year 1937: Stalin, the NKVD, and Soviet Society). Khlevniuk is presently rewriting the book for publication in this series, incorporating newly declassified documents made available since its first publication. He also works as an editor of *Svobodnaia mysl'* (Free Thought), a Moscow public affairs journal that superseded *Kommunist*.

The English-language edition of Khlevniuk's study of Ordzhonikidze and Kremlin politics represents a team effort. David Nordlander good-naturedly took up the task of translating the work, finishing a draft translation and revisions I suggested on the early chapters before he left the country to carry out dissertation research in Moscow and Magadan.

I assumed full responsibility for the project at that time, checking the entire translation against the original and editing it. I was very ably assisted by Kathy S. Transchel, who helped nurture the manuscript through several additional drafts.

It is a pleasure for me as well to thank David R. Shearer for introducing me to Oleg Khlevniuk's work, and Sheila Fitzpatrick and J. Arch Getty, who called this particular volume to my attention. I also wish to acknowledge the assistance of Susan Beam Eggers, who prepared the index. Finally, I wish to express my thanks to Patricia A. Kolb and her staff at M. E. Sharpe Inc., Publisher, for their unflagging support of this monograph series and for their sound professional advice, which made this a better book.

Donald J. Raleigh
Chapel Hill, NC

Russian Terms and Abbreviations

CC	Central Committee of the Communist Party of the Soviet Union
CCC-RKI	Central Control Commission of the Workers' and Peasants' Inspectorate
gorkom	city party committee
Gosplan	State Planning Commission
GPU (or OGPU)	the State Political Administration
ITR	Engineer-Technical Worker
Komsomol	All-Union Leninist Communist Youth League
kraikom	regional party committee
NEP	New Economic Policy
NKTP	People's Commissariat of Heavy Industry
raikom	district party committee
RSFSR	Russian Socialist Federated Soviet Republic
RSDRP	Russian Social Democratic Workers' Party
Sovnarkom	Council of People's Commissars
STO	Council of Labor and Defense
VSNKh	Supreme Council of the National Economy
VTsIK	All-Russian Central Executive Committee

IN STALIN'S
SHADOW

Introduction

Some of the most controversial questions in Soviet history concern the activities of the higher echelons of the party-state leadership, especially the Politburo. The Politburo stood at the apex of power in the USSR. This body brought together the networks of administration and made major decisions that determined the country's fate. How did this come about? Were Politburo resolutions merely the secret personal orders of the leader, the result of so-called collective leadership, or the by-product of more complex interests and conflicts among groups or individuals? The answer to such questions depends, of course, on formulating a more general understanding of the political system and how it functioned, as well as of its stages of development and logical evolution.

During the entire reign of the Communist Party, factions and groups opposed to the "general line" appeared within the party and suggested ways to reform the regime. These currents acquired real political strength, however, only if they had support in the Politburo. From this supreme body emanated all efforts at reform, from the deepening of the New Economic Policy (NEP) in the 1920s and de-Stalinization in the 1950s and 1960s, to the policy of perestroika. How and when did these reformist groups take shape, and which other currents of reform or counterreform appeared in the Politburo? These questions gain special significance in light of the fact that most of Soviet history represents the gradual and inconsistent reformation of Stalinism from above.

Many issues merit our utmost attention regarding the 1930s, the period of the so-called Stalin Revolution.* Debate revolves around several questions: When did Iosif Vissarionovich Stalin (1879–1953) assume absolute rule—at the end of the 1920s following victory over the Bukharin group, or later, as a result of the mass purges of 1937? What real power did Stalin's associates in the Politburo have? Finally, did forces exist in the Stalinist Politburo of the 1930s that had the potential to revise the general line, even if they did not institute any principal changes?

In answering this last question, many historians have focused mainly on two members of Stalin's Politburo—Sergei M. Kirov (1886–1934) and Grigorii K. (Sergo) Ordzhonikidze (1886–1937). Several versions regarding the circumstances of their deaths have long circulated. The main question that still has not been answered centers around whether there was a link between the tragic deaths of Kirov and Ordzhonikidze and their opposition to Stalin. Would it be fair to say that they represented a relatively moderate strand of party leadership, a center of opposition to Stalinist extremism and a distinctive brand of "soft" Stalinism? If this in fact was the case, then another question arises: To what extent were these associates of Stalin prepared to take decisive and independent actions in opposing the leader?

Such questions obviously require concrete answers. In this context, general arguments are inappropriate and hypothetical reflections and suppositions are of little interest. If Stalin and his associates actually clashed over differences of opinion, then it is necessary for the historian to present facts and evidence to document this. Moreover, as in historical research generally, it is obviously not enough to rely on memoirs and rumors. If conflicts actually existed, one can find traces of them in the archives even if the materials are not always informative

---

*Stalin Revolution. The period of revolutionary change that the USSR underwent at the end of the 1920s and early 1930s associated with the launching of the First Five-Year Plan. The main features of the Stalin Revolution were rapid industrialization, forced collectivization of agriculture, cultural revolution, and eventually the use of terror, as a result of which Stalin consolidated his own personal dictatorship. During the Stalin Revolution the so-called command-administrative system was established, which gave the Soviet Union its basic political, economic, social, and cultural forms until recently.—Ed.

and candid. Reminiscences must be supported by historical documents.

This work represents an attempt to do just that. In researching this project, I have collected and analyzed documents on the relationship between Stalin and Ordzhonikidze in the 1930s. These include materials from the Politburo Archive; the archives of the Council of People's Commissars (Sovnarkom), the Supreme Council of the National Economy (VSNKh), and the People's Commissariat of Heavy Industry (NKTP—which Ordzhonikidze led); and Ordzhonikidze's personal archive as well as those of his Politburo colleagues. These documents are located in the Russian Center for the Preservation and Study of the Documents of Modern History (RTsKhIDNI), the State Archive of the Russian Federation (GARF), and the Russian State Archive of Economics (RGAE). Papers in the so-called Kremlin Archive (Archive of the President of the Russian Federation, the former archive of the Politburo of the Central Committee of the Communist Party of the Soviet Union [CC CPSU]), remain closed to researchers. Something needs to be said regarding these depositories.

Judging from available information, the Kremlin Archive contains the protocols and records (stenograms were not always kept) of Politburo meetings, including decisions stored in a "special file," preparatory materials for Politburo resolutions, all Central Committee plenums, records of party congresses and conferences, and personal archives of individual party activists. At first glance, the inaccessibility of this set of documents would seem to doom any attempt at studying the history of the highest echelons of power in the Soviet party-state. However, extensive archival experience and comparison of available documents with those materials from the Kremlin Archive published periodically in the press, indicate that the classification of Kremlin archive documents as confidential serves more to satisfy the self-esteem of the bureaucrats than to interfere with the historian's task. The current availability of previously closed archival files of the Politburo, Sovnarkom, and departments of the People's Commissariats, as well as the personal papers of party leaders, and so forth, will either prove to duplicate documents in the Kremlin Archive or provide information that sheds light on a majority of the most secret acts of the country's leadership in the prewar period. For specialists, there was nothing sensational about the well-publicized excerpts from the Kremlin Archive concerning the shooting of Polish prisoners of war, the secret protocols of the Soviet-German Non-Aggression Pact, or resolutions on conducting mass arrests and executions in 1937. Of course, new documents define things more precisely, and to a certain degree dot the *i*'s, but they usually only supplement what was previously known with good and colorful examples.

Likewise, little new awaits us in the unpublished materials from the personal files of the Presidential Archive. For example, the recent publication of the correspondence between Stalin and his wife Nadezhda S. Allilueva (1901–1932) unquestionably contains many interesting details and is an important source.[1] But it does not provide answers to many critical questions—especially, what happened in the Stalin family in 1932? Did political disagreements between Stalin and Allilueva bring about her tragic death? It is clear that a complete selection of letters from 1932 does not exist. The reason for this is explained in the preface to the publication: "The journal begins publication of documents from the personal archive of I.V. Stalin. The archive was kept by Stalin. It contains documents reflecting his party and state activities from 1916 to 1931, personal correspondence, biographical materials, and photographs from 1888 to 1953." Apparently, Stalin compiled his archive from those documents that presented the great leader and his deeds in the best possible light, and conversely, those that exhibited the worst traits of his political opponents.[2] It is appropriate to remember that a search, conducted over several years in the Politburo Archives for serious evidence concerning Kirov's murder, was undertaken during the tenures of both Nikita S. Khrushchev (1953–1964) and Mikhail S. Gorbachev (1985–1991) without success. This quest only revealed that documents capable of shedding some light on this secret had been destroyed.

Of course, this does not mean that historians do not need the Kremlin Archive materials, but rather shows that they can conduct extensive research without "presidential decree" to open these party files.

It is necessary to note that previously, in spite of the complete inaccessibility of the archives, historians produced a considerable number of significant works that remain important. This is true of the topic under study. In the historical literature there are two opposing points of view regarding the conflict between Stalin and Ordzhonikidze. One is based primarily on memoirs. Its supporters believe that serious disagreements existed between Stalin and Ordzhonikidze stemming from the arrests of the latter's friends, colleagues, and relatives. According to this version, Ordzhonikidze was ready to challenge Stalin openly, and eventually paid with his life (either was driven to suicide or was murdered). Currently, this is the prevalent point of view found in numerous scholarly, popular, and belletristic works, and is most fully presented in the studies of Roy A. Medvedev, Robert Conquest, and Robert Tucker.[3]

Another less common, skeptical viewpoint is advanced by J. Arch Getty, whose interpretation is supported by several recently declassified documents. He maintains that Ordzhonikidze was not considered a serious opponent of the Stalinist Terror. Under the best of circumstances, Ordzhonikidze was prepared to defend his colleagues, but not all of them. In particular, Getty questions whether Ordzhonikidze tried to defend Georgii (Iurii) L. Piatakov (1890–1937).[4]

After studying available materials, I have come to the conclusion that both viewpoints contain some truth. Archival sources support memoir accounts concerning the existence of a serious conflict between Stalin and Ordzhonikidze, which began in the late 1920s or early 1930s. This does not mean, however, that Ordzhonikidze was ready to actively and openly oppose Stalin or seriously struggle against the so-called Great Terror. Ordzhonikidze was not an independent political figure, and almost always followed Stalin's lead. The documents show that many of the initiatives attributed to Ordzhonikidze in the literature were not his own, but Stalin's. As a Stalinist, Ordzhonikidze was not able to go beyond clearly defined limits in his opposition—he was able to argue with Stalin in private or use his power to sway some decision. In the end, he could take his own life as an act of protest, but he could go no further.

Of course, this does not mean that Ordzhonikidze wielded no influence over defining the general political line or shaping Stalin's decisions. Ordzhonikidze can be examined as a typical, in fact, most active, representative of the moderate wing of the Stalinist Politburo whose opinion Stalin had to consider to a certain degree.

Apart from the question about the nature of Stalin's conflict with Ordzhonikidze, the literature addresses several other questions connected to Ordzhonikidze's activities in the Central Control Commission of the Workers' and Peasants' Inspectorate (CCC–RKI), VSNKh, and

the People's Commissariat of Heavy Industry, and his position regarding specialists and the campaign against "saboteurs" of the Stakhanovite
movement, and so forth. My study utilizes much of this earlier work. A
critique of the ideas presented in the literature can be found in the
appropriate chapters of this book.

Chronologically, my project encompasses the period from the end of
the 1920s to Ordzhonikidze's death in February 1937. Special attention
is given, however, to the events of 1935–37, when the conflicts between
Stalin and Ordzhonikidze peaked. The first chapters survey the history
of the relationship between Stalin and Ordzhonikidze and present a
series of familiar and revealing conflicts between them throughout the
period of their work together.

The nature of the documentary materials greatly shaped the focus of
my research, which attempts to reconstruct events on the basis of well-
known and revealing documents.

Chapter 1

The Making of a "Party Professional"

"Before 1905 I was a student, and then served for several months as a medical assistant. In the remaining years before the Revolution of 1917, I was a party professional," wrote Ordzhonikidze on a party questionnaire in 1931.[1] Party professionals, dedicating their lives to the struggle with the tsarist regime and subjugating their personal interests to those of the party, constituted the majority of those who came to power in Russia in October 1917.

Despite the fact that the fate of each of these people took shape differently, there evidently existed common life experiences and circumstances that helped form the revolutionary type. As a rule, revolutionaries were forced to grow up early or had to deal with adult crises as children: they were subjected to humiliation and national oppression, and acutely felt their positions as social outcasts. The tsarist regime, whose cruelty engendered great bitterness, successfully increased the ranks of its opponents. Revolutionaries often were motivated by hatred for an all-encompassing injustice and oppression rather than by some doctrine. Often, their character and upbringing prevented them from leading quiet or normal lives. They preferred a dangerous struggle with the government to a steady rise up the career ladder. Prison, exile, flight, and emigration—these were the experiences that formed and defined their vision of the world and its specific characteristics.

The war, unleashed by the European governments in 1914, strengthened the resolve of those revolutionaries who believed that capitalism was in decline. It was a shock for a whole generation that magnified hatred and reduced the price of human life to a minimum. War brought about the revolution—the stellar hour of the revolutionaries.

Ordzhonikidze was one of those whose background and character led directly to revolution. He was born in October 1886 to an impoverished noble family in the Georgian village of Goresha. His mother died while he was still an infant, and his father when Ordzhonikidze was ten. Thanks to relatives, he finished a two-year secondary school and a doctor's assistant program. At seventeen, he joined the Russian Social Democratic Workers' Party (RSDRP), worked at an underground printshop, and distributed leaflets. It was at this point that he befriended the desperate Kamo,* apparently seeing in him a "kindred spirit." In 1905, he threw himself into the revolutionary cause by taking the most dangerous assignments. He was arrested while transporting arms that December. He spent several months in jail, where he participated in the growing hunger strike movements. His comrades still at large helped him get released on bail before he went to trial. When the threat of arrest loomed again, he fled to Germany. Soon he returned to Baku, and in 1907 was arrested once more. After a short twenty-six-day prison term, he continued to carry out party work under an alias in Azerbaidzhan, where Stalin was also serving.

In November 1907, he was arrested for the fourth time, imprisoned in a fortress, and then exiled indefinitely to Siberia. Ordzhonikidze fled after several months of exile, returned to Baku, and after a while crossed over into Persia. When revolution broke out there, the Bolsheviks in the Caucasus sent Ordzhonikidze to help Iranian insurgents direct an armed guard.

Ordzhonikidze traveled to Paris in the spring of 1911, where he met Vladimir Ilich Lenin (1870–1924) for the first time. While there, he became a student at the party school at Longjumeau, organized to prepare Bolsheviks for revolutionary work in Russia. He did not stay in school long, due to a bitter struggle in the party. Consequently, Lenin

---

*Kamo. Party name of Simon A. Ter-Petrosian (1882–1922), a protégé of Stalin's who orchestrated a dramatic seizure of funds for the Bolshevik Party in Tiflis (Tbilisi) in June 1907.—Ed.

sent Ordzhonikidze to Russia to help convene the Sixth Conference of the RSDRP. Ordzhonikidze successfully completed this assignment and was elected to the Central Committee at the Prague Conference in January 1912. He returned to Russia following the conference, and worked spreading information to members of various organizations who had been co-opted into the Bolshevik Party Central Committee at the Prague Conference. During this time he visited Vologda, where Stalin was living in exile. Together, Stalin and Ordzhonikidze left for the Caucasus. After some time they returned to St. Petersburg, where Ordzhonikidze was again arrested in April 1912.

This arrest proved to be a serious matter. The police established Ordzhonikidze's true identity, and recounted all his previous transgressions, including the transport of arms in 1905. Ordzhonikidze spent three years in Schlüsselburg prison, and in the fall of 1915 was sent to Siberia into permanent exile. It was outside Yakutsk that he learned of the February Revolution. At the end of May 1917, Ordzhonikidze returned to Petrograd with his Bolshevik comrades.

For the month that he remained in the capital, Ordzhonikidze was fully engaged in the political struggle: he joined the Petrograd Bolshevik Committee, often addressed rallies, and carried out party work at the city's largest factories. He once again worked closely with Stalin in Petrograd. At the same time, relations between Ordzhonikidze and Lenin strengthened. He accompanied Lenin to Razliv on an assignment from the Central Committee, and at the Sixth Congress he reported on Lenin's decision not to appear in court.*

In the fall, Ordzhonikidze traveled to Transcaucasia for a short visit,

---

*Sixth Party Congress. After largely spontaneous mass disturbances in Petrograd in 1917 known as the "July Days," the Provisional Government, headed by Alexander Kerensky, cracked down on Bolshevik activities. Rather than risk turning himself in to the government, Lenin fled to Razliv, a small resort town on the Gulf of Finland not far from Petrograd. Because of the repressive measures the government introduced against the Bolsheviks, Lenin and some other prominent party members did not participate in the party's Sixth Congress, held in semilegal conditions at the end of July. The congress adopted a cautious wait-and-see policy, but also, in large measure because of Lenin's insistence that the soviets were now in the hands of the counterrevolutionary bourgeoisie (Mensheviks and SRs), dropped the slogan "all power to the soviets."

Sergo Ordzhonikidze during the Russian Civil War.

returning to Petrograd before the Revolution on October 24. He was sent to Pulkovo to fight against units loyal to (the leader of the Provisional Government) Aleksandr F. Kerensky (1881–1970).

During the Civil War, Ordzhonikidze spent more than three years on various fronts. He was a special Bolshevik Commissar of the Ukraine, South Russia, and the North Caucasus, and fought in the battle for Tsaritsyn. He found himself on the western front in 1919, where Stalin was a member of the Revolutionary Council. In 1920, Ordzhonikidze was a member of the Revolutionary Military Council of the Caucasian Front and a chairman of the North Caucasus Revolutionary Committee. He entered Baku victoriously at dawn on May 1, 1920. Afterward, he became embroiled in the desperate struggle for the consolidation of Soviet power in Azerbaidzhan and the North Caucasus. When an uprising broke out in Dagestan and the Terek Oblast in October 1920, Stalin, who had arrived from Moscow, praised Ordzhonikidze's work highly in reports to Lenin and the Central Committee:

> The mountaineers have shown their best side, and in the majority of cases fought with weapons in hand alongside our partisans against the bandits; undoubtedly, Ordzhonikidze and the Caucasus Bureau have followed our policy accordingly, uniting the mountaineers with Soviet

Sergei M. Kirov (left) and Ordzhonikidze in Baku in 1920.

power. . . . A thousand volunteers (from Dagestan) fought alongside us and together with our partisans drove out the counterrevolutionary insurgents—this fact is characteristic, once again, of the correct policy of Ordzhonikidze and the Caucasus Bureau.[2]

After securing Azerbaidzhan, Ordzhonikidze and his assistants hurried to establish Soviet power throughout Transcaucasia. Armenia was annexed in December 1920. Ordzhonikidze then rushed to Georgia, and urged Moscow to intervene with the Red Army there. Moscow held back, restrained Ordzhonikidze, and demanded that he be careful. But not for long. In February 1921, the Eleventh Army entered Tiflis. For Ordzhonikidze and other Georgian Communists, this event undoubtedly had special significance.

Because of the war in Transcaucasia, Sergo Ordzhonikidze was not able to attend the Tenth Party Congress, which opened in Moscow at the beginning of 1921. Several delegates to the congress opposed Ordzhonikidze's reelection to the Central Committee. Only Stalin's, and most importantly, Lenin's intercession preserved Ordzhonikidze's place in the leading party organ. While the stenograms of this session of the congress are not available, the memoirs of Anastas I. Mikoyan (1895–1978)* provide adequate detail concerning the arguments surrounding Ordzhonikidze's candidacy:

> Several military delegates from the North Caucasus unexpectedly shouted their objections to Ordzhonikidze's candidacy from their seats. These delegates sat in the last row and made noise heard throughout the hall. One of them rose to the podium and began to say that Orzhonikidze yells at everyone, orders everyone around him, ignores the opinions of local party members, and therefore should not be in the Central Committee. This demagogic outburst influenced the mood of the delegates, many of whom did not even know Ordzhonikidze.

---

*Anastas I. Mikoyan. An old Bolshevik and member of Stalin's inner circle in the 1930s who, during his last years in office, supposedly fell under Stalin's suspicion for spying for the British and Turks. Mikoyan remained at the top of the party leadership throughout Nikita S. Khrushchev's years in office, however, and played a not unimportant role in the latter's removal from power. Mikoyan later retired from politics (of his own free will) and published his memoirs.—Ed.

Speaking in a soft, quiet voice, Stalin rose in defense of Ordzhonikidze. He provided biographical details, recounting Sergo's work in the underground and on the fronts of the Civil War. Further, he recommended Ordzhonikidze's selection to the Central Committee. It was clear, however, that he could not convince the delegates, who continued to stir up a row.

Then Lenin spoke in defense of Sergo's candidacy, offering the following summation: I have known Comrade Sergo for a long time, from the underground days, as a dedicated, energetic, fearless revolutionary. He showed his true colors in emigration, played an outstanding role in preparing for the Prague Conference in 1912, and was elected to the Central Committee. He carried out active work in Petrograd preparing for and conducting the October Revolution. He proved himself to be a brave and capable organizer in the Civil War. But the comrades who criticized Sergo correctly noted one thing; that is, he yells at everybody. This is true. He speaks loudly, but you don't know why. When he speaks with me, he also shouts. This is because he is deaf in the left ear, Lenin noted with affection. Therefore, he shouts—he thinks that nobody hears him. But one should not pay any attention to this shortcoming. . . .

This brought smiles and even good-natured laughs from the delegates. It became clear that Lenin, in supporting Sergo's candidacy, defeated all opposition . . . [and this was important] for there had been serious apprehension that many votes would be cast against him. In a secret ballot following Lenin's speech, Ordzhonikidze received an overwhelming majority of votes. Like Dzerzhinskii, he received 438 votes out of 479. . . .[3]

Ordzhonikidze undoubtedly knew what happened at the congress and was grateful to Lenin and Stalin. At the time, he belonged to a group of party leaders who unquestioningly supported Lenin in his rivalry with Lev Davidovich Trotsky (1879–1940). However, at the end of 1922 a power shuffle occurred at the highest echelons that directly affected Ordzhonikidze.

Beginning in 1921, Lenin was often ill. In his absence, a "troika" led the party and government: Lev B. Kamenev (1883–1936), Lenin's deputy in Sovnarkom and the Council of Labor and Defense (STO), presided over Politburo meetings; Stalin headed the Central Committee's apparatus; and Grigorii E. Zinoviev (1883–1936) led the Executive Committee of the Communist International (Comintern). At first, the "troika" trod cautiously and in accord with Lenin's wishes. As the party leader's health deteriorated, however, his associates began to prepare seriously for the transfer of power. Returning to work for a short time in 1922, Lenin objected to the concentration of "unlimited powers" in Stalin's hands and certain attitudes of the "troika" on many questions. Lenin decided to demote his comrades-in-arms.

He chose disagreements on the nationality question as one of the grounds for attack. Their essence is well known: Stalin suggested that the republics be made autonomous, while Lenin backed an all-union government. A major feature of this conflict was the so-called Georgian Affair, which received wide publicity and took on great significance.

The conflict lay in the sharp opposition existing between the Central Committee of the Georgian Communist Party and the Transcaucasian Regional Party Committee (*kraikom*), between the group of Budu Mdivani (1877–1937) and Ordzhonikidze. Personal rivalry and ambition collided in the arguments concerning the creation of a Transcaucasian federation. Ordzhonikidze, promoting Moscow's policy and receiving the continual support of Stalin, spoke on behalf of a federation of the three Transcaucasian republics, while Mdivani's group insisted on Georgia's independent entrance into the USSR without a Transcaucasian federation. Passions became white hot. Ordzhonikidze, incited by Stalin, acted aggressively and in a fit of anger struck one of the Georgian leaders, who called him "Stalin's asss."[4]

At the end of November 1922, the Politburo sent a special commission to Georgia under the leadership of Feliks E. Dzerzhinskii (1887–1926). Lenin closely followed this affair and the work of the commission, which accepted Ordzhonikidze's version to Lenin's dissatisfaction. "For all the citizens of the Caucasus Ordzhonikidze was the authority. Ordzhonikidze had no right to display that irritability to which he and Dzerzhinskii referred," wrote Lenin.[5] He decided to make this question a matter of principle—"to make an example out of Ordzhonikidze by punishing him," and to battle Dzerzhinskii and Stalin for supreme power. Lenin planned to do this at the imminent plenum of the Central Committee. However, feeling that his illness would not permit his participation, Lenin sought Trotsky's help: "It's my urgent request that you should undertake the defense of the Georgian case in the party Central Committee. This case is now under 'prosecution' by Stalin and Dzerzhinskii, and I cannot rely on their impartiality. Quite to the contrary."[6] The next day, March 6, Lenin sent a letter to the leaders of the Georgian Communists, Mdivani and Filip Makharadze (1868–1941): "Dear comrades! I'm following your case with all my attention. I'm indignant over Ordzhonikidze's rudeness and the connivance of Stalin and Dzerzhinskii. I'm preparing notes and a speech for you."[7]

Lenin's condemnation left an indelible mark on Ordzhonikidze's biography and seriously hurt his political reputation. The conflict was suppressed mainly through Stalin's efforts, who, while basically defending himself, nonetheless did Ordzhonikidze an important service. These general unpleasantries brought Stalin and Ordzhonikidze even closer together. Many years later, Trotsky evaluated the outcome of the "Georgian Affair" for their relationship:

> Stalin found his most faithful associates, his first comrades-in-arms, in Ordzhonikidze and Dzerzhinskii. They both were in Lenin's disfavor. Ordzhonikidze was a person of indubitable will, courage, and strength of character, but in essence had little culture and was unable to control himself. While he was a revolutionary, his courage and decisive selflessness outweighed his faults. But when he became a leading bureaucrat, he began to show a lack of restraint and rudeness. Lenin, who regarded him warmly in the past, avoided him more and more. Orzhonikidze felt this. The affair ended when Lenin proposed to exclude Ordzhonikidze from the party for a year or two for abuse of power. [This fact is not corroborated in the documents, but is supported by Lenin's decision "to make an example out of Ordzhonikidze."—O. Kh.] In 1922, Ordzhonikidze and Dzerzhinskii felt dissatisfied, and to a significant measure ashamed. Stalin quickly recruited both of them.[8]

It is unlikely that Ordzhonikidze considered himself "recruited," but Stalin indisputably counted on the gratitude of his associate. We can only imagine what Stalin felt when, within several months, Ordzhonikidze was drawn into intrigues aimed at limiting the powers of the general secretary.

As could be expected, friction and disagreement appeared in the "troika" leadership soon after Lenin had to stop working. The strengthening of Stalin's power and control over the party apparat alarmed other leaders. Wishing to weaken Stalin's position, Zinoviev and Nikolai I. Bukharin (1888–1938) vacationed together at Kislovodsk in July 1923, where they agreed to make a joint proposal about reorganizing the leading organs of the party—about abolishing the Orgburo* and adding Stalin and Trotsky to Zinoviev's Secretariat. Several other members of the Central Committee who were in Kislovodsk supported this proposal and Ordzhonikidze left for Moscow at the end of July to ascertain Stalin's and Kamenev's opinion on this matter.

The sincere intentions and mood of those who initiated the reorganization of the party leadership are clear from the letters Zinoviev sent Kamenev immediately after Ordzhonikidze's departure. "If the party is destined to endure (probably very briefly) Stalin's autocracy," wrote Zinoviev,

> let it be so. But at the least, I don't intend to hide this despicable act. The opposition speaks of a "troika," but my role in it counts for nothing. There is no such thing as a troika, only Stalin's dictatorship. Ilich [Lenin] was a thousand times correct: If a *serious* way out of the situation is not found, the struggle will inevitably broaden. Well, you know all this. You've often spoken about this. But what surprised me is that Voroshil[ov], Frunze, and Sergo think almost identically.[9]

Zinoviev probably exaggerated the degree of Ordzhonikidze's opposition (and that of other members of the Central Committee) in order to inspire a wavering Kamenev to more decisive action. Ordzhonikidze in good conscience told everything to Stalin, however, as he was supposed to have done. Stalin reacted angrily. Understandably, he regarded attempts at reforming the Central Committee as a desire to place political commissars above him, the general secretary, or even to prepare for his removal. Kamenev yielded to Stalin's pressure, and the affair ended in a compromise. The Orgburo was preserved, but expanded to include Bukharin, Zinoviev, and Trotsky. Beginning in the

---

*Orgburo. A subcommittee of the Communist Party's Central Committee, the Organizational Bureau was created at the Eighth Party Congress in 1919, when the party also established the Politburo (Political Bureau). Responsible for party personnel and for dealing with administrative problems, the Orgburo played a role in Stalin's consolidation of power.—Ed.

Old Bolsheviks Fedor Raskolnikov, Sergei Kirov, and Sergo Ordzhonikidze at a meeting in 1926.

fall of 1923, a sharp struggle with Trotsky united the "troika." In this clash, Ordzhonikidze took Stalin's side.

Ordzhonikidze also sided with Stalin in 1925, when the general secretary deflected an attack by Zinoviev and Kamenev. Following the Sixteenth Party Congress, during which the opposition suffered defeat, Ordzhonikidze left with other Stalinist supporters for Leningrad, where the position of Kamenev and Zinoviev was especially strong. Following the requisite purges in Leningrad at the beginning of 1926, a new local committee was selected. Sergei M. Kirov, a friend of Ordzhonikidze's, became the leader of the Leningrad organization in place of Zinoviev.

Scoring a victory, Stalin began to plan an attack against the opposition. Zinoviev's exclusion from the Politburo was discussed at the Central Committee plenum in July 1926. The battle over this turned into a well-known scandal. The "Stalinists" and their opponents recalled each other's numerous political sins, and engaged in a polemical exchange over intrigues and backstage squabbles. Ordzhonikidze got entangled in this mess. Zinoviev recounted the "Georgian Affair" and declared that Lenin had suggested Ordzhonikidze be excluded from the party for two years. (Is this the origin of the assertion in Trotsky's biography of Stalin?) Ordzhonikidze protested passionately. He read Lenin's letter out loud, told of the conflict, which he categorically labeled as slander, and denied that Lenin had proposed his exclusion from the party. He again repented: "What can I do? I'm a hot-tempered man—maybe when I turn fifty, I'll mellow a bit, but in the meantime I can't do anything about it."[10]

The accusation against Ordzhonikidze, however, was only an insignificant episode during the stormy plenum. More vital disclosures captured the attention of the Central Committee members. For example, the opposition sought broad publication of Lenin's "testament," which contained a harsh evaluation of Stalin. Zinoviev's declaration that a factional group of "seven" operated within the Central Committee in 1924–25, organized for the struggle with Trotsky, became a sensation. (More details about Zinoviev's confession and the possible role it played in the fate of Ordzhonikidze will be examined later.)

At any rate, the opposition's efforts no longer mattered. Relying on the Central Committee majority, Stalin achieved the shake-up in the Politburo he needed. The faithful Stalinist Ian E. Rudzutak (1887–1938) replaced Zinoviev in the Politburo. In order to increase the number of Stalin's supporters, which included Ordzhonikidze, more candidate members were admitted.

Ordzhonikidze took this post for granted. He remained silent when the younger Mikoyan and Lazar M. Kaganovich (1893–1991) emphatically withdrew their own candidacies during the elections. ("Comrades, I categorically reject candidate membership in the Politburo. I'm not qualified for this role: First, there are older and more distinguished members of the Central Committee than myself; second, I'm not prepared for this role. I repeat, I'm not qualified—therefore, I request that you select another in my place."[11] This is how Mikoyan demonstrated his humility.) Ordzhonikidze was already forty years old, which at that time was considerable. He was older than most party members, and was one of the oldest in the Central Committee. In general, Sergo could well aspire to a higher position, though he apparently was in no hurry to move to a Moscow office. But this soon happened nevertheless.

Chapter 2

At the Head of the Central Control Commission

As already mentioned, the opposition attempted to stop the Stalinists' offensive by publishing politically damaging facts at the Central Committee plenum in June 1926. The most significant was Zinoviev's statement about the existence of a majority group in the Central Committee since 1924, organized for the struggle against Trotsky. This faction, Zinoviev explained, convened its own plenum and selected a leading group of "seven," comprising six members of the Politburo (all except Trotsky) and the chairman of the Central Control Commission, Valerian V. Kuibyshev (1888–1935). "This factional seven," said Zinoviev, "was in fact the Central Committee of our party for two years. It met every Tuesday, sometimes more often."[1] The "seven" discussed all key questions in advance, and then performed according to a prearranged scenario at official meetings of the Politburo that Trotsky attended.[2]

Although Zinoviev's disclosures did not tip the scales in favor of the opposition (incidentally, Zinoviev himself did not come across in the best light in this instance), they significantly undermined the authority of the Stalinist majority. It turned out that Stalin and his supporters were the first to resort to factionalism and violate party rules. Zinoviev and other oppositionists vigorously underscored the fact that the chairman of the Central Control Commission, Kuibyshev, who was called upon by his post to be an example of impartiality, had joined the "seven."

It is possible to suggest with a great deal of certainty that this circumstance played a role in Kuibyshev's appointment to the post of chairman of the Supreme Council of the National Economy (VSNKh), vacated by Dzerzhinskii's death in July 1926. In the impending battle with the opposition, it was important that Stalin have a supporter as head of the Central Control Commission who was not as compromised as Kuibyshev. In the end, Ordzhonikidze replaced Kuibyshev. But this took place only after long-term squabbles and arguments between Sergo and Stalin, the vague traces of which are found in the documents.

The question of Ordzhonikidze's appointment to the open post of the people's commissar of the Workers' and Peasants' Inspectorate and chairman of the Central Control Commission was predetermined back in July. Stalin informed Ordzhonikidze of this and asked him "not to resist, since it wouldn't help anyway."[3] Ordzhonikidze categorically rejected the new position, however, and Stalin undertook a circuitous maneuver. On August 5, 1926, the Politburo relieved Kamenev from his post of people's commissar of external and internal trade of the USSR and named Mikoyan to replace him. A Politburo decree followed on August 30 regarding the recall of Ordzhonikidze from Transcaucasia and his appointment as first secretary of the North Caucasus Regional Party Committee in place of Mikoyan. This illogical placement (after all, the only meaningful transfer would be to a position in the capital) brought real pressure on Ordzhonikidze by offering him a choice: either Moscow or an ordinary position in the North Caucasus.

Ordzhonikidze defended himself as best he could. His supporters in the Transcaucasian Regional Committee appealed to the Central Committee on September 1, requesting that Ordzhonikidze retain his previous post.[4] Several days later, on September 4 (while vacationing in the south), Stalin informed Viacheslav M. Molotov (1890–1986) in Moscow:

> Sergo was with me for a few days. He went into a rage over the *wording* of the Central Committee resolution concerning his *recall.* He considers the *recall* punishment by the Central Committee for some unknown reason. He interpreted the phrase that Sergo should transfer to Rostov *"in place of Mikoyan"* to mean that Mikoyan is *higher* than Sergo, that Sergo is only qualified to be Mikoyan's deputy, etc. . . . I think it's important to satisfy Sergo because the accidental slip in the wording offended him. The wording can be corrected as follows:
> (1) Honor Comrade Orzhonikidze's request to free him from his

responsibilities as first secretary of the Transcaucasian Regional Committee. As such, reject the requests of the Transcaucasian organizations (the local central committee and the Transcaucasian Regional Committee) calling for the retention of Ordzhonikidze in his old post;

(2) Postpone for several months the naming of Comrade Ordzhonikidze as people's commissar of the Workers' and Peasants' Inspectorate (RKI) of the USSR and chairman of Sovnarkom of the USSR in view of Comrade Ordzhonikidze's firm rejection of a prompt transfer to Moscow;

(3) Accept the proposal (agreed to by Comrade Ordzhonikidze) of the North Caucasus Regional Committee to confirm Comrade Ordzhonikidze as first secretary of the North Caucasus Regional Committee.[5]

The Politburo adopted this decision on September 9: "The Politburo fully agrees with the statement of the Transcaucasian organizations (the local central committees and Transcaucasian Regional Committee) about the important work Comrade Ordzhonikidze accomplished as leader of these organizations. The Politburo does not find it possible, however, to rescind its decision confirming Comrade Ordzhonikidze as first secretary of the North Caucasus Regional Committee."[6]

On September 16, Stalin wrote to Molotov:

I didn't write you in detail about Sergo last time. But I must now inform you that Sergo, and especially Nazaretian [chairman of the Central Control Commission and people's commissar of the RKI of the Transcaucasian Soviet Federative Socialist Republic—O.Kh.], made a bad impression on me concerning the "recall" from Transcaucasia. I argued with Sergo, called him petty, and stopped seeing him (he's now in New Afone). The matter regarding the composition of the secretariat of the Transcaucasian Regional Committee is in need of special discussion. Nazaretian's replacement of Sergo on the secretariat won't do at this time (he's ordinary, lackadaisical, and not always honest).[7]

The reasons for Ordzhonikidze's categorical rejection of a respected and influential post that would open doors to the highest echelons of power are still unknown. Most likely, he did not really want to exchange the relatively quiet life of a provincial leader for the squabbles and messy intrigues of Moscow politics. Undoubtedly, Ordzhonikidze could well imagine the role in store for him as chairman of the Central Control Commission in connection with the upcoming decisive clash between Stalin and the opposition. This incident reveals, in any case, that Ordzhonikidze neither aspired to high leadership nor felt prepared to assume a paramount political role. Stalin got his way only with the help of crude pressure; Ordzhonikidze was forced to submit. Despite the official appointment, he did not wind up in the North Caucasus, but moved directly from Tiflis to Moscow, where he was appointed to the post of chairman of the Central Control Commission.

Just how important it was for Stalin to see Ordzhonikidze in this position is evident from the specific circumstances of the appointment, which was made during the break between the afternoon and evening sessions of the plenum of the Central Committee and Central Control Commission on November 3, the last workday of the Fifteenth Party Conference. In proposing Ordzhonikidze's candidacy, Aleksei I. Rykov (1881–1938) acknowledged that it was at odds with party regulations: the chairman of the Central Control Commission was supposed to be chosen from among its members, and Ordzhonikidze was not one. Only a party congress could appoint him to the Central Control Commission, but its convening had been postponed. Rykov offered a solution: report the violation to the conference and ask it to discuss the matter as one of vital importance. This measure violated party law because the conference could not assume the authority of a congress. Nevertheless, participants at the plenum and conference delegates learned of the appointment during the evening session the same day and agreed almost unanimously to accept the party leadership's proposal.[8]

From his first days at the new post, Ordzhonikidze demonstrated all the "charms" of his temperamental character and lack of refinement. After a month on the job, on December 3, 1926, he received a letter from one of his subordinates, Parkhomenko:

> Comrade Sergo, because of our common interests, I want to confide in you about some of the moods and reactions to your joining the RKI. . . . Following your speech at a gathering of associates . . . people believe that in you the RKI has received strong and confident leadership. . . . It's not my job to remind you that apart from strong leadership, comradely relations toward others is necessary, rather than

belittling them. . . . At the meeting of the RKI on December 2, I think that you exploded inappropriately (here's an example of when it's bad to have a temper) and cut off Peters and Miliutin. I am sure that as a result they recall Ilich's characterization of you in the affair of the "deviationists." The impression is that you terrorize comrades at work. . . . If you'll restrain this negative character trait, you have the qualities to be a good leader.[9]

Parkhomenko's letter, which to some degree was a result of the relative democratism within the party of the 1920s, appears to reflect the fact that Moscow officials still did not acknowledge Ordzhonikidze as a leader. The reminder about Lenin's criticism was very frank, as were the observations about Ordzhonikidze's rudeness and the rather straightforward observation that "you have the qualities to be a good leader" (as if someone doubted this).

In either case, Ordzhonikidze held one of the most important posts in the party and government. The Central Control Commission had significant powers at the time. Its members, like those of the Central Committee, were elected directly by the party congress. The Central Control Commission's importance increased as it became more involved in the bitter struggle for power with the party's old guard in the second half of the 1920s, an event in which the Control Commission was destined to be an arbitrator.

Ordzhonikidze responded well to the responsibilities with which Stalin entrusted him. The Central Control Commission played a direct and prejudiced role in the expulsions, arrests, and exiles of the leaders and supporters of the Trotskyite-Zinovievist Opposition,* as well as in the defeat of the so-called "Right Deviation."† Though Stalin was especially friendly toward Ordzhonikidze, their relationship occasionally became strained, due to the spontaneity of the impulsive and unrestrained Sergo.

---

*Trotskyist-Zinovievite Opposition. In 1923–24 Stalin carried out a factional struggle against the Trotskyist opposition and in 1925 against Zinoviev and his supporters. During 1926–27, Stalin battled against the "united" opposition of Trotsky and Zinoviev, which was defeated and expelled from the Communist Party at the Fifteenth Party Congress in 1927.—Ed.

†Right Deviation. Refers to Nikolai Bukharin and his supporters who sought to perpetuate the New Economic Policy and who spoke out against

A closely cropped Sergo Ordzhonikidze (left) in 1927 with Kliment Voroshilov, people's commissar of the army and navy, and chairman of the Revolutionary Military Council of the USSR.

For example, Ordzhonikidze's clumsy actions during the "resolution" of the conflict with the Leningrad leaders at the end of 1929 reveal a good deal about his character. In many respects, this was a typical clash with the "fathers" of the second capital who did not share power. A group of highly placed party officials, including the chairman of the Leningrad Soviet, Nikolai P. Komarov (1886–1937), and the

---

the use of violence against the peasantry, for which they were accused of underestimating the danger of the restoration of capitalism in Russia. The label also refers to Bukharin and his followers who, at the Sixth Comintern Congress in 1928, were reluctant to accept Stalin's formula for lumping together social democracy with fascism in Europe and the implication that Communists might ally with fascists against fellow socialists. Bukharin later accepted Stalin's view on this issue, but nonetheless was accused in 1929 of being the main inspirator of the right deviationists (this time the label referred to his "pro-peasant" policies). By the time of his arrest, of course, the right deviation had become an "opposition," as Bukharin was pilloried for being pro-kulak, anti-Bolshevik, un-Marxist, and anti-Leninist.—Ed.

Sergei Kirov and Sergo Ordzhonikidze in the late 1920s.

leader of the Regional Party Control Commission and member of the presidium of the Central Control Commission, G.A. Desov* (1884–?), turned against Kirov. They used Kirov's association with the Vladikavkaz liberal newspaper *Terek* (published from 1912 until the first half of 1917) to justify their attack. Sitting in the library, Desov compiled "compromising" materials—articles Kirov wrote that did not toe the party line.[10]

The affair spread to Moscow. As chairman of the Central Control

---

*G.A. Desov. Party member since 1902 whose fate remains unknown.

Commission, Ordzhonikidze met with Desov and strongly defended Kirov. According to Desov, however, Ordzhonikidze rashly argued that even Stalin had flirted with defensism (old party members remembered that when Stalin returned to Petrograd after the February Revolution, he backed the Provisional Government and continuation of the war, in defiance of Lenin). Fighting with all means accessible to him, Desov reported on this conversation, creating a difficult situation for Ordzhonikidze.

On December 7, 1929, following Ordzhonikidze's report, the Politburo reviewed Desov's statement and resolved to convene a session of the Politburo and Central Control Commission presidium on December 10. The secretariat of the Leningrad Regional Committee, district secretaries, and both full and candidate members of the Central Committee from Leningrad participated.[11] The result of this meeting was a special resolution drafted by a commission on December 11 under the security classification "special file." The commission was chaired by Mikhail I. Kalinin (1875–1946), and included Stalin, Ordzhonikidze, Kuibyshev, M.F. Shkiriatov, B.P. Pozern, and I.F. Kodatskii (1893–1937). Judging from the contents and style of the resolution, Stalin played a leading role in its formulation.

Stalin, as usual, fully extracted all political dividends from this conflict. The resolution contained a reminder of Kirov's mistakes committed while he worked with *Terek*, and stated that the party made Kirov a member of the Central Committee and candidate member of the Politburo because Kirov, "in spite of his past mistakes, is without question a steadfast Bolshevik and one of the experienced leaders of our party." Having reminded Kirov of his sins, and consequently of his political dependency, Stalin firmly backed his faithful associate. Desov's statement in the resolution was labeled as "deeply libelous." They accused him of rubbing shoulders with Trotskyists and Right Opportunists by hurling accusations against one of the most devoted leaders of the party. Similar accusations were made against other Leningrad leaders who either supported Desov or failed to stop the spread of the slander. The Politburo and Central Control Commission presidium resolved to ask the plenum of the latter body to expel Desov from its presidium and warned that if Desov continued to spread libelous rumors, "it would force the party to take more decisive measures." The Central Control Commission also ordered an end to the "anti-party work" of other

Desov supporters. Komarov was removed from his responsibilities as chairman of the Regional Executive Committee and the Leningrad Soviet. All of these decisions were to be conveyed to the plenum of the Leningrad Regional Party Committee.

One of the participants at the Leningrad Regional Committee plenum, M.S. Rosliakov, discussed these events in his memoirs:

> M.S. Chudov rose to speak. He reported that after a two-day discussion of the Leningrad comrades' statements, Stalin introduced a two-point proposal: "Kirov admitted his mistakes while working for the newspaper *Terek*, and he acknowledges them; but then again he had the right to work for a liberal newspaper. The comrades who read their notes evaluated Kirov and his useful work in Leningrad incorrectly. The Central Committee believes it expedient to transfer these comrades to other positions outside Leningrad."

"I.F. Kodatskii," wrote Rosliakov further,

> told a Central Committee meeting about this, which at first was rather heated. Kirov demonstrated great self-control. Meanwhile, Stalin barely spoke; he only asked questions and at the end introduced the proposal mentioned here. Acknowledging the mistakes of Kirov's position as reflected in several articles in *Terek*, Stalin took a soft yet unequivocal stance. P.I. Smorodin said there was a sudden change at the meeting after Kodatskii's intelligent speech, which was noticed by Stalin as well.[12]

Ordzhonikidze had to solve two problems in this case. While defending Kirov, he also had to justify himself against Desov's charge of disloyalty to Stalin. In a special note to the Politburo, Ordzhonikidze basically sided with Kirov, dismissed verbal attacks on him as a "partisan struggle," and concluded with the words: "Finally, I must express my strong protest against Comrade Desov's assertion that I 'made a slip of the tongue' that even 'Stalin temporarily wavered' on the question of defensism. I don't understand why Comrade Desov had to speak such lies."[13]

It is unlikely that Stalin believed this justification. Most likely, he remembered Ordzhonikidze's "tactlessness" just as he recalled for many years his conflict with Ordzhonikidze in the Lominadze Affair.

Chapter 3

The Lominadze Affair

Vissarion Vissarionovich (Beso) Lominadze (1897–1935) played a special role in Ordzhonikidze's fate. Almost ten years younger than Sergo, he did not join the party until March 1917 and always regarded Ordzhonikidze as an older comrade and patron. Their friendship deepened while working together in Transcaucasia, where Lominadze held the post of secretary of the Communist Party of Georgia in the 1920s. Apparently they shared many similar traits. Like Ordzhonikidze, Lominadze was passionate, hot-tempered, and crude. An account by one of his Transcaucasian party workers, Aleksandr F. Miasnikov (1886–1925), provides a clear portrait of Lominadze and his relationship with Ordzhonikidze. Miasnikov noted in his diary on February 5, 1924:

> It's appropriate here to say a few words about the other, third (or, one could say, first, it's immaterial) secretary of the Central Committee of the Communist Party of Georgia, Lominadze. He, too, is a young party worker and former "leftist." He has deviated quite a bit in his time. He is temperamental, impressionistic, impulsive, and highhanded. This limits him in several ways. Sergo says that Lominadze is extremely sincere. This may be true. But I have noticed that this sincerity sometimes goes to extremes, to self-flagellation, to simplification, and so they say, to leaking party and political secrets. His impetuosity sometimes reveals his unstable character. He loves to squabble and argue. But in general, he's a good [comrade]. He works like an ox, without restraint, plan, or system to the point of exhaustion, often to the detriment of himself and his personal affairs. . . . He's a valuable worker, a true democrat. . . . I don't know how he

perceives himself as a comrade. He seems vain. He's a rather good
orator, and is sufficiently witty, logical, and consistent in thought.[1]

Subsequent events basically corroborate this assessment. In the middle of the 1920s, Lominadze worked in the Comintern in Moscow.
While there he became close to the former secretary of the Central
Committee of the Komsomol, Lazar A. Shatskin (1902–1937), whose
party career by that time was fairly successful. As unconditional supporters of Stalin, they periodically shocked the country's leadership with
their uncoordinated, independent positions. According to Ordzhonikidze, they tried to play "a unique role in the party—that of mov-
ers and shakers." They articulated strong opinions on questions
pertaining to the Chinese Revolution, struggles with the kulak class,
and also proposed the creation of a special organization for the poor.*

For a time, Shatskin and Lominadze were in accord with the leadership and its initiatives. Serious problems arose, however, in the summer
of 1929 when the persecution of the "right deviationists" got into full
swing after the rout of the Bukharin group. Unconditional support of
the general line was widely propagated as the cult of a single leader of
the party, Stalin, began to take shape. Against this background,
Shatskin's article, "Down with Party Philistinism," was more than un-
timely (*Komsomolskaia pravda*, 18 June 1929). According to Stephen
Cohen, this work reflected the "growing anxiety among Stalin's followers over his social policies."[2] Shatskin's article, as well as several other
statements by his supporters, insisted that party members had the right

---

*Chinese Revolution and kulak class. Stalin's views on both these issues
became part of the power struggle in the second half of the 1920s. Stalin,
like Lenin, supported the Chinese nationalist movement and encouraged
the Chinese Communists to join forces with the nationalist movement led
by Chiang-Kai-shek. In 1927 Chiang and the nationalists massacred their
Communist allies, and Soviet advisers were forced to withdraw from China.
Trotsky took advantage of this disaster to help discredit Stalin's foreign
policy as well as Comintern policy in China.

Throughout the 1920s, the Communist Party and its factions debated
the meaning and significance of the kulak, or rich peasant, who, by
definition, harbored an inherent hatred for socialism. At the end of the
decade, Stalin took a hard line toward the kulaks, and the term came to
be used propagandistically to refer to any peasant who opposed forced
collectivization.—Ed.

to critically evaluate directives from above. It also condemned the silent voting majority.

It would appear that the Communists often discussed these issues, especially in view of an increasingly strict ideological censorship and condemnation of the slightest dissent. Lominadze fully supported Shatskin on this matter. In the middle of 1929, in response to accusations of "left deviationism," he sent a statement to the party's Institute of Red Professors:

> There's been a rather rapid expansion of a *special type of Communist* (one might call him an ideologically lacquered Communist). This type of Communist voices his opinion on any question only after he is convinced that a particular viewpoint has been recognized as correct from above. In essence, he never gives his personal views on any question, but only repeats over and over again what already has been said by others and what already has been judged to be correct by others. The fundamental trait of this typical representative of the lower party elements is fear of making a mistake, ideological cowardice, and constant trepidation that he could say something that might differ from the leadership's thinking. Of course, this fear most often leads to mistakes. Each day poses many new questions, not all of which can be addressed with prepared, stock, and previously approved answers from above. Thinking formulaically inevitably places "those afraid to make a mistake" in a dead end at every turn. They don't find solutions to life's daily problems in their limited reserve of prepared formulas. If not previously approved from above, any new thought invariably seems to them to be a deviation of the left or right.[3]

In one of his letters to Molotov, Stalin characterized the views of Shatskin, Lominadze, and their supporters as a demand for "*freedom* to revise the party's general line, *freedom* to weaken party discipline, and *freedom* to convert the party into a discussion club." It was on Stalin's initiative that strict measures were taken against the cohort, which he named "the group that slipped from the path of young comrades."[4] In particular, Shatskin was removed from the editorial board of *Pravda* and sent to do routine work in Saratov. For several months he was chastised for his crude political errors, attacked in the press, and defamed at party meetings.

Lominadze received such treatment as well. Probably at the beginning of August, he wrote a fairly harsh letter to Ordzhonikidze. Judging from Ordzhonikidze's response, which will be discussed later, Lominadze asserted that the campaign [against Shatskin] curtailed self-criticism. He maintained that within the limits of the "general line," a member of the party had the right to demonstrate initiative, and that the accusations against Shatskin and his supporters were unfair. Receiving the letter while on vacation in the Crimea, Ordzhonikidze wrote a restrained, and in places ironic, but harsh reply. One senses that he understood Lominadze's situation and tried to find words that would not further embitter Lominadze.

> You write me that you agree with the Central Committee's general line. Thank you, but it's necessary not only to say this, but to carry it out as well. Stalin is absolutely right when he rebukes you for not being involved or interested in administrative questions. . . . You and Shatskin think you're the only true proponents of the general line, possibly its initiators. Come on, guys, stop acting foolish and get down to business. In truth, you aren't leaders and nobody recognizes you as such. These views only get you in trouble.
>
> A few words about your letter. It's no good, no good at all. It's obvious that a few slaps at your brother is not a curtailment of self-criticism . . . you can't make a big deal over a few sentences. You know exactly what I'm driving at. A cat knows who feeds it. I know that you don't want to organize opposition to the Central Committee. I know that you don't want to become a deviationist. But that's not enough, Beso. . . .
>
> I didn't intend to write in such detail—we'll discuss things at length when we meet. I'll talk with pleasure. I'll be more than happy to hear that you'll stop being so obstinate. Don't be offended. I didn't show your letter to anyone; that would be shameful. While there are no party secrets between Stalin and me, I didn't even show him your letter. Of course, I don't want to turn it into a political document, but I repeat that your letter simply won't do. More about this when we meet. . . . Well, so long. All the best. As ever—Sergo.[5]

It appears, however, that Ordzhonikidze did not send this letter to Lominadze. It is preserved in Ordzhonikidze's personal archive; in a subsequent letter to Ordzhonikidze, apparently written at the begin-

ning of September, Lominadze did not say a word about Ordzhonikidze's reply to his first letter.[6]

The fact of the matter is that upon receiving the irritating and harsh
letter from Lominadze, Orzhonikidze found himself in a difficult quan-
dary. Inasmuch as this concerned the position of an influential party
worker, and one who dared to criticize decisions taken by the Politburo,
Ordzhonikidze, according to regulations, was required to make it a
"political document"—exactly what he did not want to do. Ordzhonikidze understood what the consequences of revealing the letter
would be for Lominadze and his patron. He therefore first decided to
calm Lominadze and hide the letter, as he communicated in his reply.
In reconsidering, however, Orzhonikidze felt that such a step was too
risky. He thus held on to his reply, thereby concealing the evidence of
Lominadze's "deviationist" views and the anti-party behavior of Ordzhonikidze himself.

Eight years later, at the infamous February–March plenum of 1937*
and several days after Ordzhonikidze's death, Stalin said that many
letters Lominadze had written to Ordzhonikidze were of an "anti-party
character," and that Ordzhonikidze had kept them to himself:

> We didn't know the real Lominadze; we, the Central Committee,
> didn't know how he would turn out when we promoted him. But we
> took a risk and appointed him secretary of the Transcaucasian party
> organization.
>
> If we had known about Sergo's correspondence, we would never
> have placed Lominadze in this position. But we didn't know. We
> appointed him. It turned out later that this man worked not for the
> party, but against it.
>
> It was during this period that Comrade Sergo received a particu-
> larly unfortunate, unpleasant, anti-party letter from Lominadze. Ord-
> zhonikidze stopped by my office and said: "I want to read you
> Lominadze's letter." "What does it say?" "It's not good." "Give it to
> me—I'll report it to the Politburo. The Central Committee should

---

*February–March plenum of 1937. The Central Committee plenum that,
among other things, discussed the "anti-party" activity of Bukharin and Rykov,
both of whom were expelled from the party. The complete materials of the
plenum were published in *Voprosy istorii* (Problems of History), beginning with
the no. 2–3 (1992) issue and extending throughout 1993–94.—Ed.

know about its appointees." "I can't." "Why?" "I gave him my word." "How could you have given him your word? You're the chairman of the Central Control Commission and one who preserves party tradition. How could you honor a man with your word, and not show the Central Committee a letter against it and the party? And what secrets do you share with Lominadze against the Central Committee? What does this look like to you, Comrade Sergo? How could you have done this?" "I can't take any more." He asked me several times—implored me—to read it. Apparently he wanted me to share moral responsibility for the secrets he kept with Lominadze. Of course, he didn't share Lominadze's views about the Central Committee. I would say he behaved like a feudal lord, even like a prince. I told him I didn't want to be a part of his secret, that I considered myself to be a member of the Central Committee. "Give me the letter—I'll send it immediately to Politburo members so they know what sort of party workers they have. . . ."[7]

It is possible that this conflict concerned Lominadze's letter of August 1929. More likely, it occurred later, in 1930, when a repentant Lominadze, undoubtedly with Ordzhonikidze's help, was named to the high post of first secretary of the Transcaucasian Regional Party Committee.

During his tenure there, Lominadze became close to the Sovnarkom chairman (RSFSR), Sergei I. Syrtsov (1893–1937). In the 1920s, Syrtsov had worked in the Central Committee, and then was sent as secretary to the Siberian Regional Party Committee. At the beginning of 1928, Syrtsov experienced every party functionary's dream come true: Stalin arrived in Siberia with the well-known mission to organize an emergency grain requisition. This action was a success, largely thanks to Syrtsov.[8] Soon after, he was selected as a candidate member of the Politburo and named chairman of Sovnarkom (RSFSR), a position previously held by the head of the government, Rykov. It looked like Stalin was grooming Syrtsov to take Rykov's place in Sovnarkom. The rising young official disappointed the leader's hopes, however, by seeming obstinate and too independent. Opposing the first results of the Great Change,* Syrtsov openly demonstrated his displeasure and advocated

---

*Great Change or Great Turn (*Velikii perelom*). Generally refers to the Stalin Revolution, but more specifically to an article written by Stalin and published in the fall of 1929 in which he argued that the situation in the Soviet countryside was revolutionary. In effect, this amounted to a call for full speed ahead in collectivizing agriculture.—Ed.

his own solutions for resolving the problems, whose prescriptions partially resembled those of the previously routed "right." Lominadze was also cautiously critical of Stalinist policies at this time. A rapprochement occurred between them on these grounds, and ended with accusations that they had created a factional bloc.

In the last few years, several scholarly articles have been written about the Syrtsov-Lominadze affair.[9] Judging from available documents, as on other matters of this sort, elements of real opposition to Stalin became interwoven with fabricated provocations that aggravated the situation. Syrtsov, Lominadze, and their close friends undoubtedly met and held candid discussions condemning Stalin and his policies. From the point of view of the established canons of party discipline, such activities could only be interpreted as conspiratorial. Any criticism of Stalin qualified as preparation of a coup d'état, and unofficial meetings as the forging of factional blocs. The only thing needed was an appropriate opportunity to unleash a political affair. In this case, the occasion was the denunciation by one of the members of the circle, B.G. Reznikov.*

It is difficult to say whether the accuser acted on his own initiative or under coercion; Stalin nevertheless received the necessary "support." Reznikov wrote that the Syrtsov group had formed a bloc with the Lominadze-Shatskin group, and together they met conspiratorially to denounce Stalinist policies and nurture plans to change the party leadership. Reznikov wrote that they believed mass disturbances would engulf the country—peasant agitation, worker strikes—during which they could easily remove Stalin.

Reznikov's denunciation was delivered to Stalin on the night of October 21, 1930. The next morning, Ordzhonikidze and Pavel P. Postyshev (1887–1939) were alerted (Kaganovich and Molotov were not in Moscow), and Stalin ordered that Syrtsov be summoned. They found him by nightfall. Syrtsov read the accusation, denied the charges, and stated that more detailed evidence would be officially given only to the Central Control Commission. That very evening, the Central Committee summoned other members of the Syrtsov circle. During a confrontation with Reznikov, they denied his charges and were arrested. On October 23,

---

*B.G. Reznikov (1898–?). A party member since 1917, Reznikov was a secretary of a party cell at the Institute of Red Professors.

Syrtsov began to give testimony to the Central Control Commission, and Lominadze was summoned to Moscow on October 25.

Ordzhonikidze questioned him that same day in the presence of Emelian M. Iaroslavskii (1878–1943), Postyshev, and Rozalia S. Zemliachka (1876–1947). "Beso," he began to say, "We must have a talk that won't be all that pleasant. Sit down and tell us the truth: Are you involved in any factional groups or not?" "No. I am absolutely not connected to any groups," answered Lominadze. Ordzhonikidze reached for Reznikov's statement: "Here, read this report and tell me if what's written here is true or false. Comrade Reznikov wrote this document. . . . He writes that you, Nusinov, and Syrtsov convened all sorts of conspiratorial meetings, etc." "It's untrue," repeated Lominadze. Point by point he rejected Reznikov's charges with denials and heated epithets. Ordzhonikidze was calm, even sympathetic. In the end, they decided that Lominadze would familiarize himself carefully with all the documents, and prepare a written summary for the Central Control Commission. Before long, the document was ready. Lominadze wrote that no such Lominadze-Shatskin group existed, and that he had only a nodding acquaintance with Syrtsov and Nusinov.[10]

While Lominadze prepared his reply, Ordzhonikidze attended a Politburo meeting. There he communicated the results of Lominadze's interrogation, and reported that the arrested Kavraiskii, Nusinov, and Galperin made depositions to agents of the GPU [political police].

At the end of October, Syrtsov was summoned for repeated questioning. Because of the testimony of his supporters, he acknowledged that he had sharply criticized Stalin's policies. On November 3, Lominadze filed a new statement as well. He conceded that his explanation of October 25 was mistaken, and confirmed that he had held talks with Syrtsov on political topics. But along with this, he asserted that these were only conversations between Communists, and not an attempt to create a factional bloc. He stated that he did not know the Syrtsov group existed, but that he always expressed his own views openly. If they somehow differed from generally accepted opinions, Lominadze maintained, the distinction "wholly and fully lay *within the limits* of the party's general line."[11]

In drafting a new statement, Lominadze tried as much as possible to preserve his own dignity. On the charge of plans to remove Stalin, he answered:

> I have always supported the Stalinist leadership, and never enter-
> tained thoughts of changing this leadership, for that would signify a
> clear turn to the right and away from the correct class line. I regarded
> and still regard Stalin's inflexible resoluteness in the struggle against
> the Trotskyists and the Right Opposition as a great historical service.
> . . . But at the same time, I believed Stalin had a certain empiricism,
> an insufficient ability to foresee things. . . . Furthermore, I didn't and
> don't like the fact that sometimes (most notably during his fiftieth
> birthday celebration), the press and certain individuals place Com-
> rade Stalin almost on a par with Lenin. As far as I remember, I spoke
> to Comrade Ordzhonikidze about this and provided him with sup-
> porting evidence from the press.

In conclusion, Lominadze wrote:

> I think it a serious political mistake that I conducted frank conversa-
> tions on all these problems with Comrades Syrtsov and Nusinov.
> These talks turned out to be used for factional goals and thus caused
> great political harm. I feel that through my careless conversations, I
> provided grounds for the charges that I belonged to the Syrtsov bloc.
> But I did not have this in mind, and in fact see this as absolutely
> politically unacceptable.

The accusations against Lominadze placed Ordzhonikidze in a very
difficult dilemma. His unprincipled patronage (refusal to show Lominadze's letter to Stalin) facilitated the activities of the "factionalists." In
the previously cited speech at the February–March plenum, Stalin argued that Ordzhonikidze had "sought Lominadze's execution." "Such an
extreme," lamented Stalin. . . . "We said: 'No, we'll not shoot him, nor
arrest him, nor even expel him from the party. We'll simply remove him
from the Central Committee.' "[12]

Stalin lied, however, and was able to do so because Ordzhonikidze
was already dead. Characterizing Ordzhonikidze as evil and blood-
thirsty, Stalin portrayed himself as the one who softened Lominadze's
sentence, and once again intimated that he was fair and lacked any bias.
Indeed, two choices existed in 1930: expulsion from the party, or only
from the Central Committee. Ordzhonikidze in fact had sought the
"extreme measure"—expulsion from the party. "Lominadze wasn't a
bad person, in spite of all his wavering. Many comrades who know him,
myself included, regard him as a revolutionary. Nevertheless, we can't
be patient with people who double-deal or deceive the party," said

Ordzhonikidze at a joint meeting of the Politburo and presidium of the Central Control Commission, at which the fate of Syrtsov, Lominadze, and their comrades was decided.

Stalin himself was also not interested this time in attaching too much significance to the affair. Objectively, it weakened his position and sowed doubts about the stability of the regime and the loyalty of Stalin's supporters. At a joint meeting of the Politburo and Central Control Commission Presidium on November 4, Stalin already had stated that the incident involving the Syrtsov-Lominadze bloc was not serious.[13] On November 20, 1930, the Politburo adopted a special resolution Stalin proposed, "On *Vorwärts*'s Fabrications: (a) Don't provide any refutations in our press; (b) Order TASS to indicate through the foreign press that *Vorwärts*'s report concerning a 'military plot' and the arrest of Comrade Syrtsov, Lominadze, and others represents a complete and malicious fabrication."[14]

The decision taken in regard to the affair was the most lenient of all possibilities. The list of serious charges included creating an anti-party group, unifying it in a single "left–right" bloc, violating party unity resolutions of the Tenth Party Congress as well as those of the April 1929 Central Committee plenum on observing the secrecy of the Central Committee, Central Control Commission, and Politburo decisions, and disregarding the Fifteenth Party Congress's ruling that Communists are obliged to give accurate answers to control commissions. (Each of these "articles" "set" expulsion from the party as a minimum punishment.) Despite all this, Syrtsov and Lominadze were only removed from the Central Committee, while Shatskin was released from the Central Control Commission.[15]

Stalin, however, now counted Lominadze among his enemies and concealed his hostility toward Ordzhonikidze, who dared defend Lominadze.

Chapter 4

The Head Manager

As subsequent events showed, the Syrtsov-Lominadze Affair was part of a new shake-up of cadres undertaken in the last months of 1930, known as the defeat of the "Right Opposition,"* which completed that stage in Stalin's struggle for absolute power.

In spite of the elimination of the Bukharin group from power and the Sixteenth Party Congress that consolidated Stalin's role as the sole party leader, the situation in the country did not allow Stalin to "rest on his laurels." The policies of the Great Change exacerbated problems it aimed to resolve. The violence of collectivization undermined the productive forces of the villages and led to massive unrest among the peasantry. Excessively ambitious industrial plans disrupted industry and finance, and living standards declined sharply. As a result, the urban population, including the working class that the regime considered to be its main social base, became dissatisfied. The attempt to institute violent and harsh administrative-repressive measures to obvert disorganization failed.[1]

All of this weakened Stalin's position and had a number of negative

---

*Right Opposition. Refers to Bukharin, Rykov, and Tomskii, whom Stalin defeated in 1928. Their defeat marked the removal of the last remaining obstacle to using force against the peasantry. Realignments had taken place within the Politburo and party back in 1925, when the Left Opposition, most closely linked to Kamenev and Zinoviev, denounced the idea of "socialism in one country" and stressed the inevitability of conflict with the peasantry. The Bukharin group (Right) emphasized the need for harmonious cooperation between workers and peasants.—Ed.

political consequences. First, the deepening crisis showed that the warnings of the right, which not long before had been stigmatized as opportunistic, were in many respects true. This objectively improved the chances of Bukharin and Mikhail P. Tomskii (1880–1936), in spite of their expulsion from the higher echelons of power, and preserved their reputations as renowned party statesmen.

It also benefited Rykov, who until the very end of 1930 remained chairman of Sovnarkom and a member of the Politburo. He was able to rely on many supporters within the government for a more moderate course. In this complex situation, Stalin, like any other dictator, had reasons to keep an attentive eye on his own supporters. What threatened him at this time was the growing displeasure within the party nomenklatura, the hesitancy of Politburo members who were always wavering (such as Kalinin, for example), or the relative independence of impulsive rivals who inevitably became more powerful during this period when Stalin needed their support in his struggle with the opposition.

In order to crush the last "rightist nest" and alleviate social tension, Stalin organized several widely publicized show trials (the shooting of the "Supply Wreckers," the "Industrial Party Trial," etc.).[2] A purge and reorganization of the state's economic planning administration (Gosplan) was conducted in connection with the struggle against the "wreckers" and a strident campaign to fulfill the program of the so-called "special quarter" (October–December 1930).* This culminated in Rykov's removal in December 1930, and Molotov's appointment as Sovnarkom chairman. Kuibyshev became the chairman of Gosplan in place of Gleb M. Krzhizhanovskii (1872–1959), and Ordzhonikidze transferred to Kuibyshev's former post as chairman of the Supreme Council of the National Economy (VSNKh) on November 10, 1930. Ordzhonikidze then took Rykov's place in the Politburo in December 1930.

Several circumstances apparently influenced this new turning point in Ordzhonikidze's career. The situation in industry was extremely bad,

---

*Special quarter of October–December 1930. The last quarter of 1930, when attempts were made to correct some of the most egregious errors in the First Five-Year Plan. Even though performance during this quarter did not improve, the party adopted an even more ambitious annual economic program for 1931, which called for a 45 percent increase in output.—Ed.

and it became clear that Kuibyshev was a poor economic manager.[3] Ordzhonikidze, as head of the Central Control Commission of the Workers' and Peasants' Inspectorate, had often been involved in economic matters and had the reputation of being an expert of sorts. The Central Control Commission, achieving the "apogee of its power and influence" in 1929–30, according to E.A. Rees, was not needed as much by Stalin following the defeat of all opposition groups.[4] After Ordzhonikidze, the colorless Stalin lackey Andrei A. Andreev (1895–1971) headed the Central Control Commission. A few years later, the Seventeenth Party Congress decided to transform the Central Control Commission into a powerless commission of party control under the party Central Committee.

There is a significant body of literature that investigates Ordzhonikidze's activities as the head of the VSNKh and the creation of the Commissariat of Heavy Industry (NKTP) upon the foundation of VSNKh at the beginning of 1932.[5] Research proves that during the first half of the 1930s, the NKTP was the most powerful and influential economic department in the country. Above all else, of course, this was due to the NKTP's strong potential and its paramount role in deciding key industrial questions in developing the defense industry. Ordzhonikidze's efforts were also of major importance as he strove to strengthen his commissariat. By examining Ordzhonikidze's role, it becomes clear that the interaction and collision of special group and departmental interests in the Soviet party-state determined many critical policies.

In principle, Soviet leaders at all levels of power exhibited a growing inclination toward "their own" departments to a certain degree. In Ordzhonikidze's case, however, this predilection was especially pronounced because of his high position as a Politburo member and his personality. The explosive and crude Sergo interpreted any criticism of the NKTP as a personal affront. There is a great deal of evidence showing the methods he often used in settling interdepartmental conflicts.

The main engineer of the Administration of Metallurgical Industry of the NKTP, A.S. Tochinskii, remembered how Ordzhonikidze at one of the Sovnarkom meetings hurled insults "with all his might" at Rudzutak (who, by the way, was a member of the Politburo and chairman of the Central Control Commission), a man who had criticized the

NKTP on one matter. "When Chairman Molotov tried to stop him . . . in order to soften his remarks, Comrade Ordzhonikidze became impatient, slammed his fist on the table, and shouted angrily that not enough time was given at meetings for Politburo members to say what needed to be said."[6] Nikita S. Khrushchev (1894–1971) recalled Ordzhonikidze thus: "In the 1930s, discussions on some matters were quite heated, especially when someone got emotional. . . . Once, for example, Sergo exploded (he was usually a very passionate person), pounced on Rosengolts of the People's Commissariat of External Trade, and almost hit him."[7]

In a more restrained yet no less decisive fashion, Ordzhonikidze defended his rights in conflicts with close associates in the Politburo and with his bosses—Stalin and Molotov. For example, Ordzhonikidze wrote to Kuibyshev: "Today your urgent order was given to me, hastily addressed to Union Chemical. . . . I feel that such an order through the head of the NKTP is incorrect, and think that you will agree with my request to send all necessary orders in the usual, normal fashion."[8]

Ordzhonikidze complained in one of his letters to Molotov.[9]

> From the resolutions, one gets the impression that VSNKh is composed of idiots. I don't think you want this. . . . In general, it's necessary to say frankly that things are not going all that well. We are presented almost daily with resolution after resolution; moreover, each one is more strongly worded than the next and more unfair. . . . Furthermore, the Executive Commission, that is, its leadership, intends to issue orders to factories through the head of VSNKh. Perhaps the devil only knows, but what the hell is VSNKh for and why am I a member of it? . . . It seems it will be difficult to work under such conditions, if at all,

As the documents show, there were numerous conflicts between VSNKh and NKTP, as well as other economic commissariats with control and distribution networks regarding plans for production and capital investment. In trying to lighten their load, the leaders of heavy industry tried to obtain higher capital investment targets, more moderate production plans, and lower production costs. In fulfilling their function, Gosplan, the People's Commissariat of Finance, and the leadership of Sovnarkom limited the appetite of NKTP by periodically constricting capital investment and requiring greater return from available funds. Finally, similar disputes that continually arose while compiling yearly and even quarterly plans allowed the Politburo, and Stalin personally, to be the ultimate arbiter. Advantage in various cases seemed to be held either by government agencies or by their subordinates. But most often such cases ended in compromise that in one way or another satisfied all sides.[10]

In spite of the bitterness of these conflicts, it is unlikely that they had significant consequences since typical clashes of departmental interests did not involve vital goals. Any participant might one day defend the position of his agency, then transfer to another department and on the very next day back an altogether different viewpoint. In short, it was a fight for a share of limited resources and the reputation of an influential leader, a struggle that rarely affected the system fundamentally.

Of greater importance were the aspirations of departmental leaders to strengthen their political standing, to achieve relative independence from party control and "security" organs, and to ensure their right to personally manage the careers and lives of their subordinates. Their success was mainly dependent upon the interrelationship between the real power accorded their departments (and hence themselves) in the party-state structure and the absolute rule of Stalin.

Ordzhonikidze's arrival at VSNKh coincided with the implementation of a series of inconsistent reforms that R.W. Davies has labeled "mini-reformist."[11] The most successful and vital part of this "reform" was the political change in relations between specialists and managers. After several years of active specialist-baiting ("spetsbaiting") policies,* which Ordzhonikidze as Central Control Commission chairman organized and inspired along with others, the economy had suffered such irreparable damage that the national leadership overcame its own biases and sought a rapprochement with the engineering and technical intelligentsia.[12]

---

*Spetsbaiting policy. The party's attack on specialists and managers at the end of the 1920s, especially on those "bourgeois" specialists trained before 1917. Disgruntled workers and party activists were encouraged to criticize the specialists, who were subjected to discrimination of all sorts. The party began to distance itself temporarily from these policies in mid-1931.—Ed.

One of the first official signals indicating a turn toward rapprochement was the first All-Union Conference of the Workers of Socialist Industry held in Moscow in late January–early February 1931. The country's leaders, including Stalin and Molotov, participated in this conference. Stalin spoke, but limited himself to political slogans and unconditional demands to fulfill the plan for 1931 (and once again warned of the danger of economic sabotage). The most radical proposals were presented in a speech by Ordzhonikidze, who showed more flexibility and demonstrated a knowledge of the real situation in industrial affairs. In particular, he advocated strengthening one-man management and emancipating managers from the dictates of political overseers. He also stated that the majority of specialists had nothing in common with saboteurs.[13]

This conference, along with other data, suggest that Ordzhonikidze was committed to a new course that led specialists to conclude that the People's Commissariat of Heavy Industry was the initiator of the "mini-reform."[14] Several new archival documents, however, challenge such a conclusion by showing that a retreat gradually took shape under the pressure of circumstances and was largely realized on Stalin's initiative.

On January 4, 1931, for example, the director of the Petrovsk Metallurgical Factory in Dnepropetrovsk, Gorbachev, wrote Stalin a letter complaining about constant interference from the Dnepropetrovsk party organization and press. "In order to enable the factory administration to concentrate all its efforts on fulfilling its tasks," wrote Gorbachev, "stop the constant harassment of workers at meetings. All the energy of the factory administration is wasted in refuting accusations from the party leadership, both orally and in writing, which bombard us as if from a cornucopia."[15] This letter caught Stalin's attention and he wrote the following note on it: "Comrade Ordzhonikidze, I think Gorbachev's complaint has merit. What is needed, in your opinion, to rectify the situation? Would it be enough if we simply put the party organization in its place?"[16] At Ordzhonikidze's urging, the Politburo held a special review session several days later, on January 20, 1931, to address the question raised by Gorbachev's letter. As Stalin had suggested, the Politburo defended Gorbachev and "reined in" the party organization. In addition to this, the Politburo, acting on Stalin's suggestion, gave orders to regional committees and the republic-level central committee "not to allow the removal of directors from factories of national importance without first receiving approval from the Central Committee and VSNKh."[17] This decision was of primary importance, because it marked the gradual strengthening of economic agencies and the weakening of political control over their activities.

To a certain extent, Stalin shaped the evolution of this policy from the time of the Gorbachev affair to the first All-Union Conference of Managers. Originally, his speech at the conference contained many disparaging remarks about the specialists. In preparing the speech for publication, however, he amended it substantially by removing criticism of Communist managers who demanded the help of "old tired specialists," and omitted a long passage about economic sabotage. His revised version stated that only "a few older" engineers and technicians had "slid down the path of sabotage."[18]

Of course, this does not mean that Ordzhonikidze played no role in this policy shift. Having to confront in VSNKh the destructive consequences of earlier policies, Ordzhonikidze radically altered his earlier position and called for a better-thought-out economic and political course. In doing so, he strongly relied upon the full support of the Politburo, and above all else, on Stalin. Following the Conference of Managers, the policy of reconciliation with specialists gained momentum. On March 11 and May 6, 1931, the Politburo rehabilitated "saboteurs" who had worked at the Stalingrad Tractor Factory.[19] On May 20, the Politburo, at Stalin's behest, reviewed the conviction of a shop foreman named Venchel from the Sulinskii Factory. The Politburo dropped the guilty verdict and ensured Venchel "normal conditions of work in the shop," and "proposed that the North Caucasus Regional Committee put an end to police interrogation of specialists."[20] Two weeks later, on June 3, 1931, the Politburo took a more decisive step in this direction: it carried a resolution concerning the urgent need to ensure fire-proof materials and strengthen the authority of individual bosses at the Steel Industrial Plant. The resolution forbade the police, the criminal investigation department, and the procurator's office from interfering with factory production or carrying out investigations without the presence of factory directors or higher officials. OGPU (political police) representatives were removed from the factory. The prerogatives of party organizations were substantially restricted: they could no longer cancel, correct, or delay the operational orders of factory bosses. Furthermore, a special clause in the resolution stipulated that engineers and technicians at the plant would be allocated new apartments and a full supply of food and manufactured goods.[21]

Although these measures only concerned the Steel Industrial Plant, worsening economic conditions compelled the national leadership to continue the "reforms." On June 22–23, 1931, the Central Committee convened a new conference of VSNKh managers and the People's Commissariat of Supply. This gathering differed from its predecessor back in January by reaching much more radical conclusions. (Incidentally, the only documents published from this conference were reports by government leaders that were altered beyond recognition.) Opening the conference, the chairman of Gosplan, Kuibyshev, reported that industrial output for the first five months of 1931 was "abysmal."[22]

The issue of relations with bourgeois specialists and the dynamics between managers and punitive state organs was a central theme at the conference. Participants spoke candidly about this. For example, one of the leaders in the coal industry, Rumiantsev, reported that up to half of all engineers at the Donbass mines had been sentenced to from one to eight years of forced labor. "The engineers complain: You don't pay us a salary, but force us to work. What do you expect from us?"[23] Many speakers were especially critical of the OGPU's interference in production. Government leaders readily acknowledged that the case against the "wreckers" had been trumped up. "Up until now, the OGPU was always prepared to call in some specialist for accountability," said Molotov, "and it is clear that in such instances they could fabricate a case and attain the desired result." Stalin replied, "It isn't necessary to admit that a policeman was really a technical expert in production. . . . It isn't necessary to admit that a special office of the OGPU existed at the factory, where they sit and wait to be presented with cases. When there aren't any, they concoct them."[24] (In preparing his remarks for publication, Stalin deleted this passage.) While fully justifying previous repressions against specialists, government leaders declared that the change in course was a result of the consolidation of socialist transformations and the specialists' willingness to support Soviet power. As an example of this, frequent reference was made at the conference to the Politburo resolution regarding the Steel Industrial Plant. (Incidentally, Ordzhonikidze spoke on the first day of the conference. The main ideas of his report were similar to those of other speakers.)

In implementing the decisions reached at the conference, the Politburo approved a secret resolution on July 10, 1931, entitled "On the Work of Technical Personnel in Industry and the Improvement of Their Standard of Living." It decreed an amnesty for specialists sentenced to hard labor and rescinded discriminatory policies against them in filling administrative posts at industrial enterprises. Their children were also to receive the same rights in admission to institutions of higher education as the children of industrial workers (earlier they too had been discriminated against). The final clause of the July 10 resolution addressed the expansion of measures approved by the Politburo on June 3 regarding the Steel Industrial Plant to all enterprises in the country. This signified that the organs of the procuracy, police, and department of criminal investigation were forbidden to interfere in factory production, and that the OGPU was to be removed from all enterprises.[25]

One clause of the resolution disallowed party organizations to interfere in industrial managers' work. This was of vital significance. In previous years, party organizations had relied on support from the center, including the organs of the Central Control Commission led by Ordzhonikidze, to harass managers. Now the pendulum swung the other way. Moscow authorities, stung by the destructive consequences of the party's administration of the economy, decided to strengthen the position of economic experts. This campaign was launched under the slogan of strengthening one-man authority (at the workplace), and was supported, if not initiated, by Stalin and actively carried out by the new leadership of VSNKh.

However, it proved difficult to break the tradition of party management, in spite of strong efforts to do so, especially because the party organs' leading role was not abolished. Conflicts occurred from time to time between managers and party functionaries in various regions of the country. Interfering in several of these clashes, the Moscow leadership arranged show trials aimed at discouraging violation of the principle of one-man rule in production.

For example, conflict was brewing at the beginning of 1932 in the Rostov Agricultural Machine Factory. On February 1, its director,

Nikolai P. Glebov-Avilov, wrote to Ordzhonikidze that the district party committee (which had replaced the factory party organization) had for several months earlier placed itself above the factory administration. The district party committee issued directives to shops and departments, removed and appointed their bosses, and turned several cases over to the OGPU for prosecution. Against all formalities, the committee went so far as to remove the very same Glebov-Avilov from his position. This event exhausted the patience of higher authorities. The secretary of the Azov-Chernomorskii Regional Party Committee, Boris P. Sheboldaev (1895–1937), rescinded the dismissal of Glebov-Avilov and removed the secretary of the district party committee from his post.[26] Despite the resolution of the conflict, as Glebov-Avilov reported to Ordzhonikidze, his letter was circulated among full and candidate members of the Politburo on Stalin's order. On March 17, the Orgburo of the Central Committee reviewed this matter and resolved to censure the Rostov factory's party organization for violating directives on one-man rule.[27]

This warning, however, did not achieve its full effect. Within two weeks the Central Committee had to interfere in a similar situation in the Nizhnii Novgorod Auto Factory, where the prosecution of specialists had halted production. On April 2, 1932, the Central Committee adopted a resolution, "On the Nizhnii Novgorod Auto Factory," which condemned "the illegal actions of the district party committee and party organization in replacing managers, the presence of an anti-specialist mood, and the persecution of managerial and technical personnel." The factory party organization was disbanded, and a new party committee created in its place. The secretary of the district party committee was removed from his position.[28]

In November 1932, on the initiative of the Central Committee's Resource Management Department, headed by Nikolai I. Ezhov (1895–1940), the excessive turnover of administrative cadres in the coal industry was questioned. As investigations by Ezhov's assistants showed, failure to meet coal quotas was directly related to frequent replacement of mining supervisors. On average, each manager and chief engineer in administration served six months in one place, and shaft managers averaged from three to three and a half months. Normal work conditions required placement in these positions for several years. Roughly the same was true for all engineers and technicians.

Ezhov prepared a special report on this, which the Orgburo reviewed on January 19, 1933.[29] It adopted a new system for appointing and removing managers of coal enterprises. According to the new regulations, administrators could only be appointed and removed by the Central Committee; deputy administrators by order of the NKTP; and shaft managers by order of the trust administrations, and so on. On the whole, the government sought to keep administrative staff in one place for at least three to four years. Party organizations were unambiguously instructed to "ensure the stability of the coal industry's managerial staffs . . . by protecting them from all attacks and unwarranted dismissals that harm production, and by treating them the same as directors of industrial enterprises."[30]

In April 1933, Ezhov sent a report to a Central Committee secretary, Lazar M. Kaganovich, about the arbitrary removal of four metallurgical factory directors by local managers and the Ural Oblast Party Committee. This was done without the approval of the NKTP or the Central Committee. On June 7, the Orgburo resolved to rescind that local decision and punish those responsible.[31]

Thus, together with the People's Commissariat of Heavy Industry, the party leadership, motivated by economic expediency, gradually strengthened the authority of managers. Employees of the NKTP were now among the most protected against political arbitrariness in the entire Soviet bureaucracy. The time came, however, when Stalin began to regret this policy introduced in 1931. But Ordzhonikidze held on to his earlier views and this inevitably led to a clash with Stalin.

The first of the well-known conflicts between Ordzhonikidze and Stalin, who was dissatisfied with the independent conduct of the NKTP leadership, came in August 1933. Having difficulty recovering from the crisis spawned by the Great Change, the economy was in particularly bad straits. One of the most intractable problems of industry was the poor quality of products, due in large measure to the mass production of unfinished and shoddy items. Trying to correct the situation, the government employed extreme and repressive measures, such as widely publicized trials against slipshod workers. One trial conducted against employees of a number of economic institutions and the Kommunar factory (in Zaporozhe) over an incomplete shipment of combines caused dissension in the Politburo.

At the end of July 1933, Sovnarkom received several telegrams addressed to Molotov from the provinces which said that the factory Kommunar shipped new combines with a number of the most important parts missing.[32] On the basis of these signals, Sovnarkom adopted a resolution on July 28, "On the Criminal Shipment of Incomplete Combines to the MTS and Sovkhozy." Sovnarkom demanded that the NKTP immediately halt the shipment of incomplete combines and supply the missing parts for the ones shipped earlier. It also ordered the USSR Procurator, Ivan A. Akulov (1888–1938), to arrest and immediately arraign the managers who were guilty of shipping the unfinished combines.[33]

This decision caused protests. The secretary of the Dnepropetrovsk Regional Party Committee, Mendel M. Khataevich (1893–1937), sent a special letter to several addresses: Sovnarkom, the Ukrainian Communist Party Central Committee, the NKTP (Ordzhonikidze), the Central Control Commission, and the procurators of the USSR and Ukraine. He tried to show that Kommunar worked efficiently and that the shipment of unfinished combines was caused by a desire to prevent the theft of components—several combine parts had been shipped separately in special boxes. "On the whole, the factory has more positive attributes than shortcomings. As such, the obkom considers it expedient to institute judicial proceedings against the factory leadership, in particular the factory director, Comrade Shabashvili. But it would be altogether sufficient to limit his punishment to appropriate administrative penalties," wrote Khataevich.[34] Upon receiving this letter, Molotov responded to Khataevich: "The achievements of Kommunar are well known to us, as well as the procuracy. However, this matter will be handled in a civil court because the trial has far-reaching significance, beyond the factory, and its cancellation would unquestionably be inexpedient."[35]

The trial served a didactic purpose. Leaders of enterprises and economic organizations were threatened by charges against the accused, and were reminded that they were responsible if government orders were not followed. "Every directive of the government," said the state prosecutor, Deputy General of the Procuracy (USSR), Andrei Ia. Vyshinskii (1883–1954), at the end of his two-hour summation, "is an operational order that must be unconditionally fulfilled from top to bottom. Only complete execution of orders and discipline will ensure total victory in the battle to build a socialist economy in the USSR." Striving to give greater significance to his example, Vyshinskii stated:

> The trial provides us with a basis for asking general questions about the work of Soviet economic organizations. . . . I'm talking about the People's Commissariat of Agriculture. . . . I'm talking about the People's Commissariat of Heavy Industry. . . . I'm talking about republican organs. I'm very sorry that the circumstances of the preliminary investigations don't allow us to place the main leaders of the Ukraine Combine Factory in the dock . . . and compel us to put aside this affair so as not to delay the whole trial.[36]

Such open threats disturbed Ordzhonikidze, as well as the head of the People's Commissariat of Agriculture, Iakov A. Iakovlev (1896–1938). In Stalin's absence (he was vacationing in the south), they succeeded in carrying a resolution condemning Vyshinskii's address. On August 24, one day after the publication of the deputy procurator's speech, the Politburo called his attention to the inadmissibility of his assessment "that gave grounds for incorrect accusations against the People's Commissariats of Heavy Industry and Agriculture."[37] Stalin soon learned of these events, undoubtedly from Vyshinskii, and agreed more or less with Vyshinskii's actions. Stalin was extremely irritable. "I consider Sergo's tirade against Vyshinskii as hooliganism," he wrote to Molotov on September 1. "How could you give in to him? It's clear that Sergo wanted his protest to frustrate the fulfillment of the production campaign of Sovnarkom and the Central Committee. What's the problem? Did Kaganovich bring this on? Apparently, he did. And he was not alone."[38] Stalin was so outraged that he returned to the incident several days later, on September 12, in his subsequent letter to Molotov:

> It's impossible to classify Sergo's behavior (and Iakovlev's) during the "fulfillment of production" campaign as anything other than anti-party, for it had the objective goal of defending reactionary elements of the party *against* the Central Committee. Indeed, the entire country wages war against nonfulfillment of production; the party began a campaign for fulfillment, an open, publicized, and punitive campaign; it condemned party enemies who insolently and maliciously violated party and government decrees. Sergo (and Iakovlev), who

are responsible for these violations, struck out against the procuracy instead of repenting their sins! For what? Of course, not for restraining reactionary violations of party rulings, but for morally supporting them, justifying them in the eyes of general party opinion, and disparaging the unfolding party campaign. That is besmirching the practical line of the Central Committee. I wrote Kaganovich, accusing him of assisting the camp of reactionary party elements against my expectations.[39]

These letters of Stalin's caused me to make a mistake in my book *1937: Stalin, the NKVD, and Soviet Society* (Moscow, 1992, p. 30). Insofar as Stalin expressed his opinion about the conflict in a letter dated September 1, but then returned to this matter (as if he had yet to decide) on September 12, and reported only then that he had written a letter about this to Kaganovich, I searched for a possible revision of the Politburo resolution concerning Vyshinskii in the protocols after September 1. These efforts proved unsuccessful, and I wrote in my book that the resolution about Vyshinskii was not reviewed. R.W. Davies pointed out this mistake to me a bit later. His careful study of the protocols revealed that already on September 1, 1933, the Politburo had rescinded its August 24 decision concerning Vyshinskii.[40]

But in my opinion, this fact does not refute the general conclusion about the relative independence of Politburo members (including Ordzhonikidze) at the beginning of the 1930s. First, the Politburo resolved this rather major question on the initiative of one of its members—Ordzhonikidze—and without Stalin's knowledge carried a resolution that went against his inclinations (Politburo members, including Ordzhonikidze, understood that Vyshinskii did not act independently). Second, the conflict demonstrated that divergent views were possible, and actually existed, in the Politburo. Molotov, "having conceded" to Ordzhonikidze, according to Stalin, supported harsher policies on this question (his letter to Khataevich suggests this, as does the tone of Stalin's letter). Kaganovich, who had "been put on the spot" (and "he was not alone"), began to waver and to try to mollify the conflict by ceding to Ordzhonikidze. But he then quickly corrected his "mistake" after Stalin's reprimand. Despite his extreme irritation, Stalin himself circulated an explanatory letter to his comrades-in-arms and demonstrated his anxiety by mildly reproaching them for giving in to

Ordzhonikidze, who did not wish "to repent of his sins." Moreover, he returned to this question repeatedly over the next two weeks. Several years later, this situation would have been impossible. The Politburo would not have examined such an important question without Stalin's knowledge, and he would not have had to resort to detailed correspondence with his associates in order to correct some sort of "mistake."

Finally, the circumstances surrounding the revocation of the Politburo decision concerning Vyshinskii remain unclear. Only when the actual protocols of Politburo meetings and related materials become available (at present they remain classified in the Presidential Archive) will it become clear under what circumstances the September 1 decision was taken and what the results of the vote were. It is improbable that the decision of September 1 (unless it were added in the protocols afterward) was the result of Stalin's letter to Molotov on September 1. It is possible that this letter reflected Stalin's reaction to the previously adopted decision. But then it is incomprehensible why he did not mention the September 1 decision, and wrote only of the erroneous August 24 decision, criticizing Ordzhonikidze and reproaching Molotov.

Despite similar conflicts, the general course for increasing the power of the engineers and the autonomy of enterprise leaders was preserved. This was promoted by the need, above all else, to develop industry and overcome the economic crisis, which reached its apogee during the First Five-Year Plan. Relative economic stability was attained in the Second Five-Year Plan. A gradual increase in industrial growth was largely achieved by reforming the system of management. The main change consisted of redistributing some of the powers of the people's commissariats to the enterprises. Ordzhonikidze's departments conducted the most far-reaching of these distinctive economic experiments.

It must be understood that widening the economic independence of enterprise managers strengthened their power and required legal guarantees for their relative security. Such guarantees were acknowledged from time to time. In the spring of 1934, for example, the Office of the Procurator set up a new procedure for instituting criminal proceedings against managers, engineers, and technical workers in cases relating to production. In accordance with the new rules, criminal proceedings, except in a few stipulated instances, could take place "only with the decision of the procurator of the krai (oblast), or the republican procu-

Sergo Ordzhonikidze, Stalin's head manager in the 1930s.

rator in the absence of a regional division. In these cases, preliminary agreement with appropriate economic organizations is essential." The leadership of the procuracy demanded "the assurance of systematic procuratorial supervision over investigations in these cases." Investigatory organs were allowed "to summon managers and engineers for questioning only with the sanction of the appropriate procuracy and only if such a summons would not interfere with production. The procurator would be personally responsible for unnecessary summonses of managers and specialists."[41]

Of course, such instructions and laws would have been meaningless if not for the active and even "aggressive" stand of the NKTP leadership on the question of cadres. Ordzhonikidze himself did not fully understand economic and organizational matters, and was a typical administrator of the Stalinist mold—energetic, crude, and harsh. He completely mastered only one method of leadership: putting pressure on subordinates, keeping firm control over the "economy," and promoting leaders who employed the same methods locally to ensure success. He especially valued the right to personally control the fate of subordinates.

There were numerous cases in which Ordzhonikidze sought to break up organized attempts to frame managers, even large-scale actions prepared by the NKVD (political police). For example, the Politburo immediately adopted three resolutions on December 3, 1933, concerning NKTP employees. Two of these resolutions rescinded earlier Politburo decisions on the arraignment of the heads of the Kramatorsk Factory (for a blast furnace accident) and the Pribalkhashsk Construction Plant (for disruption of construction plans). Instead of a court case, the Politburo ordered Ordzhonikidze "to punish the guilty with administrative sanctions." The Politburo also revoked the decision of provincial organs expelling from the party two construction specialists who had worked in the Far East.[42]

For Ordzhonikidze, the so-called Ural Machine Factory trial was yet another example of interference. It was conducted in the summer of 1934 at the Ural Machine Factory, after the NKVD fabricated accusations of organizational sabotage, arresting workers and charging them with damaging machinery and arson.[43] As usual, during the investigation those arrested were coerced to implicate a large group of other workers who allegedly conspired in the "sabotage." New shocking re-criminations awaiting the factory, however, were thwarted.

Ordzhonikidze arrived at the Ural Machine Factory at the end of August 1934. At a factory meeting he stated:

> I think there was a trial here not long ago of a small circle of crooks, scoundrels, and rogues—this will be the last such one here at Ural Machine Factory [applause]. . . . Comrades . . . several years ago the engineering personnel were extremely hesitant. . . . But today, when our country has triumphed on the industrial front and in foreign affairs, there of course can no longer be any talk of our engineers, with whom we built these factories, being untrustworthy.

Ordzhonikidze recalled that the defendants had given depositions against other factory workers involved in sabotage, and reported to those assembled that no new charges would be forthcoming:

> We answered that the devil knows what sort of duplicity there was. We summoned these people and said that we have testimony against them. Tell me, will you work honestly or not? [applause]. If not—we'll have another conversation. I think that this trial and this group of people will be the last in our factory. As we settle down to work, we'll curse them for causing so much trouble and harm to our efforts and the nation as a whole.[44]

In carrying out these activities, Ordzhonikidze apparently enlisted Stalin's support in some form or another. One can say with certainty that Ordzhonikidze informed Stalin, who was vacationing in the south, about his trip to the Urals. Ordzhonikidze's personal papers contain Stalin's short reply, written on September 18, 1934: "I received your letter. It's good that you were able to spend almost a month in the Urals. I am against official 'one-hour' trips—well-publicized, but fruitless visits. But I'm altogether for those trips that are *long* (for 1–2 months) and *serious*, that are useful and don't create unnecessary fanfare."[45]

At the very same time, Ordzhonikidze fought against the organization of yet another trial—at the Kuznetsk Metallurgical Combine. We can judge the nature of this conflict from Vyshinskii's notes to Molotov on October 5, 1934. Vyshinskii reported that the procurator of the West-Siberian region had conducted an investigation by order of the national procuracy regarding information provided by the newspapers *Pravda* and *For Industrialization*, as well as by complaints of a number of factories about poor-quality products from the Kuznetsk complex. Verification of this revealed the mass production of worthless goods. As a result, charges were brought against several engineers and technical workers, some of whom already had received previous convictions for sabotage. The head of the main administration of the NKTP metallurgical industry, A.I. Gurevich, reviewed this matter with the national procurator in Moscow and agreed with the charges. The affair, however, soon reached a standstill. "Comrades Ordzhonikidze and [Robert I.] Eikhe (1890–1940) [secretary of the West-Siberian regional party organization—O.Kh.] objected to conducting this trial," Vyshinskii reported to Molotov, along with a request for instructions. Molotov's response reads: "To comrades Zhdanov and Kuibyshev. We must discuss this in the Central Committee."[46]

Of course, the fact that Ordzhonikidze had to constantly defend his workers and intercede on their behalf with the punitive organs proves that even in the best of times, the People's Commissariat of Heavy Industry was not immune to repression. Hopes for serious support, however, clearly inspired confidence in NKTP workers. Many enterprise managers remained sufficiently independent and did not hesitate to challenge representatives of the punitive organs. The documents provide evidence of clashes with the procurator involving several highly placed people in the southern metallurgical factories, including Ordzhonikidze.

In November 1933, the national procuracy, in executing the special resolution of the Central Committee and the Council of Labor and Defense (USSR), ordered the transport procurator of the southern railroads to conduct investigations into the downtime and damage to rolling stock at the Rykov and Voroshilov factories. Verification confirmed a significant downtime in transport affairs and a barbaric handling of equipment (unloading, for example, was sped up by making holes in the floor of train cars). The investigation got bogged down, however, owing to the opposition of the directors of both factories. As the national procurator, Akulov, reported to the chairman of the Central Control Commission, Rudzutak, on November 26, 1933:

> The directors of the factories, Comrades Puchkov and Prapor, not only fail to cooperate with the procuracy in exposing the criminal attitude of the guilty parties toward transport, but actually hinder the

investigation. . . . Comrade Prapor forbade the transport shops of his factory to give necessary evidence for the procurator's investigation, didn't permit legal experts on the factory grounds, and blocked the police from fulfilling the procurator's order to arrest the deputy head of the transport shop . . . who refused to appear for questioning at the investigator's summons.

Comrade Puchkov gave orders not to allow procuracy employees on factory grounds, and forbade anyone from giving any evidence about downtime and damage to train cars to the procuracy. He also commanded the deputy director of commercial affairs, . . . the head of the towing service, . . . and other people summoned for questioning, not to appear. . . . Moreover, Comrade Puchkov threatened the assistant procurator of the southern railroads . . . and ordered the factory security forces to shoot the police if they showed up at the factory on order of the procuracy.[47]

Akulov asked Rudzutak to call the directors to account to the party and simultaneously complained to Ordzhonikidze.

On November 27, Ordzhonikidze sent Akulov (with a copy to Rudzutak) the following reply:

After your oral report to me at the Sovnarkom meeting, I gave specific instructions to Comrade Shleifer of the Steel Plant and the technical director of the Rykov Factory, Comrade Butenko (who returned yesterday), to cooperate with investigative authorities and the procuracy in all cases.

At the same time I'm enclosing a clipping from the newspaper *For Industrialization* from November 27 that includes demands from the deputy procurator of transport of the southern railroads, Comrade Grankin. Please pay close attention to these absurd demands.[48]

The enclosed material, under the heading "A Document Remarkable in Its Own Way," contained Grankin's letter to the management of the Enakievskii Metallurgical Factory with demands for a detailed report on the condition of railroad cars and locomotives (according to a detailed inventory). An accompanying editorial stated:

What will the factories do if they have to respond to the pettiest demands from the transport procurator, who keeps burdening them with impossible accounting procedures? It should be well known to the transport procurator that repeated decisions by the government and organs of the Workers' and Peasants' Inspectorate have freed managers and enterprises from superfluous and harmful bookkeeping.

After running into opposition from Ordzhonikidze, Akulov complained to the Politburo. On December 5, 1933, the Politburo was polled and carried a resolution consonant with Akulov's note concerning the enforced idleness and damage to the rolling stock at NKTP factories. The resolution, however, was mild: "We propose that Comrade Ordzhonikidze punish the guilty with administrative sanctions in the case of enforced idleness and damage to the rolling stock at the Voroshilov, Rykov, Kramatorsk, and Magnitogorsk factories."[49] True, Ordzhonikidze several weeks later demonstrated objectivity in this affair. On January 1, 1934, the Central Committee Secretariat adopted Ordzhonikidze's proposal on firing the director of the Voroshilov Factory, Prapor, "for failure to cope with his work."[50]

As in most conflicts, this episode contains many barely discernible and "informal" realities. Above all, attention must be paid to the extremely independent position of factory directors who readily battled the public prosecutor and threatened the police with their own armed security. Local procurators were practically powerless. The only course open to them was to complain to Moscow. But directors were not obliged to do what the national procurator ordered. He could only seek help from the Central Control Commission of the Workers' and Peasants' Inspectorate, and complain to Ordzhonikidze. In spite of Ordzhonikidze's positive reply to the procurator, he actually again defended his subordinates. He not only failed to punish the accused, but presented Akulov with counter charges against the procurators for their arbitrariness. (There is some suspicion that the publication *For Industrialization* referred to by Ordzhonikidze was prepared solely for this case. The editorial commentary appended to the transport procurator's letter noted that the newspaper had already written about his order in its November 22 issue. Meanwhile, the NKTP newspaper had criticized procurator Grankin's actions twice in the course of several days. It is unlikely this would have happened if it had not been for Akulov's appeal to Ordzhonikidze.) Finally, the Politburo, clearly at Ordzhonikidze's request, also adopted the mildest of possible resolutions.

The large number of facts of this sort strongly suggests that the active protection of the NKTP's employees was one of Ordzhonikidze's chief concerns and the principal foundation of his policies. This does not mean, of course, that the People's Commissariat of Heavy Industry was completely shielded from all repressions. Arrests, dismissals from work, and impositions of party penalties were so widespread at this time that it was practically impossible to control every case and intervene in all disputes. Ordzhonikidze himself often dealt severely with guilty subordinates. But reserving this right for himself, he reacted angrily to the interference in commissariat affairs by numerous party-state control boards and punitive organs. Both the heads and staff of these organs and Ordzhonikidze's subordinates knew this. In a system where laws were mere formalities and real power and influence counted for everything, Ordzhonikidze's position proved to be decisive.

Chapter 5

Ordzhonikidze and Kirov

During the Khrushchev thaw,* an account based on the memoirs of Old Bolsheviks appeared that spoke of the existence of a group of highly placed party leaders who aspired to remove Stalin from the post of general secretary in 1934. After reaching a preliminary agreement in January 1934 at the Seventeenth Party Congress, they allegedly tried to propose Sergei M. Kirov as general secretary. He refused. Learning of this, Stalin took measures to prepare reprisals against delegates to the congress, especially Kirov.[1] In several memoirs, Ordzhonikidze is named as one of those who apparently took part in these plans against Stalin. Roy A. Medvedev maintains that it was in Ordzhonikidze's apartment that the decision was made to back Kirov at the Seventeenth Congress.

To what extent does this actually correspond with the facts? Were Kirov and Ordzhonikidze allied against Stalin? There is no reliable evidence apart from the memoirists' assertions. All that is apparent is that Kirov and Ordzhonikidze were on friendly terms at the time. It is well known that Kirov, Ordzhonikidze, and Stalin carried on a lively corre-

---

*Khrushchev thaw. The relaxation of controls over society in the aftermath of Stalin's death resulting in a brief but impressive bloom of literary and artistic creativity that delved into formerly taboo subjects. The period takes its name from a novella by that title authored by Ilya Ehrenburg and published in 1954. Khrushchev promoted the thaw for his own reasons and encouraged public discussion of the Stalin question with his "secret speech" at the Twentieth Party Congress in 1956, in which he publicly condemned Stalin.—Ed.

spondence, and it is likely that these letters were removed and presumably destroyed after Kirov's death. In any case, a commission created in the 1950s to investigate Kirov's murder was unable to find them.[2] What seems unusual, of course, are the circumstances that prevented Ordzhonikidze from meeting with Kirov on the eve of his murder, but then took him to Leningrad as a member of the Politburo commission investigating the causes of the tragedy.

Anatoly N. Rybakov's acclaimed novel *Children of the Arbat* contains the following scene: Moscow, November 1934—a plenum of the Central Committee discusses abolishing ration cards. Kirov meets Ordzhonikidze in the foyer during a break. Stalin approaches them. Not looking at Kirov, Stalin coldly utters a few words and moves on. The experienced Sergo becomes worried: "Today, in the course of a two-minute conversation with Stalin in the foyer, Ordzhonikidze clearly understood the true nature of the relationship between Stalin and Kirov. Ordzhonikidze knew Stalin, knew what it meant when Stalin talked to someone but didn't look at him."

Ominous premonitions that had gnawed at him for some time and warning signals that bombarded him from all sides came together at that moment and made Ordzhonikidze realize that danger threatened Kirov. "There is only one thing to do: stall for time. It's necessary to detain Kirov in Moscow for at least several days or even a week. It's necessary to think everything over, consult with comrades, and perhaps persuade Kirov to transfer to Moscow. The main problem is that Kirov's unexpected delay in Moscow would put Stalin on guard, and he might possibly go back on his word," thought Ordzhonikidze. But he resolved not to tell Kirov about his apprehensions. In order to detain his stubborn comrade, he had to be cunning. Ordzhonikidze ordered his driver to make sure Kirov was late for the train. The chauffeur, however, staged a "breakdown" in an inappropriate place—at a tram stop. Kirov leapt onto the tram's running board and got to the train a minute before it departed. He was murdered two days later.

This scene in Rybakov's novel was most likely based on several sources. The main source was probably Stanislav Krasnikov's book titled *Sergei Mironovich Kirov: Life and Work*, which describes Kirov's departure from Moscow after the November 1934 plenum as follows: "Sergei Mironovich leapt onto the 'Red Arrow' after the train had already started moving. Chudov, Kodatskii, and other Leningrad participants in the Central Committee plenum anxiously met him on the train's platform, worried that something had happened to him en route to the station.

"'No, nothing's wrong. Sergo wanted me to stay with him another day. . . .' "[3]

Another source is the brief memoirs of Zinaida Gavrilovna Ordzhonikidze, published in *Izvestia* on the anniversary of Sergo's death on February 18, 1939. Ordzhonikidze's widow described how Sergo had once wanted Kirov to stay with him, and actually ordered his driver to remain in Moscow. Zinaida Gavrilovna does not report in which year this event happened, but provides vital information several lines later: Having fallen ill in Tbilisi, Ordzhonikidze arrived in Moscow in November 1934 only after Kirov's departure. Rybakov ignores this evidence in his well-known version, and in fact blends elements from Krasnikov's book with contradictory material from Zinaida Gavrilovna's memoirs. After the appearance of Rybakov's novel, Krasnikov's suppositions were resurrected and gained currency as firmly established facts.[4]

It is possible that Rybakov had grounds for doubting the accounts of Ordzhonikidze's widow, especially since they were published in the official Soviet cant of the late 1930s. Although Krasnikov's version lacks any references to sources, it was based (judging by context) on memoirs that appeared during the "thaw" and therefore could lay claim to great authenticity. The fact that Ordzhonikidze tried to delay Kirov, even though Krasnikov does not comment on it, is significant. It is generally well known that Kirov and Ordzhonikidze were friends and trusted each other. When he arrived in Moscow from Leningrad, Kirov typically stayed at Ordzhonikidze's apartment and held conversations with him lasting many hours. ("Kirov always stayed with us when he was in Moscow. He usually notified us the night before that he would arrive the following morning, and Sergo would always wait to have breakfast with him. After this, they both went to work and then met again late in the evening. They ate dinner and then settled in the dining room or study. Sergo rested on the couch, while Kirov sat beside him as they began a long and intimate conversation," wrote Zinaida Gavrilovna.)

It is altogether possible that the experienced Ordzhonikidze could have suspected that something was amiss. In general, it is natural to question the nature of the last conversation between Kirov and Ord-zhonikidze. Interest in their final meeting was sparked for an obvious reason: the Central Committee plenum met in Moscow between November 25 and 28, and Kirov and Ordzhonikidze could have had extensive contact for several days prior to the tragic murder. What was discussed at these meetings? Did they speed up preparations for Kirov's murder in Leningrad? Asking these questions, however, is useless because Ordzhonikidze was not in Moscow, and did not meet with Kirov. This is just one more of those errant suppositions based on numerous misunderstandings and suspicious coincidences surrounding December 1, 1934, which, at the very least, we need to untangle.

On November 1, 1934, Ordzhonikidze left for Makhachkala on business, intending to continue on to Baku and Tiflis. The next day, Ordzhonikidze's assistant, Semushkin, sent him an urgent telegram stating that the Politburo would extend Ordzhonikidze's vacation until November 15.[5] It seemed logical since the celebration of the October Revolution was imminent, and it was better to spend the holiday in his native Georgia than somewhere on the road. Moreover, it was necessary to return to Moscow by the 20th, before the plenum began. In the company of the Transcaucasian party secretary, Lavrentii P. Beria (1899–1953), Ordzhonikidze arrived in Baku on November 3. He spent the next several days at numerous meetings and visits to oil refineries, which the local press reported on in detail. On November 6, following dinner at the apartment of the first secretary of the Central Committee of the Communist Party of Azerbaidzhan, Mir D. Bagirov (1896–1956), Ordzhonikidze (as Zinaida Gavrilovna wrote at the end of the 1950s) suddenly fell ill—his temperature rose, and he got the chills. In spite of this, he left with Beria by special train for Tiflis.[6] On November 7, Ordzhonikidze and Beria went directly from the station to take part in a parade commemorating the anniversary of the October Revolution. But on the night of November 7, while staying at Beria's apartment, Ordzhonikidze began to have serious intestinal bleeding and acute stomach pains. According to his medical diagnosis, he subsequently suffered a "serious heart attack aggravated by underlying myocarditis and food poisoning" on the morning of November 11. Local doctors decided to request help from Moscow,[7] and three professors from the Kremlin clinic came to examine Ordzhonikidze. Judging from the reminiscences of one of the Tbilisi doctors, I.S. Frangulian, as well as entries from a notebook of Ordzhonikidze's assistant, Semushkin, the commissar's illness confounded the specialists, who could not establish its causes or character.[8]

Ordzhonikidze soon recovered. Thanks to painstaking care and a strict diet, his condition improved. Archival documents show that he already started back to work by November 16 and transmitted orders to Moscow.[9] Against his doctors' wishes, Ordzhonikidze apparently intended to return to the capital. This became known in Moscow. On November 19, Tiflis received a coded telegram:

> Decipher quickly. Tiflis. Transcaucasian VKP [Communist Party]. Deliver to Ordzhonikidze and Beria. Reporting the Central Committee resolution of November 18: (1) Comrade Ordzhonikidze must strictly fulfill his doctors' instructions and not return to Moscow before November 26 without their permission. (2) It is decided that Pletnev and Fronshtein will depart for Moscow, while Levin remains in Tiflis with the local doctors to treat the patient and then accompany him to Moscow. (3) Forbid the NKTP from pestering Comrade Ordzhonikidze with routine questions. Secretary of the Central Committee of the Communist Party, Stalin.[10]

In addition, Stalin sent a personal telegram on November 20:

> Tiflis. Transcaucasian VKP. Deliver to Ordzhonikidze. It is better to wait until the twenty-sixth. Don't take your illness lightly. Regards. Stalin.[11]

Ordzhonikidze was not able to ignore this command. Despite his recovery, he busied himself with trivial matters in Tiflis, such as visiting the construction of a hospital unit, as Frangulian recalled, rather than return to Moscow early.

Ordzhonikidze carried out Stalin's orders and arrived in the capital on November 29. The Central Committee plenum had concluded the night before, but its participants, including Kirov, had already left for home in order to discuss the plenary decisions among party activists, as was customary. Judging from Zinaida Gavrilovna's memoirs, Kirov told Sergo's chauffeur before his departure: "I have not seen Sergo for a long time. I badly want to see him!" Ordzhonikidze himself often told his wife in Tiflis that "he would like to see Kirov, because it had already been three months since he had done so, and he missed him." Upon returning to Moscow, Ordzhonikidze immediately called Kirov in Leningrad.[12]

Two days later, news about Kirov's murder reached Moscow. In the obituary, published on December 2 in all newspapers, Ordzhonikidze's signature appeared second after Stalin's. This broke the usual hierarchy (Sergo typically signed after Molotov, Kalinin, and Voroshilov) and demonstrated the special nature of Ordzhonikidze's relationship with Kirov. Ordzhonikidze was not, however, included in the group of national leaders who quickly left for Leningrad. Stalin, Molotov, Voroshilov, and Kirov's replacement, Andrei A. Zhdanov (1898–1948), departed on the morning of December 2. Some accounts contend that Stalin had opposed the inclusion of Ordzhonikidze. Apprehensive that Ordzhonikidze's presence in Leningrad would upset his plans, Stalin allegedly told him: "It's impossible for you to go with your weak heart."[13] No documentary evidence concerning discussion of Ordzhonikidze's trip has been found. If this matter had been raised, then Ordzhonikidze's illness surely might have been used as an excuse to prevent him from traveling to Leningrad.

Ordzhonikidze took Kirov's death very hard. According to Semēn Z. Ginzburg (b. 1897), who at the time held a responsible post in the NKTP, Ordzhonikidze did not show up at work for several days, and when he did, colleagues "did not recognize the typically enthusiastic and vivacious Sergo. He had turned gray and aged noticeably. He often seemed lost in thought, with a face heavy from grief."[14] "Something in him had clearly snapped; he became withdrawn, grew reticent and even more lost in concentration," noted Ginzburg in later publications.[15] In the words of another of Ordzhonikidze's colleagues, A.V. Ziskind (as recounted by I.N. Kramov), Ordzhonikidze in those days "was seriously ill, deathly so. He collapsed from a heart attack when he learned that Kirov had been shot. . . . When I entered his Kremlin apartment, Pletnev was examining the ill Sergo. He left Sergo in a somber mood, and said: 'It's serious—his heart can't take it . . . his funeral might not be far off.' "[16]

Ordzhonikidze, however, gradually improved. "He soon was another person."[17] But he did not appear at the funeral service in Red Square on December 6.

Did Ordzhonikidze have any doubts about the official version of Kirov's murder? Did he believe Stalin, who accused the Zinovievites of this terrorist act? The questions will never be answered in full. But to categorically reject the possibility that Ordzhonikidze wondered about the real reasons for the events of December 1 would be wrong. He was a sufficiently experienced politician who had passed through the Stalinist school of power struggles. Yet this did not mean that he was prepared for what took place.

Ordzhonikidze was soon to receive yet another blow—the fall of Lominadze.

Chapter 6

Lominadze's Suicide

After Lominadze's fall from grace at the end of 1930 (see chapter 3), his political standing slowly but surely improved owing mostly to Ordzhonikidze's support. At first, Lominadze worked as head of the scientific-research sector of the People's Commissariat of Supply. Ordzhonikidze then took him under his own wing and succeeded in getting Lominadze appointed secretary of the party committee of Moscow Factory No. 24, a plant that made airplane engines. This position had many advantages. Ordzhonikidze could now directly support Lo-minadze. Nikita S. Khrushchev, working at the time as secretary of the Moscow City Party Committee, recalled:

> Sergo called me several times at the Moscow committee when he had questions. One day, he asked: "Comrade Khrushchev" (he spoke with a strong Georgian accent), "why don't you ever give Lominadze peace of mind instead of always criticizing him?" I answered: "Comrade Sergo, you know, after all, that Lominadze is one of the most active oppositionists, even an organizer of the opposition. We demand precise accounts from him, but he responds vaguely and invites criticism of himself. What am I to do? After all, this is a fact." "Listen, Comrade Khrushchev, you just do whatever it takes to harass him less."[1]

Moreover, rapid advancement in the aviation industry, which enjoyed the special attention and patronage of higher powers, allowed for more public exposure and more rapid career promotion than if one were engaged in the less prestigious "supply front." In August 1933,

Lominadze was awarded an Order of Lenin and soon received a promotion—he left Moscow to become the secretary of the city party committee in Magnitogorsk.

Positions such as this were unique in the party hierarchy. Along with the People's Commissariat of Heavy Industry, the Magnitogorsk party organization was responsible for developing and completing a gigantic metallurgical project that was the symbol of the nation's industrial might. It was a rare day when newspapers did not write about the Magnitogorsk Combine. The Kremlin followed his work closely, especially Stalin. Magnitogorsk city leaders also watched closely. It was easy to fail under the burden of such heavy responsibilities and immediately lose everything. But then, every successful or merely decisive move was noticed, too. Success in Magnitogorsk turned into national fame and glory, providing potential career advancement. Not many disgraced oppositionists encountered such a propitious change of fate, and Lominadze tried honestly to take advantage of this second chance.

"In Magnitogorsk, the first day of his arrival," witnessed John Scott,* who labored at the Magnitogorsk Combine for five years, "Lominadze worked like a beaver. An excellent orator, he made speech after speech to functionaries, engineers, and workers, explaining, persuading, cajoling, and encouraging. He demanded the greatest sacrifices from his subordinates. These, incidentally, he tended to choose from a circle of personal friends, many of whom had, like himself, at one time or another been associated with some opposition group."[2]

At the end of January 1934, Lominadze arrived in Moscow for the Seventeenth Party Congress. Like other disgraced oppositionists (Kamenev, Zinoviev, Rykov, Bukharin, Tomskii, Karl Radek [1885–1939], and Evgenii A. Preobrazhenskii [1886–1937]), Lominadze had to stand before the congress tribune to repent past transgressions and to glorify Stalin. Admitting his undeniable participation in the "right–left bloc," he enumerated and condemned his mistakes in detail while

---

*John Scott. An American college student who during the Great Depression left the University of Wisconsin in 1931 for the Soviet Union, where he worked as a welder in the new city of Magnitogorsk, known as the Soviet Union's Pittsburgh. Scott's memoirs of his experience in Red Russia were first published in 1942 and were later reissued by Indiana University Press in 1973, and again, with a new introduction by Stephen Kotkin, in 1990.—Ed.

acknowledging his failure to understand the "brilliantly simple, pro-
found, clear, and rich theoretical contents of Comrade Stalin's thesis
that the destruction of classes takes place in the process of fiercest class
struggle. . . . The right–left bloc," said Lominadze,

> comprised a variety of opportunistic oppositions during the new stage
> in the struggle and, like any opposition, inhibited the party from
> moving forward. . . . It was smashed, routed by the party's principled
> irreconcilability that distinguished its fight against all deviations from
> the Leninist line. In the struggle with the "right–left bloc," Comrade
> Stalin evinced the same severe impatience that had set Lenin apart in
> his battle with oppositionists, an impatience that he—Stalin—inher-
> ited from Lenin.[3]

Despite the unpleasantries of having to criticize and disparage himself, Lominadze took the invitation to participate in the work of the
congress as a reassuring sign. Unlike others, Lominadze was invited to
the congress not simply to repent, as were Zinoviev, Kamenev, and
Preobrazhenskii, but to serve as a delegate, albeit a nonvoting one.
Lominadze spoke not only as a former oppositionist, but also as a representative of one of the most important party organizations. He spoke
confidently and at great length as he put forth several proposals.

Soon afterward, it appeared that the congress had been especially
fortuitous for Lominadze. The successful resolution of a conflict between Lominadze and the head of the Magnitogorsk Metallurgical
Combine, Avraamii P. Zaveniagin (1901–1956), underscored Lominadze's
fortunate turn of fate.

Clashes in the provinces between managers and party leaders were
common in the 1930s. Both possessed real power. Managers controlled
material resources and could provide or withhold money, personnel,
and transportation. Party leaders claimed power as "bosses," utilizing
the levers of party discipline. The resolution of such conflicts, which
were often drawn-out and bitter, mainly depended upon the direction
of the general line. In the first years of the Great Change, when
"spetsbaiting" flourished and every manager was labeled a potential
"wrecker," the power of party organs reached their peak. Secretaries of
party committees often took on the day-to-day management of enterprises, and interfered in resolving key problems. The negative conse-

quences of this, as already mentioned, prompted the launching of a new campaign—"the strengthening of one-man management." From then on, Moscow usually sided with factory directors. Direct interference in production cost more than one district or city secretary his post. In general, if Lominadze had been an "average Joe" or if Stalin had wished to intervene, then the secretary of the Magnitogorsk City Party Committee would have faced serious difficulties. But Ordzhonikidze once again got involved in the affair.

Hostility between Zaveniagin and Lominadze erupted immediately after the latter's arrival in Magnitogorsk. Impatient and thirsting for recognition, Lominadze fervently set to work and immediately violated certain "limits" that Zaveniagin—with good reason—considered within his own domain. Passions flared. Zaveniagin complained to Ordzhonikidze, but his attempts to squelch the conflict were unsuccessful. At the end of January 1934, Zaveniagin again wrote Ordzhonikidze:

> Lominadze wants to be completely in charge at Magnitka [Magnitogorsk], and isn't inhibited by any bounds or party instructions. My report to you, your directives, my repeated conversations with him and my rebuffs, delicate but firm, achieved nothing. Moreover, on theoretical grounds he is violating the principle of one-man management. The question has been raised for discussion at party meetings. It was also discussed at a party conference in accordance with the secretary's instructions and the encouragement of the party organization. As a result, in spite of my harsh remonstrations, reprimands, and daily exhortations, discipline at the factory and construction sites is not being strengthened, but is actually weakening. The threat of collapse grows every day. . . . It's clear to me that you must remove both of us, or at least one of us. As far as I'm concerned, I would prefer to be removed rather than witness this kind of deterioration.

Zaveniagin's letter began with these harsh words and provided many supporting facts. He wrote that without prior agreement, combine workers were named to positions in the city's party committee, and that the leader of the city party control commission "literally harassed all shops and administrative employees with dismissals, arraignments, reprimands, and affronts to party collegiality, etc." Furthermore, Lominadze encouraged managers who did not get along with Zaveniagin to ally with him and interfere with drafting plans.

Zaveniagin understood that his position was strong, and therefore took the offensive. But also knowing about the special relationship between Lominadze and Ordzhonikidze, he crafted the letter diplomatically:

> My letter to you might seem tendentious and caustic, and even an exaggerated account of the true situation. For this reason, I waited ten days before sending it to you. The facts about which I speak are of such importance, however, that it would be a big mistake to downplay them or remain silent. I'm aware of your good relations with Lominadze, and it appears that you are close to Stalin also. This makes it more difficult to raise these concerns with you. It's worse, though, to let an illness go untreated and ruin things.[4]

Ordzhonikidze found himself in difficult straits for the umpteenth time. He did not want to openly take sides. As the people's commissar of heavy industry, he supported the directors in similar situations. To do otherwise now would demonstrate bias and lack of principle. But Ordzhonikidze could not condemn Lominadze because, in contrast to Zaveniagin, he knew the real nature of Stalin's relationship with Lominadze. Cognizant of the fact that in the given situation Lominadze should back down, Ordzhonikidze summoned him and appropriately reprimanded him. Beso yielded, at least verbally, and upon returning to Magnitogorsk he attempted to amend his relationship with Zaveniagin. "As a result of conversing with him," Lominadze reported to Ordzhonikidze,

> I'm convinced that all misunderstandings between us are settled. The next day I called a meeting of the key employees of Magnitka (ten people), patiently waited two and a half hours for Zaveniagin to arrive, and informed those present of my trip to Moscow and discussions with you and Kaganovich. I then raised the question of the improper activities of the city control commission [control commission of the party city committee—O.Kh.], the GPU, etc. Things went calmly and well, and we left the meeting with the impression that our relationship had been put right.[5]

The truce, however, did not last long. Zaveniagin went to Moscow and again complained to Ordzhonikidze about Lominadze. Allies of Lominadze reported this in Magnitogorsk. Beso was outraged and wrote Ordzhonikidze a scathing letter. He reiterated his attempts at reconciliation, denied all charges, and described Zaveniagin in the following manner: "Nobody likes him because he's a man in a shell, withdrawn, anti-social, and an armchair employee. Nobody respects him because he's weak."[6]

Ordzhonikidze answered with a letter that reproached and needled Lominadze. He wrote that "the problem needs to be resolved quickly." Lominadze agreed with these demands, although he once again revealed his true self. He was polite after Zaveniagin's return, but wrote in reply to Ordzhonikidze that if Zaveniagin behaved as before, and "it appears that he is about to disrupt things," then "it will be necessary to appoint a more pliable secretary here."[7]

In general, the tension was only slightly alleviated and grounds for a new quarrel quickly arose. Lominadze convened the regularly scheduled plenum of the city party committee, but several members, including Zaveniagin, did not show up. Lominadze viewed this action as a violation of party discipline, and had Zaveniagin penalized. The conflict was reported in the press, and the Politburo's attention was drawn to the Magnitogorsk affair. Zaveniagin and Lominadze were summoned to Moscow. On June 9, 1934, in the presence of practically all members of the Politburo—Stalin, Kliment E. Voroshilov (1881–1969), Kaganovich, Kalinin, Kuibyshev, Ordzhonikidze, and Mikoyan—they both reported on the situation at the combine. Each spoke about construction projects, as well as technical, financial, personnel, and social problems. They did not neglect the conflict between the city committee and combine director, and listened to each other's position.

From the beginning, Ordzhonikidze helped prepare this issue for the Politburo. He made a report and proposed his own draft resolution. Review of the conflict ended peacefully. The decree, confirmed two weeks later, read:

> [The Politburo] takes into consideration the statements of Comrades Lominadze and Zaveniagin that they are ending the outstanding friction between themselves through friendly cooperation, and that they ensure the fulfillment of this Central Committee resolution. Considering the city committee's decision to be correct, the Central Committee agrees that a number of party members who failed to appear at the plenum violated party discipline. The Central Committee takes

into account Comrade Zaveniagin's statement that he could not attend the city committee meeting due to work-related pressures at the factory. In connection with this, it also takes into consideration Comrade Lominadze's statement that the city committee reconsider its own resolution in regard to Comrade Zaveniagin.

The Politburo resolution satisfied Lominadze's request to name as his assistant Mazut, who had worked with Beso in the Comintern. Both of these points—the cooperation between Zaveniagin and Lominadze and the appointment of Mazut—were written on the draft resolution by Ordzhonikidze.[8]

Lominadze returned to Magnitogorsk and immersed himself in his responsibilities. By involving himself in the affairs of the city party organization and combine, he maintained regular contact with Moscow. Lominadze sent one of his last letters to Stalin and Ordzhonikidze on November 21, 1934. He wrote about financing industrial construction, housing, and other needs in Magnitogorsk for 1935. He complained that the Politburo estimate of 250 million rubles for the main administration of the NKTP's metallurgical industry had been reduced to 220 million, and asked Stalin and Ordzhonikidze to restore the previous figure.[9]

Lominadze and Ordzhonikidze soon became convinced, however, that Stalin neither forgot nor forgave anything. Following Kirov's murder, the NKVD, on Stalin's instructions, began to fabricate cases concerning the participation of former oppositionists in terrorist acts. Despite the lack of any proof, many arrests took place. "Evidence" was forced from those arrested in an attempt to create an appearance of conspiracy on the part of deviationists. Hundreds of people were sacrificed in this operation—including Lominadze.

Lominadze had found out earlier that the NKVD had received reports about his participation in a "counterrevolutionary organization" in 1932. He wrote Stalin a letter trying to prove his innocence. There was no reply. Repressions began in Magnitogorsk. On December 31, the wife of one of Lominadze's closest associates, who had been expelled from the party and sentenced to exile for "Trotskyism," committed suicide.

On January 16, 1935, a special session of the NKVD sentenced nineteen people accused of conspiracy in the fabricated "Moscow Center"

case to various terms of incarceration. Zinoviev, Kamenev, G.E. Evdokimov, I.P. Bakaev, and other long-term members of the party received
from five to ten years. On the same day, the NKVD also handed down
sentences for the so-called "Leningrad Counterrevolutionary Zinoviev-
ite Group." Seventy-seven people, among whom were such party luminaries as G.I. Safarov and P.A. Zalutskii, were sentenced to camps or
exile.[10]

After these punishments were meted out, Lominadze no longer harbored any illusions. On January 18, he left in his automobile for
Cheliabinsk upon a summons from the local regional committee there.
Several hours passed of agonizing vacillation. He had already traveled
120 kilometers from Magnitogorsk when Lominadze ordered the driver
to turn around. Lominadze apparently wrote his last letter in the vehi-
cle, and then shot himself in the heart with a Browning only seven or
eight kilometers from his home.

The shot was not initially fatal. Lominadze was still alive when they
brought him to his house. But on the night of January 18, an operation
failed to save him and Lominadze died the next morning.[11] Earlier, his
deputy, Mazut, dictated Lominadze's letter to Moscow by telephone. At
12:45 A.M. on January 19, Ordzhonikidze's assistant, Semushkin, received the following text from Magnitogorsk:

> Comrade Mazut. I request that this message be passed on to Comrade
> Ordzhonikidze.
>
> I decided long ago to choose this ending in the event that no one
> believed me. Scoundrels such as Safarov and others apparently spread
> slander against me. I was ready to prove the absurdity and complete
> lack of truth in this libel, to justify myself and attempt to persuade
> others—but even then I wasn't sure they would believe me.
>
> Please convey all this, as I now cannot.
>
> I did nothing wrong in 1932. I explained my actions accurately to
> Comrades Stalin and Ryndin [secretary of the Cheliabinsk regional
> organization—O.Kh.]. Apparently, that wasn't enough. An ordeal
> awaits that I am in no condition to endure.
>
> In spite of all my mistakes, I have devoted my entire adult life to
> the Communist cause, to the affairs of our party. I only regret that I
> didn't live to see a decisive struggle in the international arena. It isn't
> far off.
>
> I die fully believing in the victory of our cause.

Convey to Sergo Ordzhonikidze the contents of this letter.
Please help my family. Beso.[12]

At first, there was no official reaction to Lominadze's death. Local
newspapers published a short report on his sudden demise and funeral.
All waited for Moscow to decide how the suicide would be interpreted—
as the desperate act of a slandered man or an attempt by an exposed
enemy to shirk responsibility. An explanation came at an emergency
plenum of the Magnitogorsk city organization: Lominadze was a traitor.
At this plenum, Mazut was removed from his post, and repressions
befell other Lominadze associates. Having beaten corroborative evidence out of those arrested, the NKVD fabricated a case about a counterrevolutionary group in Magnitogorsk headed by Lominadze.[13]

In killing himself, Lominadze obviously tried not only to avoid arrest,
but also to remove his wife and son from the threat of arrest. He wrote
his final letter for this reason. But the subsequent charges against the
dead Lominadze completely dashed these hopes. Harsh repercussions
awaited the family of the leader of this "counterrevolutionary group."
Lominadze's family, however, remained untouched while Ordzhonikidze still lived. Moreover, the government gave his wife a pension
"for the revolutionary service of her husband." Nina A. Lominadze received this pension from 1935 to 1937. Following Ordzhonikidze's
death, the pension was rescinded, and Lominadze's wife was arrested
twice—in 1938 and again in 1950 as "a family member of a national
traitor."[14]

Chapter 7

Stakhanovites and "Saboteurs"

The sharp turn in the political course after Kirov's murder did not bypass the employees of the People's Commissariat of Heavy Industry. Many of them became victims of the "strengthening of vigilance" policy, and were arrested or expelled from the party. The Stakhanovite movement* that began in the fall of 1935 was accompanied by a new campaign of persecution and repression in industry. These events caused conflicts between managers and politicians.

There is a significant body of literature on the Stakhanovite movement. In evaluating this phenomenon and its consequences, researchers have reached a variety of conclusions that bear testimony to its complex character.[1] But without doubt—and on this point specialists are in agreement—this campaign "intensified the class struggle," became a root cause of numerous conflicts at the workplace, and was used as a new method to purge cadres. It is also common knowledge that Ordzhonikidze was behind the movement, while the NKTP constituted a distinctive experimental field upon which different types of Stakhanovite initiatives were "broken in." A logical question pertaining to this topic therefore arises: To what extent did Ordzhonikidze take

---

*Stakhanovite movement. Named after coal miner Alexei G. Stakhanov, who in August 1935 set a new record for hewing coal, launching a nationwide campaign to rationalize and raise industrial production. The government introduced an array of incentives to increase output.—Ed.

part in organizing the new purge, and do his Stakhanovite initiatives signify an attempt to follow the distinct course, initiated after Kirov's murder, of preparing for the Great Terror, and to demonstrate loyalty to Stalinist tactics of repression?

In Ordzhonikidze's large commissariat there were two especially complex and key subdivisions—ferrous metallurgy and coal mining. Despite countless party and state resolutions, threatening warnings, and the efforts of conscientious managers, shortages of coal and metal continued to plague the economy. But toward 1935 the situation in ferrous metallurgy improved. Attempts to revamp this industrial branch, including experimentation with the widespread use of economic stimuli and the rejection of ambitious plans for smelting millions of tons of cast iron and steel, produced results. The coal miners, however, could not boast of similar achievements and once again thwarted fulfillment of the plan for the first half of 1935.

Inspired by the successes in ferrous metallurgy, Ordzhonikidze decided to assign a more active role for the Donbass—the main coal center in the country. A typical exchange between Ordzhonikidze and the head of the Donetsk Artem Trust Mines, Z.E. Zorin, at a conference of the People's Commissariat of Heavy Industry on May 11, 1935, demonstrated which methods he intended to use in clamping down on the miners. Ordzhonikidze listened to Zorin's hackneyed complaints of poor supply, lack of mechanization, and so on, and then laid into him:

> You tell me you have fine workers at the mines who produce three, four, five times more than the Donbass average. What have you done here?
>
> *Zorin:* First, these are the best and most qualified workers.
>
> *Ordzhonikidze:* What do you mean by the best workers?
>
> *Zorin:* Workers with excellent qualifications.
>
> *Ordzhonikidze:* Those like Telnykh.
>
> *Zorin:* He works in Kadievugol, not for me. He's a highly qualified worker.
>
> *Ordzhonikidze:* Murashko.
>
> *Zorin:* He's a qualified worker, and physically very strong.
>
> *Ordzhonikidze:* Is Telnykh very strong?
>
> *Zorin:* Telnykh doesn't work for me. Second, these are class-conscious workers.
>
> *Ordzhonikidze:* You have only one class-conscious Telnykh?

> *Zorin:* They are brigade leaders—the same Murashko and Riaboshapko instruct the other workers.
> *Ordzhonikidze:* There are probably hundreds, thousands of such workers that you only need to find and place in position.[2]

Ordzhonikidze was possessed with the idea of drawing to the coal mines a higher number of "leading workers." He left for a vacation in Kislovodsk at the beginning of August 1935, and met with the secretary of the Donetsk Regional Committee, S. Sarkisov, and Zorin en route in his train car. After hearing their complaints of insufficient funds and materials, Ordzhonikidze promised to help, but once again ordered them to pay attention to the work of "leading" miners, and to identify "thousands" of such outstanding workers in the Donbass.[3]

A month passed. On September 5, while in Kislovodsk, Ordzhonikidze read a short notice on the last page of *Pravda* about the record set by a miner named Stakhanov, and immediately ordered the central newspapers to organize a corresponding propaganda campaign. On September 6, he sent a letter to the secretary of the Donetsk Regional Committee, Sarkisov, that sheds light on Ordzhonikidze's intentions:

> The situation is bad, Sarkisov, with regard to coal and fuel in general. . . . Today, the following became clear to me: There's poor economic leadership at Main Coal and the trusts. The vast majority of managers are of the old system. They will either be compelled to change their ways and adapt to modern methods, as we did with the metallurgists, or we will replace them with younger men. . . . After all, there's no escaping the fact that there are hundreds and thousands of such heroes in the lower ranks of laborers in the Donbass who do outstanding work. It's necessary to shift these heroes to jobs managing mines and trusts. We have to act boldly. The experience of metallurgy fully justifies this. . . . We can't get by without a large shake-up in the coal industry. We can't revamp salaries and reposition workers without a shake-up.[4]

Thus, according to Ordzhonikidze's thinking, it was necessary to conduct a "shake-up" of cadres in the coal industry, promote younger and more enthusiastic workers, and clamp down on the "old timers." Simple and usually effective, this method was utilized quite often during those years, including at the People's Commissariat of Heavy Industry.

But this time the reassigning of cadres from the very start threatened to turn into a political purge. It seems that in preparing this action, Ordzhonikidze did not realize the danger; but when it became real, he tried to neutralize it.

On September 14, 1935, the newspapers published a telegram Ordzhonikidze sent to the secretary of the Donetsk Regional Party Committee, Sarkisov, and the head of Donbass Coal, V.M. Bazhanov. Ordzhonikidze clearly wanted to make a point: "I won't hide the fact that I'm deeply worried that this campaign will encounter narrowminded skepticism on the part of several backward leaders, which in this case would amount to sabotage. Such excuses for leaders need to be dismissed quickly." But *Pravda*, in commenting on the telegram in its lead article, exaggerated Ordzhonikidze's comparatively moderate statement to conform to the new turn in the general line in politics: "The first days of the Stakhanovite movement have already provided more than one example of the most malicious sabotage and wrecking." This situation was then repeated. Ordzhonikidze removed managers for not fulfilling the plan and for not actively supporting the Stakhanovite movement, and appealed to the "commanders" of industry to lead the initiative.[5] Meanwhile, *Pravda* periodically staged political attacks against managers in its lead articles, and maintained: "People who don't help the Stakhanovites are not our people."[6]

It has already been noted in the literature that during the first months of the Stakhanovite movement, the NKTP leadership occupied a special position regarding the campaign against "saboteurs and wreckers." The commissariat's newspaper, *For Industrialization*, and numerous speeches by leaders of the department, consistently depicted resistance to Stakhanovite methods in an apolitical way, and examined it primarily from a technical and organizational point of view. The sluggishness and mistakes of engineers and managers grew out of their conservatism, poor preparation, and, of course, laziness; but never out of any intentions to wreck things (it was characteristic that Ordzhonikidze's deputy, G.L. Piatakov, used the word "resistance" [to the Stakhanovite movement] in quotation marks). All this differed significantly from the statements of many other leaders of the country aroused by the "horrors of wrecking."[7]

Resolution of this conflict obviously depended primarily on Stalin.

He actively campaigned for the new movement, causing it to spread widely and acquire state support. Stalin's reasons soon became apparent. The campaign was consciously used to strengthen the new direction embarked upon after Kirov's murder. Contrasting the Stakhanovites to "saboteur-wreckers" played an essential part in creating an atmosphere of vigilance in the struggle against enemies. Meetings between leaders and the Stakhanovites were conducted on a scale previously unseen in order to demonstrate the unity between the country's leadership and common people. Addressing an All-Union Conference of Stakhanovites on November 14, 1935, Stalin assumed the role of defender of the workers against bureaucrats and manager-saboteurs, and made appeals that were reminiscent of the Shakhty Show Trials.* Maintaining that the Stakhanovite movement "originated and developed to a large extent despite the wishes of enterprise managers, and even in opposition to them," Stalin evoked the intensification of class struggle, called on engineers and technicians to apprentice themselves to the Stakhanovites, and promised to give the obstinate ones "a little slap on the face."[8]

The December (1935) plenum of the Central Committee, convened to examine the Stakhanovite movement, continued in this vein. It resolved "to break the remaining resistance to the Stakhanovites from conservative managers, engineers, and technical personnel," and to expose class enemies trying to "undermine the Stakhanovites."[9] It was characteristic that the main report at the plenum was given by a Central Committee secretary, Andrei A. Andreev, and not by any leader of administrative departments. Having received reports from the NKVD on counterrevolutionary resistance to the Stakhanovites while preparing his presentation,[10] Andreev stated at the plenum: "Stakhanovite norms represent the victory of socialist labor over capitalist norms of production, and eradication of the last remnants of capitalism in our production. It is therefore clear that such a movement cannot avoid determined resistance from our class enemies."[11] Other plenary partici-

---

*Shakhty Show Trials. In 1928 fifty-five engineers from the Donbass mines were accused of sabotage and collusion with the forces of international capital. The affair triggered the widespread arrest of "wreckers" and "saboteurs," in which many bourgeois specialists suffered.—Ed.

Stalin and Ordzhonikidze in 1935.

pants peppered their speeches with accounts of the intensification of class struggle. Stalin also repeated his earlier directives concerning resistance to the Stakhanovite movement.[12]

The politics of a "total Stakhanovization" to overcome sabotage had destructive socioeconomic consequences. Fearing accusations, industrial bosses began to falsify statistics and create a semblance of efficiency by making a fuss over the records of individual Stakhanovites. Rush jobs involving all workers were practiced extensively, providing a temporary illusory effect which inevitably ended in failure. Feverish attempts to set new records violated technical regulations, led to wear and tear on the machinery, worsened quality, and increased the number of accidents. Production records were attained by producing simple items. The resultant lack of a wide selection of goods became a serious problem, as did growing shortages of materials needed to complete partially finished products.

Blame for the failures fell upon the managers, while hysterical statements in the press triggered numerous repressions. Stigmatizing industrial bosses while extolling the innovation of the working class became mandatory. As usual, violence against engineers and technicians led to a weakening of discipline, a decline in responsibility, and the desire to play it safe.

The payoff from such a high price for success turned out to be ephemeral. From the beginning of 1936, administrative disorganization and neglect of mining drifts resulted in a decline of coal extractions in the Donbass. A spurt in production of ferrous metals was achieved at the expense of numerous furnace explosions and mass production of an unnecessary amount of metal good only for the attainment of a record gross tonnage. The situation was similar in other industrial branches.

Such overt breakdowns gave the heads of economic departments additional grounds to challenge the new course.[13] One of the signals for a temporary retreat was a lead *Pravda* article, "Lesson of the Donbass," published on June 7, 1936. The newspaper wrote that the average daily extraction of coal in May had declined significantly from that of December 1935, and for the first time in many months, openly acknowledged the reasons for this—"rushed work," the blind pursuit of records, and the persecution of engineers and technicians. "If one is to believe the Donetsk press and numerous speeches delivered in the Donbass," the editorial stated, "then one can get the impression that the majority of engineers and technicians are saboteurs and conservatives. . . . There are many good specialists in the Donbass whom we must patiently help liberate from their conservatism. Instead, they are cursed at and 'worked over.' Dozens of engineers, shaft managers, and party workers received reprimands. . . . Their spirits have been broken, and they walk with their tails between their legs."

In view of the nature of politics in the 1930s, it is all but certain that the statement in *Pravda* was sanctioned at the highest levels of power. Inasmuch as the question concerned the NKTP, Ordzhonikidze would have had to have been involved in the matter. Stalin apparently yielded to him and agreed to restrain organizers in the struggle against "saboteurs." Another piece of evidence supporting such a conjecture is the materials of a conference of the People's Commissariat of Heavy Industry, which met soon after the appearance of *Pravda's* lead article, from June 25 through 29, 1936.

Representing a sort of supreme collective leadership organ of heavy industry, the conference signaled a retreat from official encouragement of record-setting and came to the defense of the managers.

It was already clear on the first day of the conference that there would not be any frank discussions about the difficult situation of engineers. Orators spoke carefully, dropping only a few hints. The deputy head of Main Coal and head of Donbass Coal, V.M. Bazhanov, stated that "the core of engineering and technical personnel in the Donbass is strong and is in a position to cope successfully with the tasks presented to it." Further, he held that only 8 percent of shaft engineers and technicians, in accord with investigations already carried out, were to be removed and demoted."[14] The chief administrator of Kadiev Coal Trust, L.Ia. Vysotskii, reported on the high turnover of shaft management and the sharp decline in wages of engineers resulting from the introduction of a new system of remuneration—in the event of nonfulfillment of the plan, bosses did not receive their full salaries. To a leading question from Ordzhonikidze, "Tell us, how do you explain the high turnover of engineers?" Vysotskii answered carefully: "My views are as follows: We needed to teach people, but teaching people to work is more difficult than firing them. In most cases, the trusts and mines continue as before by replacing old people with young ones, apparently on the assumption that we didn't need to teach the newer ones."[15] The chief administrator of Shaktantratsit Trust, A.M. Nepomniashchii, was also cautious: "I will touch in passing upon one mistake in our trust: enthusiasm. The technical staff of our trust wasn't sufficiently prepared to accept the Stakhanovite movement, and fell behind. Unfair attempts were made to charge the engineers and technicians with sabotage. This made them uncertain too. Now we are immediately rectifying the situation."[16]

The conference continued along these lines until the chief administrator of the Stalin Coal Trust, A.M. Khachaturiants, rose to the tribune. After a brief introduction, he got to the point: "The main reason for our trust's failures to fulfill the production program is the unsatisfactory work of management." Khachaturiants maintained that Stalin's and Ordzhonikidze's instructions on the slack pace of engineers conformed to the situation during the early period of the Stakhanovite movement, but a mistake was committed and the leaders' instructions were extended to the entire administration. "Instead of patiently helping to introduce Stakhanovite methods of work and thereby helping management to understand these methods, as Comrade Stalin instructed, we declared any mistake or misunderstanding an act of sabotage." In the heat of passion, Khachaturiants accused the press of "compounding this by several degrees."

Khachaturiants harshly criticized the consequences of such policies:

> Why did the system break down, and why did so many obstructions occur? This is the result of poor inspection. Management doesn't work intensively, as a result of the charges that have been made against it for a long time. . . . Instead of thinking how to introduce an innovation or Stakhanovite method, engineers are afraid of being accused of sabotage or conservatism and try to do everything by the letter of the law:
>
> "Saboshkov's system? Please, here you have Saboshkov's system."
>
> "Do you need individual piecework? Please, here you have individual piecework." And so on. . . .
>
> Most managers reason as follows: If I don't extract coal from the mines, don't lower costs, and don't complete preparatory work—they'll remove me. But if I don't introduce Stakhanovite methods, they won't just remove me, but arraign me on charges of sabotage as well. They've bureaucratized the movement.[17]

In spite of his reservations, Khachaturiants in fact criticized policies that were initiated, as everyone knew, by Stalin. Concluding the conference, Ordzhonikidze gave high marks to the comments of the chief manager of Stalin Coal. "I think that Comrade Khachaturiants more accurately than anyone else explained all that happened in the Donbass," Ordzhonikidze stated. But he tried nonetheless "to smooth over" Khachaturiants's speech by overemphasizing the mistakes the same Donbass leaders made at the start.[18] Ordzhonikidze, moreover, made known his attitude toward the charges of sabotage against engineers and technical workers. Dismissing them as trifling, he exclaimed:

> Saboteurs! In the nineteen years Soviet power has existed, we have educated more than one hundred thousand engineers in our schools and colleges, and an equal number of technical workers. If all of them, including the old engineers whom we retrained, turned out to be saboteurs in 1936, then we should congratulate ourselves on our success. Saboteurs! They aren't saboteurs, but good people—our sons, our brothers, our comrades, who back Soviet power. They will die on the fronts for Soviet power if necessary [stormy and prolonged applause].[19]

Ordzhonikidze then proposed a new, apolitical way of explaining the specialists' mistakes: "It's not sabotage—that's nonsense—but their lack of skills that impedes fulfillment [of the plan] . . . Now there can be no talk that the engineering and technical personnel view the Stakhanovite movement negatively. Their problem is that they still haven't learned to work in the Stakhanovite way."[20]

Judging from similar statements from leaders of other economic commissariats on the need to maintain cadre stability at this time, such as those of People's Commissar of Communications Lazar M. Kaganovich,[21] the Politburo must have agreed with this in one way or another. This conclusion is supported by the fact that, in spite of the drastic worsening of the political situation, Ordzhonikidze succeeded in pushing through a resolution defending the employees of his commissariat. (On July 9, 1936, the Central Committee adopted a secret resolution "On the Terrorist Activities of the Trotskyist-Zinovievite Counterrevolutionary Bloc," demanding a more active struggle against enemies. Furthermore, during August 19–24, a show trial transpired in Moscow at which a large group of former oppositionists, including Kamenev and Zinoviev, were sentenced to be shot.)

On August 28, 1936, Ordzhonikidze read a letter from the director of the Kyshtymskii Electrolyte Factory (Cheliabinsk Oblast), V.P. Kurchavyi, who asked to be reinstated in the party and for help against persecution from local party organizations. He also reported that the newspaper, *Cheliabinsk Worker*, had played an active role in this campaign, accusing him of sympathizing with the Trotskyists. Kurchavyi appended to his letter an article from the newspaper. Ordzhonikidze responded positively to this complaint: "Comrade Ezhov [Nikolai I. Ezhov was then involved in party expulsions—O.Kh.]. I request that you look into this."[22]

Ordzhonikidze undoubtedly recalled Kurchavyi's letter the next day, when he read a piece in *Izvestia* from August 29, "An Exposed Enemy," by the Cheliabinsk correspondent of the newspaper, Dubinskii. The notice described an analogous situation: the director of the Satkinskii factory Magnezit, Tabakov, was expelled from the party for aiding and abetting Trotskyism. A quick check showed that *Cheliabinsk Worker* had played a decisive role in Tabakov's fate, since it provided information about the Magnezit director upon which the *Izvestia* correspondent hastily prepared his article.

The Tabakov Affair was addressed at breakneck speed as a matter of exceptional significance. On August 31, the Politburo reversed the resolution of the Magnezit factory party organization that expelled Tabakov from the party, informed the editor of *Cheliabinsk Worker* that he had committed a mistake in publishing the decision to expel Tabakov without verification, and approved the *Izvestia* editorial board's dismissal of the Cheliabinsk correspondent who had written the article on Tabakov.[23] The newspapers published reports the next day, "In the Central Committee," which presented the Politburo's decisions.

On August 31, the Politburo also adopted a resolution on the Dnepropetrovsk regional organization in Ukraine. One of its clauses concerned the fate of the director of the Zaporozhe Metallurgical Combine, Ia.I. Vesnik, whose name had often appeared recently in the newspapers, and who was now accused of conspiring with Trotskyists and expelled from the party. The Politburo repealed this decision. The secretary of the Krivoi Rog city party organization, who had expelled

Vesnik from the party, was himself fired.[24] On September 5, *Pravda* published information on the plenum of the Dnepropetrovsk regional party organization, which examined questions raised in the Politburo resolution. The plenum made necessary statements about intensifying the struggle with enemies and "decisively warned" "against taking things too far in the future, . . . against unfairly accusing party members of being Trotskyists or their accomplices without sufficient and serious grounds."

While members of the Politburo voted on a decision regarding the Satkinskii factory and the Dnepropetrovsk regional party organization on August 31, Ordzhonikidze was still trying to make sense out of a letter from the director of the Magnitogorsk Metallurgical Factory, A.P. Zaveniagin. He reported that an accident had occurred on May 26 in the machine room of the coke shop, which resulted in twenty-six people receiving burns, of whom four died. In Zaveniagin's opinion, those guilty of the accident included the head of the machine room, Babin (who died that day), and the skilled craftsman Panov. The procurator, however, arraigned other employees—the head of the coke shop, Shevchenko, his equipment deputy, Farberov, the chief machine room engineer, Bulgakov, and the engineer for technical safety, Bykov. Zaveniagin wrote that they were not involved in the accident. "I consider it my obligation to appeal to you to support our petition—not to implicate those not responsible for the accident, Comrades Bulgakov and Bykov, and especially the department head, Comrade Shevchenko, and his equipment deputy, Comrade Farberov." Ordzhonikidze sent a letter to the procurator of the USSR, Vyshinskii, with the following instructions: "I back Comrade Zaveniagin's request, and ask you to handle it accordingly."[25] Vyshinskii carried out Ordzhonikidze's order. On October 16, Vyshinskii reported that he had examined events involving the workers of the coke shop at the Magnitogorsk Combine and stopped the criminal investigation against Shevchenko and Farberov. "I don't think it is possible to curtail the case against Bykov and Bulgakov. Considering the characterization Zaveniagin gave of their recent work, I instructed the procurator to seek punishment that wouldn't prevent Bykov and Bulgakov from remaining at the factory." Vyshinskii, who adjudicated this case, reported the results of the judicial review to Ordzhonikidze on December 16: "Bulgakov is sentenced to one year of corrective labor at his workplace, while Bykov will serve six months. Thus, both can remain at their posts."[26]

Apart from all this, in August 1936 Ordzhonikidze helped to prevent the arrests of the construction chiefs at the Nizhnii Tagil Coach Factory, L.M. Mariasin and Sh.S. Okudzhava, which will be discussed later in more detail.

In general, available documents allow us to conclude that Ordzhonikidze tried to block repressions connected with the preparation and implementation of the first major Moscow Show Trial. There is no exact data on how he viewed the case against Kamenev and Zinoviev. What is known is only that in the fall of 1937, M.D. Orakhelashvili, who had once befriended Ordzhonikidze and was later arrested, gave the following deposition:

> From the beginning, I slandered Stalin as a party dictator, and considered his policy to be excessively harsh. Sergo Ordzhonikidze greatly influenced me in this regard. Speaking with me in 1936 about Stalin's attitude toward the leaders of the Leningrad Opposition (Zinoviev, Kamenev, Evdokimov, and Zalutskii), Ordzhonikidze argued that Stalin's excessive cruelty was causing a split in the party and was leading the country into a dead end.[27]

It is impossible to verify how much of Orakhelashvili's testimony was true. There are serious grounds for asserting, however, that relations between Stalin and Ordzhonikidze worsened precisely at this time, in August 1936.

As is well known, the first accusations of enemy activity were officially levied at the August Moscow trial against the former "right"—Bukharin, Rykov, and Tomskii. Trying to defend himself and enlist some support, Bukharin wrote to Stalin and other members of the Politburo to deny the charges, arguing they were absurd. Although Bukharin sought an official reply, none came. Stalin acted more subtly: Voroshilov spoke out against Bukharin, and gave his "own" unofficial response. Bukharin sent a personal letter to Voroshilov on September 1, 1936. Voroshilov immediately publicized it, circulating it to Stalin, Molotov, Kaganovich, Ordzhonikidze, Andreev, Vlas Ia. Chubar (1891–1939), and Ezhov. On September 3, undoubtedly at Stalin's prompting, Voroshilov drafted a crude response to Bukharin that included the following: "If in your letter you wish to charge me with your complete innocence [the text reads as such—O.Kh.], then convince me of that: restrain yourself hereafter, regardless of the results of the investigation into your case; if you don't refrain from writing vile epithets in addressing the party leadership [Bukharin's letter does not contain any "vile epithets," yet Voroshilov undoubtedly "discerned" them with Stalin's help—O.Kh.], then I'll consider you a scoundrel." That day, September 3, Voroshilov circulated his retort to the same group of associates.[28]

Voroshilov's reply revealed that Stalin was not absolutely certain that his actions against the "rightists" had the full support of all members of the leadership. Hiding behind Voroshilov's "opinion," Stalin remained on the sidelines, stayed impartial, and did not make any official promises. Of course, he had also formed his own opinion of Bukharin's statements. After receiving Voroshilov's response, Stalin wrote on the accompanying letter: "Comrade Molotov. Voroshilov's answer is good. If Sergo had done the same and rebuked Mr. Lominadze, who had written him even more scurrilous letters against the Central Committee, then Lominadze would still be alive, and possibly a good man to boot. I. Stalin."[29]

As with all such observations made by the leader, Stalin's remark was clearly intended not only for Molotov, but for others as well. It was aimed at Ordzhonikidze. But it is unclear what prompted Stalin. Had Ordzhonikidze defended Bukharin? Or was Stalin aware of Sergo's conversations regarding the trial of Kamenev and Zinoviev? Or, was it Stalin's reaction to Ordzhonikidze's attempts to prevent arrests in his commissariat? In any event, one thing is certain: Stalin was dissatisfied with Ordzhonikidze. The cunning nature of Stalin's attack against Ordzhonikidze captures our attention. Stalin did not blame him for defending enemies, but for his unprincipled intercession, which destroyed "his own" by not giving them the chance to rectify themselves. This was a clear hint: nobody planned to annihilate Bukharin, but rather to save a lost soul.

Moreover, the attacks on Ordzhonikidze were linked with preparations to arrest the first deputy of the People's Commissariat of Heavy Industry, G.L. Piatakov.

Chapter 8

Piatakov's Arrest

Georgii (Iurii) Leonidovich Piatakov belonged to that group of party activists whom Lenin felt compelled to characterize in his famous "Letter to the Congress [Last Testament]."* Lenin considered Piatakov one of the "most outstanding of our youngest members," and referred to him as a man of "outstanding will and outstanding ability," but too easily carried away with "administrating and the administrative side of work to be relied upon in a serious political matter."[1] Of course, Lenin had good cause for these evaluations. Piatakov had actively spread the "sickness of leftism" among revolutionaries.[2]

Piatakov was born to the family of the director of a sugar factory in the Kiev region. He was repeatedly expelled from school, and gravitated toward the anarchists. He then joined a Kiev terrorist group planning the murder of the governor-general, Sukhomlinov. Still later, he joined the Marxist camp. He was arrested, and fled abroad from exile. It was there that he learned of the February Revolution. During the October Revolution, he was chairman of the Kiev Revolutionary Committee. He

---

*Letter to the Congress [Last Testament]. First published in the aftermath of Khrushchev's Secret Speech in 1956, the document refers to Lenin's attempt to evaluate the qualifications of the most prominent party members most likely to succeed him. Lenin dictated the first part of his testament on December 23, 1922, and a few weeks later added a postscript in which he urged the party to remove Stalin from the post of general secretary. For a post-Soviet examination of the political intrigue surrounding the writing and suppression of the document, see Yuri Buranov's *Lenin's Will: Falsified and Forbidden* (Amherst, N.Y., 1994).—Ed.

did not agree with Lenin on the question of the Brest-Litovsk Peace, however, and left to fight in Ukraine. Piatakov had a particular score to settle with Bolshevik opponents: In the very first months of the Civil War in Kiev, his brother was brutally murdered. "The corpse was in horrible condition—it was obvious that they had tortured him terribly before his death; suffice it to say that in place of his heart was a deep hole, apparently made by a saber. His hands were also completely cut off; as the doctors explained, his heart had been eviscerated while he was still alive, and he convulsively clutched the gnawing blade of the sword,"[3] Piatakov later wrote. While serving on various fronts of the Civil War, Piatakov drew close to Trotsky. At the Fifteenth Party Congress in December 1927, Piatakov was expelled along with other opposition leaders. But he soon made an official break with Trotsky, and was readmitted to the party. Piatakov, however, was not allowed back into politics, but was appointed chairman of the Gosbank [State Bank] and a member of the presidium of VSNKh. In 1931, Piatakov became Ordzhonikidze's deputy, in which capacity he remained until his arrest in 1936.

Piatakov, whom Stalin never forgave because of his former opposition, saw in Ordzhonikidze not only a boss, but also a patron capable of defending him in difficult times. In dealing with Sergo, Piatakov therefore always emphasized his respect and diligently demonstrated his devotion to Ordzhonikidze. "It is because you are not only a boss and *senior* comrade, but also a man whom I have always regarded with the deepest love and respect, that your leadership was, and is, for me not only the formal tutelage of a superior, but also the leadership of a comrade whom I personally respect deeply. All this causes my blunder to distress me greatly." This is a typical excerpt from a letter of Piatakov to Ordzhonikidze that eloquently reflects their relations.[4]

Ordzhonikidze accepted the role of patron as his due. He valued Piatakov's intelligence and organizational abilities, and well understood, even if he did not demonstrate this understanding openly, that his own success as commissar of heavy industry owed much to his first deputy commissar. In general, their mutual affection was strengthened by an interest in one another. Piatakov was Ordzhonikidze's right-hand man in the commissariat, and often stood in for him or acted on his behalf.

By Stalin's order, the NKVD began collecting evidence against Piatakov in the summer of 1936. Those arrested in the case of the so-called Unified Trotskyist-Zinovievite Center, L.B. Kamenev, G.E. Evdokimov, I.I. Reingold, and E.A. Dreitser, "confessed" to the alleged existence of another Parallel Anti-Soviet Trotskyist Center, led by Piatakov. Piatakov's wife was arrested on the evening of July 27, 1936, and quickly forced to sign a confession regarding her tie with Trotskyists.

At the time, Piatakov was on vacation and knew nothing about his wife's arrest. He apparently received word from Ordzhonikidze only at the very beginning of August. Piatakov replied by telegram from Sukhumi on August 3: "Your notification struck me hard. I tried to recall details from the last nine years. I can't understand a thing. If they disclosed some connections [with] counterrevolutionary Trotskyism (that I'm unaware of), then the authorities acted properly. In view of my total incomprehension, I'll get a ticket and leave for Moscow on the next available train. I'll let you know when I leave."[5]

Several days later, he read the classified letter of the Central Committee "On the Terrorist Activity of the Trotskyist-Zinovievite Counterrevolutionary Bloc" and the affidavit of his wife Ditiatevaia. He wrote Ordzhonikidze on August 7:

> Sergo! I read the confession and classified letter. The base and heinous behavior of these people is unprecedented. I am outraged beyond belief. I am unbearably ashamed that such despicable things took place right under my own nose. I'm not speaking of the leaders of this gang [as Piatakov referred to Kamenev, Zinoviev, and the others arrested—O.Kh.]—their role and physiognomy have long been clear to me. But it was terribly unbearable for me to read about Ditiatevaia. After all, this is a triple or quadruple betrayal of me. If such heinous acts are possible, then we have no future.
>
> I'm personally aggrieved. But I assure you that all these dirty tricks instill in me only hatred toward these scoundrels, and compel me to fight even harder and with greater determination for the concerns of Stalin and the party.[6]

Charges were not levied against Piatakov himself, in spite of the fact that the NKVD already had at its disposal Reingold's testimony on the "counterrevolutionary activity" of Iurii Leonidovich in the Parallel Anti-Soviet Trotskyist Center. Stalin, who knew about these affidavits, apparently felt that they were insufficient. But when a telegraph arrived from Kiev on August 10, reporting that the arrested N.V. Golubenko "acknowledged" that Piatakov had headed a "Ukrainian Trotskyist Center," Stalin immediately gave the order that the case be sped up.

Ezhov summoned Piatakov the next day, read him the affidavits of Reingold and Golubenko, and informed him of the Central Committee's decision to remove him from the post of deputy commissar and appoint him head of Chirchik Construction. Judging from Ezhov's report to Stalin, Piatakov denied these depositions as the libel of Trotskyists. He acknowledged that he was only guilty of not paying attention to the counterrevolutionary work of his wife. He agreed with the decision to remove him from the post of deputy commissar, and stated that he should have been punished even more harshly. In trying to prove his innocence and loyalty, Piatakov, according to Ezhov, asked "to grant him any form (at the discretion of the Central Committee) of rehabilitation. In particular, he proposed that he be personally allowed to shoot all those sentenced to death at the trial, including his former wife, and to publish this in the press." "Despite the fact that I pointed out to him the absurdity of his proposal," reported Ezhov to Stalin, "he insistently requested that the Central Committee be informed of this."[7]

Ezhov's report, published in connection with Piatakov's rehabilitation in 1989, substantially impairs the historical reputation of Iurii Leonidovich. Willingness to become an executioner, all the more so of one's own wife, testifies to the complete breakdown of his character. While acknowledging a grain of truth in such an evaluation, however, we should not rush to make judgments. I do not think that Piatakov intended to pick up a revolver (which is exactly what Ezhov meant when he mentioned the absurdity of Piatakov's suggestion). His insane proposals and oaths of fealty fully mesh with the rules of the crazy game of "life and death" Stalin proposed to Piatakov. To stigmatize enemies with whatever words, and to humiliate them by making them demonstrate absolute obedience to the supreme leader, were part of the rules, and under certain conditions could save one's life. This was illusory, but represented a chance, nonetheless. Not everyone could refuse or proudly pass up such a chance. In any event, Piatakov could not.

Piatakov apparently was left alone after his first interrogation by Ezhov. It is possible that the leader yielded because of interference by Ordzhonikidze, who might have used Piatakov's desperate refutation as an argument in conversation with Stalin. The resolution on Piatakov's removal as deputy commissar mentioned by Ezhov had not yet been put in motion. It became clear several days later, however, that Piatakov's fate was sealed. At the trial of the Unified Trotskyist-Zinovievite Center on August 22, Vyshinskii stated that in considering the affidavits of the accused, he would begin an investigation of another group of people, including Piatakov. Everyone in the People's Commissariat of Heavy Industry continued to hope that Ordzhonikidze would defend his deputy. The following fact, for example, testifies to this mood.

After Vyshinskii's statement at the show trial in Moscow, leaders of the Bliavinskii Copper Smelting Combine in Orenburg Oblast organized a meeting of workers who demanded the removal of Piatakov's name from the enterprise. This initiative was consonant with the spirit of the times and suggests that ordinary workers well understood the essence of "routine politics." This time, however, the case was impeded. At the end of August, A.P. Serebrovskii, head of nonferrous metallurgy in the NKTP Central Directorate, arrived at the combine. He summoned the mine director, Tsivin, who had initiated the measure, and reprimanded him: "You're the ringleader in the movement to remove Piatakov's name and portrait, but did you know that only the Central Committee can do this?" Serebrovskii convened a meeting of the engineering and technical staff, where he said that an investigation was under way, that Piatakov might turn out to be innocent, and that Trotskyists might have entangled him in this case. In fact, Serebrovskii added, Piatakov himself had explained the situation to him when they met recently in Sverdlovsk. Piatakov, according to Serebrovskii, had said "he'll arrive in Moscow, and give them [the Trotskyists—O.Kh.] a real fight."[8]

Piatakov was actually on a work-related trip in the Urals at this time, and apparently still hoped that this case would be resolved. He wrote Ordzhonikidze a letter on September 9. Piatakov reported to the commissar about the results of his inspection of the copper industry, and complained to him that political accusations raised at the Moscow trial were interfering with his normal routine: "I can't deny the fact that in comparison with past trips, my work has suffered significantly. . . . I encountered a great amount of wariness and confusion in party organizations. . . . The shadow of suspicion that fell after Comrade Vyshinskii's pronouncement has greatly weakened all my efforts." At the end of his letter, Piatakov appealed for help:

> Of course I'll continue to work. But if a short notice were to appear that these scoundrels, traitors, and rogues had slandered me (as is indeed the case), then my work in the Urals would undoubtedly be enhanced.
>
> Sergo. Imagine all those party comrades with whom I have had to meet both one-on-one and at meetings. After all, they don't know that these counterrevolutionary murderers are slandering me in a final malicious strike. These party comrades simply don't know what to do with my instructions, statements, demands, etc. I perfectly understand that once a declaration of this sort was made at the trial, Comrade Vyshinskii had to announce a forthcoming investigation. . . . But inasmuch as this is actually a despicable lie, and insofar as I was and am a person devoted to the leadership of our party and our country . . . and since the shadow of suspicion literally constrains the party organizations from helping raise the output of the copper industry, something must be done to diffuse the tense suspicion. . . .
>
> You're not only a member of the Politburo and a people's commissar to me, but also a comrade to whom I am personally attached with all my heart, and with whom I always share everything. Therefore, I've allowed myself to write about the difficult position I'm in. If I'm wrong—tell me. After all, there's no one to advise me except you. Iurii.[9]

But Ordzhonikidze was no longer able to help, and in fact turned Piatakov over to Stalin. On September 10–11, the Central Committee members polled agreed with a Politburo proposal to expel Piatakov from both the Central Committee and party. While on vacation, Ordzhonikidze sent the following coded message on September 11: "I fully agree with and vote for the Politburo resolution to expel Piatakov from the Central Committee and the party. Ordzhonikidze."[10] On September 11, the Politburo resolved to remove Piatakov from the post of deputy commissar of heavy industry; he was arrested on the night of September 12. The wording of the Politburo's resolution is worth noting: "To remove Piatakov, Iu.L., from the post of deputy commissar of heavy industry of the USSR (without mention in the press until further notice)."[11]

For the first thirty-three days of his arrest, Piatakov categorically denied his guilt. Recent research reveals how those arrested in the case of the Parallel Trotskyist Center were subjected to cruel interrogations: the so-called conveyor belt [continual interrogation for hours and days at a time—Ed.], endless hours "standing at attention," and physical tortures. NKVD investigators tried any methods to get confessions. They often fabricated "affidavits" themselves and forced prisoners to sign them.[12] Like many other unfortunate comrades, Piatakov could not endure the torture and made the required "confessions."

After this, copies of the transcripts of Piatakov's interrogations were routinely sent to Ordzhonikidze. Two of them are preserved in Sergo's personal papers—from November 14 and January 4.[13] What could Ordzhonikidze have learned from these documents? They indicate that wrecking over the course of many years was responsible for the numerous problems besetting heavy industry and the economy in general. Piatakov confessed that under his leadership, managers improperly estimated output, commissioned incomplete projects, allowed worker social services to decay, damaged the means of production, organized "work delays," and impaired the development of various branches of industry, such as copper smelting. It is unlikely that Ordzhonikidze, who knew all too well the real state of the economy and reasons for the collapses and mix-ups, could take this testimony seriously. After all, in his many speeches he himself addressed these problems and gave them a completely "materialistic" explanation. Ordzhonikidze often signed off on impossible plans that he knew required the employment of projects yet to be completed. He himself strove for quantity, while closing his eyes to quality. He himself asked people to put off improving living conditions until better times and to build temporary barracks. Ordzhonikidze could not help but understand that the numerous "consequences of wrecking" enumerated by Piatakov were the results of actual economic practices. In general, Ordzhonikidze could every bit as much see himself and other leaders of the country as saboteurs.

It cannot be ruled out that Piatakov hoped that Ordzhonikidze would see things this way. In any event, it was as if he sent Ordzhonikidze faint signals of his innocence, in places giving contradictory testimony. This is especially clear in the transcripts from November 14 (Piatakov had only just begun to give evidence, and the investigators apparently were still not on top of things). Piatakov acknowledged wrecking activities and suddenly stated: "But I must say in the majority of cases that I was unsuccessful. . . . Projects and plans were fulfilled and all our so-called 'intentions' crumbled like a house of cards."[14] To the investigator's question: "But why didn't you say anything about the wrecking activities you personally conducted at the People's Commissariat of Heavy Industry," Piatakov replied: "I can't say anything about this, because I wasn't able to do anything. The situation in our commissariat and my type of activities didn't give me the opportunity to do anything of the sort."[15]

It turned out that the "consequences of wrecking" were present, while the "intentions" to wreck never amounted to anything. The man was a deputy commissar, and for several months on end was completely in charge of the commissariat, but he could not "do harm." It is possible that Ordzhonikidze paid attention to these passages. In any event, they are highlighted in the preserved copies of the transcripts.

One of the most important questions is whether Ordzhonikidze believed in Piatakov's guilt. As in many other instances, it is not possible to answer this question with assurance. Circumstantial evidence exists, however, that allows us to assume that Ordzhonikidze most likely wavered and did not take a definite stance in the matter.

While speaking in the commissariat at a meeting of workers from the synthetic rubber industry on December 3, Ordzhonikidze rambled on, clearly not speaking from prepared notes: "Moreover, in spite of all the unpleasantries, major unpleasantries caused us by Piatakov, Rataichik, and other scoundrels, I personally spent many sleepless nights after this took place, wondering how this could happen. After all, this person worked with me, was a member of the Central Committee, and was my deputy. We gave him a chance to work as he pleased, and everything else he wanted. Yet in the end, he turned out to be a scoundrel."[16] In this "unpolished" and, incidentally, unpublished speech, it seems that doubt was present in equal measure with condemnation of the "scoundrels." How could this have happened?

On the next day, December 4, Bukharin recounted his conversation with Ordzhonikidze at a Central Committee plenum: "Sergo asked me at his apartment, tell me, please, what is your opinion of Piatakov? I literally told him that Piatakov impressed me as a man who was so tactful that he didn't realize that he spoke the truth out of tactical considerations." Ordzhonikidze retorted from the hall: "That's correct."[17] This fact can be attributed to Ordzhonikidze's wavering. How can it otherwise be explained that he suddenly asked Bukharin about Piatakov?

The confrontation between Bukharin and Piatakov that took place in January 1937 in the presence of Politburo members may have reinforced doubts. Bukharin's wife, Anna M. Larina, had this to say about Nikolai Ivanovich's version of the event:

> Piatakov's appearance stunned N.I. more than his preposterous slander. These were the living remains, as N.I. expressed, "not of Piatakov, but of his shadow, a skeleton with its teeth knocked out." Piatakov spoke with his head lowered, trying to cover his eyes with his palms. N.I. thought that bitterness could be felt in Piatakov's tone against those who listened to him without interrupting the absurd spectacle or stopping the unheard-of arbitrariness.
>
> "Iurii Leonidovich, explain," asked Bukharin, "What compelled you to slander yourself?"
>
> There was a pause. At this point, Sergo Ordzhonikidze looked intensely and with astonishment at Piatakov, shaken by the exhausted appearance and testimony of his accomplished assistant. Ordzhonikidze placed his palm to his ear . . . and asked him:
>
> "Is your testimony voluntary?"
>
> "My testimony is voluntary," answered Piatakov.
>
> "Absolutely voluntary?" asked Ordzhonikidze again with great surprise. But there was no answer to his repeated question.[18]

In general, there were substantial grounds for Ordzhonikidze to doubt the confession. His long association with Piatakov, ample knowledge of the actual situation in industry, and experience over many years of conflicts with the OGPU–NKVD regarding unfounded accusations of wrecking against managers made it difficult for him to believe in the sincerity of the NKVD materials. Disagreeing with the charges, however, would be tantamount to entering into an open conflict with Stalin and other Politburo members who fully supported Stalin's intentions ("Yes . . . your deputy turned out to be a swine of the first class. You must already know what he told us, the pig, the son-of-a-bitch!" wrote Klim E. Voroshilov to Ordzhonikidze on October 16, 1936).[19] Apart from this, numerous testimonies about Piatakov's "treason" actually existed from which it was not always easy to separate the truth from half-truths and lies. It is also the case that Ordzhonikidze renounced Piatakov. In turning over Piatakov and a number of other NKTP leaders to Stalin, Ordzhonikidze tried to save remaining cadres and, of course, himself.

In conclusion, it is appropriate to examine the account of Piatakov's fall put forth in the well-known book by a former NKVD officer, Alexander Orlov. In this version, Ordzhonikidze convinced Piatakov, who had remained silent, to give Stalin the necessary depositions. Ordzhonikidze allegedly twice visited Piatakov in prison, where he told him that in exchange for his repentance, Stalin promised to spare his life. Ordzhonikidze was the odd guarantee of this promise. Piatakov believed this and fulfilled all conditions. But Stalin deceived both Piatakov and Ordzhonikidze. Piatakov was shot, and this became the main reason for the bitter conflict between Stalin and Ordzhonikidze.[20]

Orlov's assertions are often repeated in scholarly accounts as immutable fact, without any reservations. In reality, much of Orlov's book is based on rumors and second-hand reports. To date, no concrete data exist that would even indirectly back his version about Piatakov and Ordzhonikidze. Anna M. Larina's reminiscences on the behavior of Ordzhonikidze at the confrontation between Bukharin and Piatakov contradict Orlov's evidence. It also seems that Orlov's data do not match the context of the well-known facts of the relationship between Stalin and Ordzhonikidze after Piatakov's arrest. Clearly preparing a strike against Ordzhonikidze (soon after Piatakov began to provide testimony, Sergo's brother was arrested—a bit more on this later), it is unlikely that Stalin would have ordered him to try to persuade Piatakov to repent. In essence, such an order would imply that the investigation lacked sufficient evidence. Moreover, Stalin had numerous other means to get Piatakov to talk. After all, defendants who were as strong as Piatakov also gave evidence. As subsequent events revealed, Piatakov was not simply a target of Stalinist intrigue, but was simultaneously a card in the leader's game with Ordzhonikidze. It is therefore difficult to believe that Stalin decided to play this card with the help of Ordzhonikidze himself.

Finally, there is one more circumstance worth mentioning. At the time of Piatakov's arrest, and for the thirty-three days after his arrest when Piatakov refused to acknowledge his guilt, Ordzhonikidze was on vacation in Kislovodsk. There is not even circumstantial evidence that he returned to Moscow at some point during this period.

Chapter 9

An Unhappy Birthday
(Ordzhonikidze and Beria)

On September 4, 1936, the Politburo granted Ordzhonikidze a vacation from September 5 to November 5.[1] On the first day of his break, Ordzhonikidze managed to read a letter from the head of the blast furnace shop at Zaporozhe Steel who had been expelled from the party, M.Ia. Gorlov. "I entreat you, Comrade Ordzhonikidze," wrote Gorlov, "to personally, or through Comrade Ezhov, clarify my immunity from such a serious charge as Trotskyism." Ordzhonikidze left instructions: "Comrade Ezhov, please look into this."[2]

Ordzhonikidze apparently left for Kislovodsk that very day. He continued to work there, constantly receiving information on the commissariat's work, issuing departmental orders, resolving contentious issues, and handling complaints.[3]

On September 25, Stalin and Zhdanov, while vacationing not far from Ordzhonikidze in Sochi, sent a telegram to Moscow for Kaganovich, Molotov, and other Politburo members attending to the "economy" in the capital: "We consider it absolutely necessary and urgent to appoint Comrade Ezhov to the post of people's commissar of internal affairs. Iagoda is clearly not up to the task of exposing the Trotskyist-Zinovievite Bloc. The OGPU was four years behind on this case. All party workers and the majority of NKVD regional representatives concur." On September 26, the Politburo approved Ezhov's appointment, and on September 29 adopted a resolution "On Treatment of the Counterrevolutionary Trotskyist-Zinovievite Elements," which contained a directive bolstering the struggle with "enemies" by dealing expediently with the arrested and previously exiled "Trotskyist-Zinovievite scoundrels."[4]

Stalin informed Ordzhonikidze of these decisions. Ordzhonikidze then most likely went to Sochi for the purpose of discussing them with Stalin. We have no details on their conversations. The only evidence we have about them is a sentence in a letter from Kaganovich, which he sent from Moscow to Ordzhonikidze in Kislovodsk on September 30: "I'm not writing you in regard to the counterrevolutionary affairs, because you were with the boss and read and discussed everything. There's nothing new to add to what you already know."[5] We can conclude from these words that at the time when Politburo members remaining in Moscow appointed Ezhov, Stalin most likely showed Ordzhonikidze recent transcripts from the interrogations and explained to him the thinking behind the change in the NKVD leadership. It is not known whether Ordzhonikidze objected to Stalin at this point. But the following circumstance is worth noting: In the previously mentioned letter from September 30, Kaganovich insistently, even a bit too enthusiastically, supported Stalin's telegram, not sparing plaudits and words of praise: "Our main news," he wrote,

> is Ezhov's appointment. This remarkable, wise decision by our father matched the attitude of the party and country. Iagoda turned out to be unquestionably weak for this role. To be an organizer of construction—that's one thing. But to be politically mature and uncover enemies *in good time*—that's another. The OGPU was already behind on this case by many years, and didn't warn of the heinous murder of Kirov. Ezhov will certainly handle things well. According to my information, the majority of Chekists [members of the NKVD—Ed.] have welcomed the change of leadership. Iagoda himself is apparently deeply upset about his dismissal, but that can't bother us where matters of state are concerned.[6]

It thus appears that Kaganovich purposely demonstrated his unconditional support for these decisions to Ordzhonikidze, as if to convince him not to argue with the "boss."

Soon afterward, in a letter from October 12, Kaganovich once again informed Ordzhonikidze of his strong approval of the actions of the new NKVD leadership. "I can reiterate that Comrade Ezhov is handling things well. He's taken care of the situation in a Stalinist manner. He's dispensed with the bandits of the counterrevolutionary Trotskyists in Bolshevik fashion. History hasn't known such base double-dealing and deceit from provocateurs, and therefore revolutionary punishment must correspond to the crime."[7] While hearing this, Ordzhonikidze continued to defend "his" people. For example, he twice sent telegrams on October 13 and 15 to the Supreme Court chairman of the RSFSR: "I request that you familiarize yourself with the case of the former director of the Kalinin Factory, Comrade Danilenko, and inform me of your findings."[8]

Ordzhonikidze celebrated his fiftieth birthday on October 24, 1936, in Kislovodsk amid a mass campaign of congratulations and reports. He also received news at this time that his older brother Papulia (Pavel) had been arrested in Georgia.

When Beria was shot following Stalin's death in 1953, rumors circulated that Beria himself had been responsible for Ordzhonikidze's death. Beria allegedly slandered Sergo in front of Stalin and organized his brother's arrest. "Several days before his own death, Sergo," stated Anastas I. Mikoyan at the July 1953 plenum, "twice said in conversation with me:

> "I don't understand why Stalin doesn't trust me. I believe in him 100 percent; I don't want to fight with him, but rather support him, yet he doesn't trust me. Beria's intrigues play a major role here, for he feeds Stalin lies, and Stalin believes him." "I recall," corroborated K.E. Voroshilov in his speech at the same plenum, "how it was well known at the time to Comrades Molotov, Kaganovich, and especially the Tbilisi Georgians, in particular those present here, that Beria played a despicable role in the life of the outstanding Communist, Sergo Ordzhonikidze. He did everything to slander and ruin the reputation, in Stalin's eyes, of this truly innocent person and Bolshevik. Seeing Beria as the real enemy, Sergo Ordzhonikidze said terrible things about him to me and other comrades. He stated that Beria was an insolent enemy who has yet to reveal his true self." "Beria set Comrades Stalin and Ordzhonikidze at loggerheads, and the noble heart of Comrade Sergo didn't hold up; this is how Beria disabled one of the best leaders of the party and friends of Comrade Stalin," said A.A. Andreev at the plenum.[9]

In the investigation that followed, Beria was charged with arresting

Ordzhonikidze's relatives and those Transcaucasian Communists close to him. The fact that Beria had used torture to garner testimony compromising Sergo was highlighted.[10] This version dating from 1953 was concocted by a political order—to move Stalin out from under attack and transfer all blame for the so-called "cult of personality" to Beria. To what extent do the known facts allow us to cast Beria as the main culprit for the clash between Stalin and Ordzhonikidze?

For a long time, the relationship between Ordzhonikidze and Beria was the kind one would expect between one of the top "leaders" and the head of a union republic who had only recently made his career. They held altogether different positions in the party-state hierarchy. And Beria secured the patronage of Ordzhonikidze because of this. Beria's situation was complicated by the fact that many old Caucasian Bolsheviks were well received at Ordzhonikidze's house in Moscow, and they did not like the "upstart" Beria and used any opportune moment to discredit him in Ordzhonikidze's eyes. Beria tried quite earnestly to demonstrate his devotion to Ordzhonikidze and refute the slander of his enemies. Beria's letters to Ordzhonikidze, which are preserved in Ordzhonikidze's personal papers at RTsKhIDNI, testify to this. "Sergo," he said in one of these letters dated December 18, 1932,

> you have known me more than ten years. You know all my faults and all my abilities. I never tried to undermine either the Central Committee or you, and I am sure I will not do so in the future. I devote all my time to work, hoping to justify the party's and the Central Committee's faith in me. . . . I ask you only one thing—don't believe anyone. . . . Verify all these stories so as to put an end to the incessant provocations.[11]

Judging from well-known facts, Ordzhonikidze actively protected Beria and maintained good relations with him right up to the middle of the 1930s.[12]

Even if we assume that Ordzhonikidze's patronage was a burden on Beria and that he wanted to dispense with it, it is possible to maintain that Beria would not have begun to "dig" at Sergo of his own volition. Feelings of self-preservation would have prevented Beria from doing this: The hot-tempered Sergo was not to be trifled with; neither was Stalin, who might not have reacted benevolently to them if he had really thought well of Ordzhonikidze before Beria's intrigues. Beria likely understood this. It was another matter, however, if Stalin had instructed Beria to do so (which cannot be ruled out) or had given even a hint or slight signal. Only in this case could Beria have risked arresting friends and relatives of a powerful Politburo member.

The supposition that Beria had shown the initiative in Ordzhonikidze's case is not persuasive, because Stalin in the future turned the arrests of close relatives into a traditional method of "educating" his comrades-in-arms. This was a way of verifying their absolute loyalty. As a rule, Stalin's circle successfully endured this test without protest, and often—as a manifestation of their utter devotion—actively assisted in the reprisals. This did not happen in Ordzhonikidze's case. He reacted painfully to his brother's arrest and tried to protect him from harm.

According to the 1953 testimony of Mir D. Bagirov, who was the first secretary of the Central Committee of the Azerbaidzhan Communist Party in 1936, Ordzhonikidze summoned him by telephone to Kislovodsk when he learned about his brother's arrest. "Ordzhonikidze drilled me about Beria, and spoke of him very negatively. In particular, Ordzhonikidze said that he couldn't believe in the guilt of his brother Papulia, recently arrested by Beria. . . . Beria learned through his own people that Ordzhonikidze had summoned me to Kislovodsk, and he asked me the reasons for it over the telephone. I answered that Ordzhonikidze was interested in issues concerning oil drilling."[13] Bagirov most likely did not accurately describe his role in this affair. But Ordzhonikidze's behavior testifies to the fact that he searched for a way to help his brother and tried to learn something of the case through roundabout ways. According to contemporary accounts later collected by Anton Antonov-Ovseenko, Ordzhonikidze repeatedly appealed to Stalin on his brother's behalf, tried to prove his innocence, and proposed summoning Papulia for questioning in Moscow. Stalin categorically refused.[14]

These events affected Ordzhonikidze's health in a critical way. After a period of relative improvement, associated with the visit of Professor Noorden from Austria, Ordzhonikidze's condition deteriorated.[15] On November 9, 1936, he suffered a bout of cardiovascular failure, accompanied by a brief loss of consciousness.[16]

How much did Ordzhonikidze himself believe that Papulia's arrest was a result of Beria's intrigues? On the one hand, it was convenient to believe this. In conversing with Stalin, for example, Ordzhonikidze could refer to Beria's machinations without leading to a serious argument by transferring the blame to Stalin himself. But on the other hand, it is difficult to believe that at the bottom of his heart, Ordzhonikidze did not understand Stalin's true role and the degree of Beria's independence. The conflict that soon flared up in Tbilisi involving Ordzhonikidze's other brother, Valiko, indirectly supports this view and serves as grounds for speculating about the relationship between Ordzhonikidze and Beria during this period.

Valiko (Ivan) Ordzhonikidze worked as a budgetary inspector in the financial department of the Tbilisi Soviet. At the beginning of November 1936, one of his colleagues filed a statement with the party committee charging that Ivan Konstantinovich insisted upon the innocence of Papulia Ordzhonikidze and denied he fraternized with Trotskyists. The party committee of the Tbilisi Soviet issued a denunciation. Valiko was called "on the carpet," and not only confirmed everything written in the statement, but added: "Papulia Ordzhonikidze couldn't go against his brother, Comrade Sergo Ordzhonikidze, nor the leader of our people, Comrade Stalin, whom he personally knows. . . . It's impossible to believe such accusations against Papulia Ordzhonikidze—they're all untrue." To the members of the party committee, Valiko protested: "You can be sure of the innocence not only of my brother, but of others who will be freed in a short time." For such impertinence, they expelled him from the group of party sympathizers, and fired him.

Sergo then got involved in the case. In the middle of December he phoned Beria and asked for help. Beria showed remarkable concern this time: He spoke with the accused and sought an explanation from the chairman of the Tbilisi Soviet. Sergo received a package within a week that contained an explanatory letter from the same chairman, Nioradze, and a cover letter from Beria. Beria wrote: "Dear Comrade Sergo! After your call I quickly summoned Valiko; he told me the story of his dismissal and roughly confirmed that which is expounded upon in the enclosed explanation from the chairman of the Tbilisi Soviet, Comrade Nioradze. Today, Valiko was restored to his job. Yours. L. Beria."[17]

This event merits close attention. Sergo, who apparently believed that the repressions against his friends and relatives were affairs exclusively of Beria's making, nonetheless called his enemy and asked him for help. Is this because he understood that Beria acted on orders, and that if he had none regarding Valiko Ordzhonikidze, he would have to help? Beria's reaction was curious. It was as if he signaled through such quick and unambiguous actions, "I'm always ready to serve you, Comrade Sergo. I have nothing against your family; and if I have to cause you grief, I'm not to blame." It is important to note Valiko Ordzhonikidze's behavior, of course, and his assurance that Papulia and "others" "will be freed in a short time." Could he have heard these promises from Sergo?

Conflict over the arrest of Papulia Ordzhonikidze and other Georgian Communists close to Sergo strained his relationship with Stalin. The leader's marginalia in a book, *Sergo Ordzhonikidze: Biographical Outline,* preserved in Stalin's library, testifies to the growth of his enmity toward Ordzhonikidze. Compiled by the former secretary of the Transcaucasian Regional Party Committee and deputy director of the Institute of Marx, Engels, and Lenin, Mamia (Ivan) D. Orakhelashvili (1881–1937), this work was published on Ordzhonikidze's fiftieth birthday (typeset on October 20, 1936, published on October 27). It represents a typical analysis by an old party member who knew the history well and preferred silence to outright falsification. In contrast to other works, dedicated almost exclusively to Stalin, Orakhelashvili's, while not forgetting the leader, dealt extensively with Ordzhonikidze in glowing terms.

Eulogizing Ordzhonikidze displeased Stalin greatly. He made numerous notations in the book. For example, Stalin highlighted the following passage on events in Persia from 1909: "The authority of Comrade Ordzhonikidze among the local Persian democratic population was immeasurable. They named him 'Mushtekhidom,' which means 'holy,' 'omnipotent.' "[18] He also underlined Orakhelashvili's assertion about Ordzhonikidze's systematic correspondence with Lenin, Ordzhonikidze's key role in convening the Prague Conference, and his contributions during the October Revolution and Civil War, and so on.[19] In the margins opposite statements on Ordzhonikidze's dedicated service under Stalin's leadership in the period of the July Crisis of 1917, Stalin wrote: "What about the Central Committee? The party?" "Where's the Central Committee?"[20] Stalin also paid attention to a quote from Ordhzhonikidze's report to the Sixteenth Party Congress: "Today we lavish Comrade Stalin with trust, and boldly move forward with him, knowing that he's leading the party along a Leninist path." Stalin highlighted this quote and underlined the word "lavish."[21] In Ordzhonikidze's report to the Sixteenth Congress, there were other, more "correct" pronouncements about Stalin, such as: "In Comrade Stalin, the party has a steadfast defender of the general party line and the best pupil of Vladimir Ilich [applause]. Our party and working class therefore correctly identify Comrade Stalin with the general line of our party, which leads the USSR from victory to victory."[22] But Orakhelashvili had selected the most provocative quotation, reminding readers that Stalin had become leader thanks to the support of his comrades-in-arms. It seems that Stalin understood this hint.

On the last page, Stalin underlined the book's press run: "First edition—one hundred thousand copies." Such a circulation for a biography of only one of Stalin's associates was inordinately large.

Stalin's displeasure with Orakhelashvili's book (the author, by the way, was soon to be repressed) once again shows that Stalin was threatened by the group of Old Bolsheviks who did not wish to forget the actual history of the party and acknowledge Stalin as the first among equals. The desire to get rid of them was one of the reasons for the organization of the Great Terror.

Chapter 10

Rout of the Economic Cadres

After his return to Moscow from Kislovodsk, numerous problems and unpleasantries befell Ordzhonikidze. Stalin's plans became even more definite—and Ordzhonikidze's position more precarious. The so-called Kemerovo Trial was a new blow inflicted on the People's Commissariat of Heavy Industry.

This open trial was conducted at the end of November 1936 in Novosibirsk, and widely publicized in the press. For several days, newspapers published trial records along with commentary. "Theoretical" articles followed with general lessons on "sabotage." Careful study of this case readily shows that it was in fact a rehearsal for the second Moscow Show Trial—against Piatakov and his comrades—which took place two months later, in January 1937. The reason for the organization of this trial in Kemerovo was an explosion at the Kuzbass mine Central on September 23, 1936, in which ten miners died and fourteen others were seriously injured. At the time, mine accidents occurred frequently, caused by poor equipment in the coal enterprises, rushed work, and the violation of safety rules. On December 28, 1935, at Central, for example, there was a terrible catastrophe in which, thanks only to a fortunate coincidence, two people died rather than dozens.

As a rule, such accidents were thoroughly concealed, and unhappy miners were forced to remain silent. The September tragedy at Kemerovo, however, was not covered up. A special commission was sent to the Kuzbass. Its members spent two weeks in the local NKVD building, but never even visited the mines. By dictate of the Chekists, the experts did not investigate the crux of the matter (as a review of the case at the end of the 1950s later revealed), but characterized the accident as an act of sabotage, rejecting all other accounts. In turn, NKVD agents quickly carried out arrests. It proved more than coincidental that the main engineer of the Kemerovo mine was Peshekhonov, who had been sentenced in 1928 to three years of exile in the Shakhty Affair. Engineers who formerly belonged to the Trotskyist opposition were linked to him. They even found a German specialist, Shtikling, at a neighboring shaft who had vacationed in Germany, which meant that he was a "German spy." NKVD agents arrested several other local economic managers, and concocted an "organization" that allegedly operated under the directives of the Unified Trotskyist-Zinovievite Center and received orders from Piatakov. The Kemerovo "spies" and "wreckers" were charged with artificially lowering the extraction of coal, poisoning workers with toxic gases, organizing the explosion of September 23 on orders of German fascists and, finally, attempting to murder the Sovnarkom chairman, Molotov, who had come to Kemerovo in 1934. All of these were fabrications, woven as usual only on "confessions" beaten out of people. Nevertheless, all nine of the accused were shot.[1]

The wave of state terror stimulated the strengthening of "vigilance" and a stream of denunciations, an example of which was the report of a rubber trust administrator sent to Ordzhonikidze on November 13, 1936. "I consider it my duty to report to you," it reads,

> that the systematic work stoppages in the rubber industry are rooted, above all, in the anti-Soviet technical leadership of the main engineer and deputy head of the Central Directorate, Mr. L.M. Gorbunov. I became convinced of this as a result of my observations of his work over three years. Unfortunately, I don't have any factual evidence to expose this evil. But on November 10, 1936, in an evening gathering with Comrade Bitker [head of the rubber industry in the NKTP Central Directorate—O.Kh.], . . . Mr. Gorbunov made a typical anti-Soviet statement that revealed his true class nature. He said: "*A healthy pissimism* [wording in the text—O.Kh.] *makes for technical progress.*" From today's perspective it is clear that, guided by just such an anti-Soviet principle, Gorbunov stifled any new innovation in the rubber industry, causing rubber factories to produce a huge number of defective

products, which has repeatedly come to light and is coming to light now."

Reporting to Ordzhonikidze about the other "sins" of Gorbunov, the manager continued:

> I was outraged by Gorbunov's negative statements, which were contrary to a Communist's convictions, but characteristically they weren't rebuffed by Comrade Bitker, who intimated with an unfriendly smile that one mustn't speak in such a way. I don't know how the other comrades present at this meeting will react, . . . but they all noticed the harmful attack against our *party's* policies, founded upon a *positive optimism, on a firm assurance of our strengths, on a firm assurance in victory.*
>
> I entreat you, Comrade Sergo, to pay attention to this note. The matter is more serious than it might appear at first. Produced in duplicate, I typed it myself, and retained the copy.[2]

This denunciation was such an obvious settling of accounts by an ignorant newcomer with his insufficiently "proletarian" boss that Ordzhonikidze appears to have simply ignored it. But he did not always act this way. Reacting to numerous "signals," Ordzhonikidze, more often than before, behaved cautiously and made compromises. In November 1936, for example, he received a letter from two employees of his commissariat, B. Levin and I. Gorskii, which reads:

> In connection with Piatakov's exposure as a Trotskyist scoundrel and counterrevolutionary wrecker, we consider it necessary to report to you the following facts. At the end of 1932 or the beginning of 1933, I, B. Levin, then the director of Chemical Factory No. 1 (Poison Gas), in my regular report to Piatakov . . . was given the task at Chemical Factory No. 1 to produce a gas so highly toxic that even the smallest dose would kill a person without leaving any noticeable traces in the body. This [gas] is supposedly needed for our struggle with enemies abroad. This work at Chemical Factory No. 1 was not carried out, but was limited to a study of the appropriate scholarly literature.
>
> In 1935 or the beginning of 1936, Piatakov, during our report . . . talked at length about methods and means he read about, used in the Middle Ages, by which people were poisoned with a highly toxic gas (by putting on gloves, turning pages of a book, etc.) that went undetected. The point of all this was that the chemical factory had to produce such a gas if it hadn't already done so.

On November 26, Ordzhonikidze forwarded this letter to Ezhov at the NKVD.[3]

On January 21, 1937, the Dnepropetrovsk regional committee secretary, Mendel Khataevich, sent a letter to Stalin, Ordzhonikidze, and Ezhov in which he maintained: "For several years now, all revelations regarding an array of spy and saboteur groups in our region, especially in Zaporozhe, point to the technical director of the factory combine Kommunar, and award-holder, P.I. Dik." Khataevich wrote that Dik finished engineering school in Germany in 1908. He began work in Zaporozhe before the revolution and remained at the factory after it was nationalized. In the 1920s he went to Germany to purchase equipment. Khataevich asserted that a number of arrested "counterrevolutionaries" fingered Dik as the organizer of an underground group at Kommunar in 1931–33. "According to sources, he is one of the main organizers of spy and espionage groups for the German fascists. But the People's Commissariat of Heavy Industry has not sanctioned his arrest." "The NKVD organs," concluded Khataevich, "have insisted on arresting Dik as a spy-saboteur for five years, but up until now have not received permission. . . . I request that you order the appropriate agencies to arrest Dik and strip him of his awards." Having familiarized himself with the letter, Ordzhonikidze did not defend Dik directly, but tried to stall for time. "Not once have the NKVD organs raised the question of Dik's arrest before the NKTP," he wrote.[4]

Even in those cases when Ordzhonikidze tried to help his employees, he was not nearly as successful as he had been earlier. Leaders of the punitive organs, such as the procuracy, no longer responded as before to Ordzhonikidze's requests. Following the new trend, Vyshinskii ordered in November 1936 that all criminal cases concerning major fires, accidents, and production of shoddy goods be reviewed within a month. His goal was to reveal their true counterrevolutionary, wrecking nature, and he acted in the spirit of this directive.[5] The case regarding the production of defective motor chambers at the Yaroslavl Rubber-Asbestos Combine serves as a characteristic example.

It began in September 1936, when Vyshinskii ordered an investigation following the publication of critical articles in the central press. Procuratorial investigators revealed that the Yaroslavl factory, "as a result of the criminal negligence" of responsible people, shipped worthless products to consumers. Charges were levied against the head of tire production, P.N. Borodavkin, the main engineer, Ia.K. Vecherkovskii, and other enterprise chiefs. Vecherkovskii appealed to Ordzhonikidze, maintaining that "production mistakes were inevitable because we were learning to handle new kinds of raw materials." Ordzhonikidze asked Vyshinskii to close the case.

On December 9, 1936, Vyshinskii, who previously had honored similar requests by Ordzhonikidze, refused. Wishing to somewhat soften his negative response, Vyshinskii wrote:

> Taking into consideration, however, your indication of objective difficulties at the combine in attempting 100 percent mastery in handling Soviet rubber at the combine, I have instructed the Yaroslavl regional procurator to carry out the most objective and thorough examination of this case by taking stock of the peculiarities and difficulties faced by factory workers accused in this affair. Following a thorough review of this case in court, I'll once again check on this and report back to you.[6]

Ordzhonikidze was unhappy with this reply, and personally talked it over with Vyshinskii. The procurator yielded and promised not to bring the case to court. A bit later, however, he wrote again to retract this promise: "Today I have received word that the NKVD organs have arrested the director of tire production, Borodavkin, as a Trotskyist. The combine director, Comrade Vasilev, reported to the Yaroslavl regional procurator that the main engineer of tire production at the rubber-asbestos combine, Vecherkovskii, was dismissed for poor leadership. In view of these facts, and by virtue of considerations set forth in the letter of December 9, 1936, I consider it impossible to stop this case from proceeding. Please, Comrade Sergo, don't object." Ordzhonikidze read this letter on December 21, and responded to Vyshinskii the next day: "I don't object."[7]

That it was the political aspects of the case that served as obstacles Vyshinskii could not overcome is evidenced by the fact that several days later he refused, on his own initiative, to launch a criminal investigation in an analogous situation. On January 9, 1937, he sent Ordzhonikidze a letter, in which he reported that the Leningrad regional procurator had forwarded materials to Moscow that apparently implicated a number of enterprises subordinate to the NKTP for shipping substandard products to the Red Nailmaker Factory throughout 1936. "Believing it expedient to initiate a criminal investigation against the heads of these factories (Red October, Elektrosteel, Makeevsk, Magnitogorsk, Petrovsk, and Izhevsk factories, etc.), I'm placing these materials at your disposal," wrote Vyshinskii. Ordzhonikidze ordered his associates to resolve the problem.[8]

In spite of Ordzhonikidze's efforts, the NKTP, like other commissariats, lost a critical number of cadres by the end of 1936. Some of the results of this purge concerning the number of nomenklatura employees dismissed from work, expelled from the party, and arrested were summed up by the Information Department of the Central Committee. According to that department, out of 823 people classified as belonging to the NKTP nomenklatura (deputy commissars, chiefs of major divisions, trust administrators, enterprise directors, construction bosses, and party organizers at defense plants), 56 people were dismissed from work in 1935–36. Of them, only one nomenklatura employee of the NKTP was fired, expelled from the party, or arrested during the verification of party cards from the end of 1934 to the end of 1935, whereas 11 were fired (9 of whom were expelled from the party and arrested) during the exchange of party cards in the spring and summer of 1936, and 44 were fired (37 of whom were expelled from the party and 34 arrested) after the exchange of party cards in the last months of 1936.[9]

Among those dismissed and arrested were well-known and deserving administrators who received numerous awards and were in Ordzhonikidze's special favor. Apart from Piatakov, those arrested included the head of the Chemical Industry Administration, S.A. Rataichak; the head of Siberian Machine Construction, M.S. Boguslavskii; the director of the Rostov Electric Machine Factory, N.P. Glebov-Avilov; the director of the Slavianskii Isolator Factory in the Donetsk region, I.P. Khrenov (whi, indicentally, is the hero of the famous poem by Mayakovskii, "Khrenov's Tale of the Kuznetsk Construction Site and the People of Kuznetsk"); the head of construction at the Orsk-Khalilovskii Combine, S.M. Frankfurt, who not long before this was the chief of Kuznetsk Construction and author of well-known memoirs on the construction of the Kuznetsk Combine, and many others.

In the previously mentioned files of the Information Department, the Central Committee also kept a list of nomenklatura workers of the NKTP "who in the past had taken part in the opposition and had wavered." Among them were the Deputy Commissar of Heavy Industry, A.I. Gurevich (who during the trade union controversy of 1921 had sided with Trotsky's platform); the celebrated director of the Makeevsk Metallurgical Factory and a favorite of Ordzhonikidze, G.V. Gvakharia (who, in 1928, had been expelled from the party and sent to Kazakhstan for belonging to the Trotskyist Opposition, but thanks to Ordzhonikidze's efforts, was reinstated in the party in 1930); the head of the Chemical-Plastic Trust, M.I. Frumkin (described in one document as, "one of the leaders of the Right Opposition"); the director of Factory No. 12 (Moscow region), S.I. Syrtsov, and many others—sixty-six people in all.[10] All were subsequent victims of the purges, which Ordzhonikidze could not have failed to realize. He quite possibly had discussed many of the arrests.

Ordzhonikidze could also have known about the impending arrests in his commissariat, judging by other materials preserved in his personal papers. One such document was entitled "Information on the Personal Composition of the Central Apparatus of the People's Commissariat of Heavy Industry as of December 1, 1936," and was signed by the head of the Administrative Department of Managerial Affairs of the NKTP, Bobrov. Bobrov reported that of the 743 full and candidate members of the party who worked in the central apparatus of the NKTP, 42 had incurred party penalties (including 12 for participating in the Trotskyist Opposition), while 80 had once belonged to other parties (former Mensheviks, SRs, Bundists, and Anarchists). Of the nonparty employees, 160 had been expelled at one time from the party, and 169 had belonged to other political parties. Among those employees in the commissariat's central apparatus, there were 71 former officers of the White Army, 287 officers of the tsarist army, 31 people who had worked in various institutions on the territory occupied by the Whites during the Civil War, 94 convicted of counterrevolutionary activities, and 41 convicted of malfeasance in office. There were 131 individuals who had been born to families of merchants and industrialists, 133 to the nobility, and 73 to clerical families.[11]

The trial of the so-called Parallel Anti-Soviet Trotskyist Center, held in Moscow during January 23–30, 1937 (the second major Moscow Show Trial), sped up the repression of managers. In fact, this was a trial

Ordzhonikidze with his economic cadres in the mid-1930s.

of the NKTP. Ten of the seventeen defendants were top officials in the
NKTP—G.L. Piatakov; the head of Siberian Machine Construction in
Novosibirsk, M.S. Boguslavskii; the head of the NKTP's Main Chemical
Industry, S.A. Rataichak; the head of the Kemerovo Chemical Combine
Construction, B.O. Norkin, and his deputy, Ia.N. Drobnis; the adminis-
trator of the Salairsk Zinc Mines in Kemerevo Oblast, A.A. Shestov; the
chief engineer of the Kuzbass Coal trust, M.S. Stroilov; the senior econo-
mist of the Production-Technical Department of the NKTP's Main Chemi-
cal Industry, I.I. Grashe; the deputy chief engineer of the Main
Chemical Industry and chief construction engineer of the Rionskii Ni-

trogen Fertilizer Combine in Georgia, G.E. Pushin; and the manager of the Supply Department at the Prokopevskii and Anzherskii Mines in the Kuzbass, V.V. Arnold. The press regularly published trial reports. The defendants' confessions concerning "wrecking" bred further suspicion and encouraged the search for new "wreckers."

Trying to protect his commissariat from attack in such difficult times, Ordzhonikidze compromised. He argued that there actually were and will be enemies, but the secret police had for the most part already exposed them. In keeping its honest employees, the commissariat had to overcome the negative consequences of sabotage through conscientious efforts. Ordzhonikidze consistently repeated this message in one form or another during the last months of his life. The new director of the Rostov Electric Machine Factory, D. Kartashov, remembered how at the time of his appointment, Ordzhonikidze encouraged him "to review management cadres carefully, preventing wholesale disparagement of them, expelling only true enemies of the people." "In order to fire people," Kartashov said, repeating Ordzhonikidze, "no special skill is necessary. But to find real enemies and expel them requires Bolshevik vigilance and Bolshevik tact."[12] On February 1, 1937, in one of his last speeches, made at a reception for employees of the oil-refining plants, Ordzhonikidze once again publicly disagreed with the assertions of widespread wrecking, reasoning as he had since the June 1936 conference at the People's Commissariat of Heavy Industry:

> Our engineer . . . is building his own home in his own Soviet Union. He devotes all his energies and knowledge to the construction of socialism. . . . I dare state we have such individuals in our country; at least 90 percent of the enormous number of engineers belong to this category [applause]. It can't be otherwise. These are our own sons and brothers whom we raised. During the last ten years, our institutes of higher learning trained about one hundred thousand engineers and technicians who are the flesh of our flesh, our blood, our sons, our friends, our comrades, [I repeat] our sons.[13]

Incidentally, those present understood the real intention of this statement, made a day after the trial against Piatakov and other leaders of industry ended, and showed their support by applauding Ordzhonikidze's attempt to set up a distinct quantitative limit beyond which the repressions must not extend.

It cannot be ruled out that Ordzhonikidze made similar arguments in quarrels with Stalin over the devotion to socialism of the overwhelming majority of specialists.

In defending the cadres of his commissariat, Ordzhonikidze relied not only on his powers as a Politburo member backed by a sufficiently influential economic nomenklatura, but also on the support of a significant number of local party leaders. Stable cohorts of the ruling elite, joined together by common interests, formed in the provinces. Apart from party and soviet officials, they included the directors of large industrial establishments who had significant financial power as well as connections in Moscow. The main concern of the regional bosses was maintaining stability locally, keeping the peace between rival chiefs. Conflicts and squabbles, especially those reaching the center, had the most unfortunate consequences that led to cadre reshuffling and "resolution by the punitive organs." Each regional party secretary tried to surround himself with "his own" people. A general desire to preserve their position and avoid unpleasantries tended to unite all leaders into a comparatively friendly association.

Living under the continuous threat of purges and arrests, local leaders tried their best to limit "exposures" and restrain the most zealous NKVD agents. Because each arrest entailed new accusations, or at best charges of "political short-sightedness" and "lack of vigilance," they reacted negatively to repressions against their "own" in the provinces. Regional party secretaries often formed united fronts with the leaders of economic departments to defend enterprise directors located within their region. The most open attempts by local leaders to resist the repressions took place at the end of 1936 and the beginning of 1937, during active preparation for the Great Terror. Events in Nizhnii Tagil also involving Ordzhonikidze can serve as a characteristic example.

Nizhnii Tagil was the site of one of the most ambitious projects of the Second Five-Year Plan, the Ural Coach Construction Factory, built and operated by the People's Commissariat of Heavy Industry. Its building involved the usual feverish haste, enthusiasm, use of repression and lack of sufficient preparation. The enterprise began operation in 1936, but soon the leadership of the factory was charged with sabotage and destroyed. This was yet another blow against Ordzhonikidze, who in this case tried to defend his employees to the very end.

The head of construction, L.M. Mariasin, was appointed at Nizhnii Tagil in June 1933 after successfully building the Magnitogorsk Coke Combine. Like other "captains of industry," Mariasin was a dynamic and coarse man who ruled without indulgence and sought to fulfill an order from above at any price. Like other managers, he often received penalties for not meeting goals that were frequently unobtainable. These unpleasantries were insignificant, however, in comparison with the attacks he periodically endured for his "Trotskyist past," that is, for his support for Trotsky's position in 1923. Although Mariasin had repeatedly repented since then, the stigma of political unreliability continued to haunt him.

The same was true for the secretary of the Nizhnii Tagil City Party Committee, Shalvy Stepanovich Okudzhava. He had joined a group of young Social Democrats under the leadership of the Kutaiss Bolsheviks when he was sixteen, immediately after the February Revolution in 1917. He then held the post as manager of the Organizational Department in the Central Committee of the Georgian Komsomol, studied in Moscow, and once again returned to carry out party work in his native land. In 1932, Okudzhava left the post of secretary of the Tiflis City Party Committee to become secretary of the party committee at the Ural Coach Construction Factory (there is evidence that he did not get along with Beria). In 1935, he was selected secretary of the Tagil City Party Committee. But while in Moscow back in 1923, as he himself wrote in his autobiography, his loyalty to the party line "wavered."[14] Besides this, two brothers of Shalvy Stepanovich were Trotsky supporters. The older one was a member of the party, and from 1903 to 1923 worked as a secretary of the Central Committee of the Georgian Communist Party. He was then expelled from the party; after repenting, his membership to the party was restored and he remained in Tiflis. Okudzhava's other brother refused to repent, and was exiled in the 1930s. This kinship magnified his own "sins" and caused Okudzhava constant trouble, from which Ordzhonikidze repeatedly saved him.

At the end of 1935 and the beginning of 1936, for example, Okudzhava was beset by problems stemming from statements made against him by a certain Klekovkin. Klekovkin reported that while vacationing in Sukhumi, he learned from the head of the regional party committee's Department of Culture and Propaganda of Abkhazia that

Okudzhava was an oppositionist in the Caucasus, and that his brother even led "anti-party groups." After receiving this denunciation, the secretary of the Sverdlovsk Regional Party Committee, I.D. Kabakov, set events in motion. The Tiflis city committee was asked to provide a copy of Okudzhava's registration form, and excerpts from meetings of party colleagues of the Transcaucasian Regional Control Commission. No new compromising evidence turned up against Okudzhava. Ordzhonikidze's interference also played a role, and the case was closed.[15]

Enjoying some support, Okudzhava, in turn, tried to impede repressions in the Nizhnii Tagil party organization. He defended those expelled from the party, and toned down accusatory campaigns.[16] This soon got him in deep trouble.

As the political course grew more severe, the situation of Mariasin and Okudzhava worsened. The next flare-up of "exposing" campaigns took place in August 1936 in connection with a discussion in the party organization of a secret Central Committee letter "On the Terrorist Activities of the Trotskyist-Zinovievite Counterrevolutionary Bloc." Fulfilling Central Committee instructions, the Nizhnii Tagil city committee also held a meeting of party activists. Okudzhava was worked over at this gathering, which recalled his Trotskyist past. The question of his party membership hung by a thread. Okudzhava's expulsion from the party, however, was prevented by a member of the Sverdlovsk Regional Committee Party Bureau, Uziukov, who was present by order of the regional leadership. Addressing the tribune, Uziukov stated that regional party committee members knew Okudzhava as an irreproachable Communist and trusted him. This resolved the problem.[17] (Incidentally, this speech together with other faults soon got Uziukov himself in trouble. Not waiting for the inevitable arrest, he committed suicide.)

Roughly at the same time, the leadership of the Sverdlovsk Regional Party Committee admirably managed to ward off a blow to Mariasin. It happened as follows: The instructor of the regional party committee, Maslennikov, visited the Ural Coach Construction Factory on an inspection trip. Upon returning, he submitted a report consistent with the spirit of the times that charged Mariasin with wrecking. The regional party bureau examined this memorandum, and thanks to the efforts of Kabakov and the party committee's second secretary, Pshenitsyn, rejected demands to expel Mariasin from the party and arrest him.[18] (Pshenitsyn would also soon be charged with abetting enemies, and committed suicide. Kabakov was shot.)

Moscow played its own games at this time. The NKVD fabricated evidence of Mariasin's "Trotskyist" activities, and in September 1936 received permission to arrest him. At the end of January 1937, charges were levied against Mariasin at an open trial in the case of the Parallel Anti-Soviet Trotskyist Center. Interrogated at the very beginning of the judicial session, Piatakov said that "in the Urals, there were two main establishments where wrecking activities were concentrated. One was the copper industry, and the other—the Ural Coach Construction Factory."[19] In the words of Piatakov, Mariasin was a participant in the Ural Trotskyist group, and personally carried out sabotage: He wasted funds on materials and equipment unnecessarily, dragged out construction, and made it difficult to get enterprises operating. The defendant, I.D. Turok, who before his arrest had worked as the deputy head of the Sverdlovsk Railway, maintained that Mariasin not only recruited him into the organization, but ordered wrecking on the railroad lines.[20] On April 1, 1937, Mariasin was sentenced to be shot (his legal and party rehabilitation came twenty years later, in April–May 1957).

Mariasin's arrest put Okudzhava in an extremely difficult position. Trying to save the life both of himself and his family, Okudzhava repented, recognized his mistakes, and swore allegiance to the general line. "The guilt of the Tagil city committee is tremendous," he said, for example, at a meeting of party activists in Nizhnii Tagil not long before his arrest.

> We didn't expose Mariasin's heinous gang of bandits and others, who caused harm to the people and planned to murder leaders who came to help us in our work. As leader of the party organization, I was instructed to direct and organize the masses to be vigilant. I failed to carry out this responsibility, and admit my grave mistake. This is especially difficult for me. I must take into account the fact that I have made Trotskyist mistakes in the past, and that my brothers are counterrevolutionaries.[21]

The previously mentioned party activists of the Nizhnii Tagil organization met on February 9–10, 1937. In spite of the fact that two months had passed since Mariasin's arrest, the Sverdlovsk Regional Party Committee leadership did not touch Okudzhava. As before, Kabakov waited for the Central Committee to decide. Lacking a Central Committee decision, Stalin and Ordzhonikidze apparently held conversations about Okudzhava's fate. At the beginning of February, Ordzhonikidze sent his own inspectors to the Ural Coach Construction Factory, responsible NKTP employees, S.Z. Ginzburg and I.P. Pavlunovskii, and ordered them to investigate the charges of sabotage (more detail on this will be provided in the next chapter). The denouement came not long before Ordzhonikidze's death. On February 15, the Sverdlovsk Regional Party Committee decided to dismiss Okudzhava from his responsibilities as city party committee first secretary, initially "in connection with a transfer to another job." Okudzhava was soon arrested, however, and expelled from the party as a Trotskyist.[22]

At the imminent February–March plenum of the Central Committee, statements would be heard that assailed Ordzhonikidze for actively interfering in the Okudzhava Affair. Reporting on wrecking in heavy industry, Molotov said (quoted from the published account):

> Other examples of sabotage that were not fully exposed can be found at the Ural Coach Construction Factory. This is a matter concerning the largest coach factory, which in the near future is to produce the lion's share of modern cars. A most active wrecker, Mariasin, has headed construction for several years, while the wrecker-Trotskyist Shaliko Okudzhava has been the secretary of the party committee at the Ural Coach Construction Factory. These saboteurs were exposed several months ago.[23]

Thus, the official account maintained that Okudzhava was "uncovered" "several months" before the plenum. It is unlikely that this was simply a slip of the tongue, since Molotov left this assertion in the widely published version of his report. Most likely, he made this claim to hide the fact that several months had passed between Mariasin's arrest and the Okudzhava case. Stalin explained how this had happened to plenum participants (granted, this section was never published). In his aforementioned closing speech at the plenum, Stalin said about Ordzhonikidze: "How many times has he annoyed us by defending all those scoundrels, as is now apparent, like Vardanian, Gogoberidze, Meliksetov, and Okudzhava? The case in the Urals is now closed. How many times has he caused unpleasantness for himself and how many times has he caused unpleasantness for us?"[24]

The attention devoted at the plenum to the Nizhnii Tagil affair was not accidental. Arrests at the Ural Coach Construction Factory while preparations for the plenum were being made caused arguments between Stalin and Ordzhonikidze, and became a special matter for the NKTP leadership.

Chapter 11

Preparing for the Plenum

During his last days, Ordzhonikidze's main concern was preparing for the Central Committee plenum that would take place without him and go down in Soviet history as the sinister "February–March Plenum of 1937." Hovering over the plenum—as if all the problems tormenting Ordzhonikdize for many long months had come together—was his estrangement from Stalin. For Ordzhonikidze, the plenum was one of the last chances, more illusory than real, to apply the brakes to Stalinist policy. For Stalin, it was perhaps the last plenum for which he had to prepare thoroughly and expect attacks that in all probability would be weak, but nonetheless would be aimed at him.

On January 28, 1937, the Politburo members decided to convene the plenum. They proposed that it open on February 20 and that the agenda include the case of Bukharin and Rykov, preparing party organizations for a new election system to the Supreme Soviet of the USSR, and discussion of the sabotage, diversion, and spying of the Trotskyists.[1] On January 31, the Politburo confirmed the speakers: on the first matter—Ezhov; on the second—Zhdanov; and on the third—Ordzhonikidze, Kaganovich, Ezhov, and Andreev, each of whom had to address "wrecking" in his respective department (the People's Commissariats of Heavy Industry, Communications, Internal Affairs, and the party). All speakers had to submit their draft proposals by February 5.[2]

Ordzhonikidze received this directive and began to prepare. He based his draft resolution on the previous premise that enemies had been uncovered for the most part, so the main task was to liquidate the consequences of sabotage. He fashioned the document in a relaxed tone. While formally alluding to wrecking, he devoted his primary attention to politically neutral technical and economic problems. He began his draft report referring to the successes that were—here Ordzhonikidze repeated his favorite line—"achieved thanks to our cadres of engineers, technicians, and administrators, promoted by the party from the sons of the working class and peasantry."[3] One of the points in his draft resolution stipulated that "the NKTP report to the Central Committee within ten days about conditions at the Kemerovo Chemical Combine, the Ural Coach Construction Factory, and the Middle Ural Copper Construction Plant, after indicating specific measures to liquidate the consequences of sabotage and diversion at these sites in order thereby to guarantee the starting up of these enterprises according to the fixed date."[4] As further events revealed, this point had vital significance, for Ordzhonikidze tried to legalize the NKTP's right to independently verify secret police materials that "exposed" so-called wrecking organizations in the places enumerated above.

Ordzhonikidze most likely wrote this draft resolution by February 5, as had been stipulated by the Politburo decision of January 31. On February 5, the Politburo confirmed the final order of speakers at the plenum. Ezhov would speak on the Bukharin and Rykov case; Ordzhonikidze, Kaganovich, and Ezhov would speak on the "lessons of the sabotage, diversion, and spying by Japanese-German-Trotskyist agents"; Stalin would speak on the third point of the agenda, "concerning the political education of party cadres and measures taken in the struggle against Trotskyists and other double-dealers in party organizations;" and Zhdanov would speak on the fourth, concerning preparation for the elections.[5]

The matter, however, was apparently not limited to formally adopting a resolution. It seems that on February 5 itself, Ordzhonikidze and Stalin held a conversation about sabotage in industry and how to prepare this issue for the plenum. Stalin's notes on Ordzhonikidze's draft resolution reveal the true nature of this discussion. Judging from them, Stalin remained unhappy. He scribbled comments and retorts all over the document, expressing irritation with Ordzhonikidze's attempts to soften things by limiting himself to streamlined verifications. Stalin highlighted the following point, for example, in Ordzhonikidze's document:

> The manager, engineer, and technician, whether a party member or not, can't be apolitical and concerned only with his own "technology," but along with mastering technology . . . should be concerned with politics and clearly aware of who the friends and enemies of Soviet power are [here Stalin inserted that "he himself should also be a political worker"]. But party organizations with all their means must aid the political [Stalin corrected this word to "Bolshevik"] education of the economic, engineering, and technical cadres.

Opposite this point, Stalin added: "State this more directly and make it a central issue." Stalin also "politicized" the neutral point about substituting 75 percent of employees in crucial and dangerously explosive units with people having special secondary technical educations, and added that these must be workers "who are proven friends of Soviet power," and so forth.

Stalin's general instructions ran as follows: "(1) state with facts which branches are affected by sabotage and exactly how they are affected; and (2) mention reasons for idlers (the apolitical, narrowminded selection of cadres, and absence of politically educated cadres)."[6]

One other document, which to a certain extent allows us to characterize Ordzhonikidze's mood and the nature of his conversations with Stalin, is the unabridged stenogram of Ordzhonikidze's speech at the conference of the heads of the NKTP Central Directorate on the same day, February 5. As is clear from his introductory remarks, Ordzhonikidze was very late for the conference (the reason for being late to such an important gathering could only be a delay at a still higher level, such as the Central Committee). In spite of this, Ordzhonikidze gave his subordinates a "dressing-down." Clearly agitated, he spoke incoherently, jumping from topic to topic. Ordzhonikidze also reported that he would address the issue of sabotage in heavy industry at the plenum scheduled for February 20.

Ordzhonikidze began with reproaches for the serious situation in industry and for nonfulfillment of the plan, and dedicated a significant part of his speech to charges of not struggling sufficiently enough with wrecking:

> We've learned nothing from this trial [the January trial of Piatakov and others—O.Kh.]. Here you sit, heads of the Central Directorate.

You should have bombarded me with proposals about what to do in various industrial branches. But I've received nothing from you. None of you believes this matter concerns him. The only reason that it doesn't concern you is that you didn't get involved as you should have. You'd think that if I had a first deputy, a man like Piatakov, who worked for a decade and a half in industry and had vast contacts, that he couldn't slip one or two people on us? Of course, he could and did slip some on us. We found several of them, but not all.[7]

Must I answer alone for all of you? There is sabotage at the factories—Ordzhonikidze is guilty—nobody else. Do you tell me how you'll end the wrecking and which measures you'll adopt? You don't tell me anything. . . . No, comrades, search everywhere, for we certainly have large and small party cells that have been spoiled. . . . A curious question has been nagging me—How could this have happened? We've worked together so many years, and indeed not so badly. The results have been quite good, and we even fulfilled the Five-Year Plan in four. How could it be that Piatakov was in our midst and nobody noticed a thing? You'll reply that he was my deputy, that I didn't notice, and that you have nothing to do with it. That's not right. If a Kemerovo worker were to say this, he would be correct, but if you say it, it's wrong, because many of you worked with Piatakov for more years than with me, and many of you regarded him with open sympathy. This isn't a reproach, but stems from the fact that a man worked among us as if he were helping. That's how it was. Why did this happen? Were we really so blind to it all? You must ask yourselves this question. Even if we aren't taken to court, we must ask our own conscience how this could happen. That's because we didn't pay enough attention to what was going on around us. Apparently, it's because many of us rested on our laurels.[8]

The accursed Piatakov, Rataichak, etc. played many dirty tricks on us. But their downfall came. We caught them, arrested them, and forced them to tell everything that happened. This should open our eyes. . . . Apparently we have entered into a period when it's once again necessary to rebuild our ranks, our leadership, and run things in a new fashion. The hell with it, but without any shake-up, we'll begin to rust.[9]

Ordzhonikidze's speech, never previously published, provides grounds for several observations. It definitely shows that by February 5, at the latest, he was not in a mood to quarrel with Stalin on the question of exposing sabotage but, on the contrary, demonstrated his loyalty and answered Stalin's criticism regarding his lack of vigilance. That Ordzhonikidze's speech was prompted by his conversations with Stalin is clear by Ordzhonikidze's use of Stalin's slogans concerning the tranquillity bred by success and the necessity of shake-ups and restructuring the ranks and leadership. Stalin would develop these ideas in detail at the upcoming February–March plenum. It seems that Stalin also charged Ordzhonikidze with packing the NKTP with saboteurs, and reminded him of Piatakov. This was the origin of Ordzhonikidze's remark that he was not alone to blame for the lack of vigilance.

After reacting to Stalin's criticism, Ordzhonikidze nonetheless reminded the heads of the Central Directorate about the need to defend employees from unfair accusations and ensure a peaceful state of affairs at enterprises:

> There are directors at several factories today who, in connection with the trial of the scoundrels, feel that they themselves are under attack as if they are criminals, and everyone must answer for Piatakov and the others. Nothing of the sort. They must be told directly that they're not criminals, they're our cadres. We caught the criminals, shot them, and we'll catch future criminals and shoot all the scum we find. We're not talking about them, but about the enormous mass of cadres, fine ones trained by us. This is what we need to say to them. We must not ignore the gossip among workers at the factories [linked to the strengthening of the specialist-baiting campaign—O.Kh.], but raise labor productivity and regulate affairs at the factories.[10]
>
> When you go to the directors and help them, they'll respect you more and take you more seriously. But if you only curse them, nothing will come of this. They're left to their own devices. They're put on the spot and harassed by the party organization because of the trial. It's necessary to approach them, to talk with the workers, to talk with the directors, and to help and encourage them.[11]

These words were not simply a repetition of those already spoken repeatedly. Real deeds stood behind them. That very day, February 5, Ordzhonikidze ordered one of his employees, Professor Galperin, to investigate charges of wrecking at Kemerovo. The directives Galperin received from Ordzhonikidze did not leave any doubt as to the goal of the mission. According to Galperin, Ordzhonikidze said:

Take into account that you're going to a place that was one of the more active centers of sabotage. All honest workers there—and they're the overwhelming majority—are very upset by what happened. You yourself were probably also affected by the most recent trial. Remember that the fainthearted or insufficiently conscientious people might wish to blame everything on sabotage in order to hide their own mistakes in the trial on wrecking. We simply can't allow this. We wouldn't get an exact picture of what happened, and consequently we wouldn't know how to correct it. You must approach the matter as a technician, trying to distinguish conscious sabotage from involuntary mistakes—this is your main task.[12]

Similar instructions—to make an objective financial and technical examination of evidence fabricated by the NKVD—were seditious in and of themselves. After all, official agencies unanimously demanded that all economic problems and breakdowns be evaluated from a political point of view, as a result of wrecking.

Galperin's commission carried out its mission in complete conformity with Ordzhonikidze's wishes. Molotov addressed the commission's findings in his concluding remarks at the February–March plenum on March 2, 1937: the commission "led by Professor Galperin and members Lubov, Rodionov, and Olkhov went to Kemerovo and submitted a forty-five-page report on the results of their work. Could one possibly expect not to read the words 'sabotage' or 'saboteur' in this report? But the commission submitted just such a report, where, in spite of the well-known confessions of wreckers such as Norkin, Drobnis, and others, the commission presented the usual sort of conclusion about shortcomings in construction, but missed one point—sabotage."[13]

We learn about another NKTP commission from Molotov:

This commission, led by the deputy commissar, Comrade Osipov-Shmidt, and comprised of engineers Ivanov, Shneerson, Abramovich, and Solovëv, investigated the case in the Donbass coke industry, where the Trotskyist gang led by the infamous Logunov was active. It also submitted a written report on the results of its work. Its findings detailed the great losses of ammonia and benzol last year that were caused by neglect of chemical-processing equipment and prematurely starting up chemical works at a number of factories. But there's not a word concerning sabotage or saboteurs in this report.[14]

Information about the work of the third commission, comprised of
the head of NKTP's Main Construction Industry, S.Z. Ginzburg, and the
NKTP deputy commissar, I.P. Pavlunovskii (apart from that previously
mentioned in Molotov's report), is preserved in the testimony of Ginzburg, the only participant of those events alive today. Ginzburg recalled:

> In the beginning of February 1937 Sergo told me about events at the
> Ural Coach Construction Factory at Nizhnii Tagil. . . . He proposed
> that Pavlunovskii, who was in charge of the NKTP defense industry,
> and I go there as soon as possible in a commissariat train car and
> conduct a detailed investigation of the nature of the arrested
> builders' wrecking activities. . . . Upon arrival in Tagil, I immediately
> went to the construction site in order to look into the situation in
> detail. . . . I studied the shops and buildings for several days, and then
> with utmost attention checked construction estimates and expenses
> for each item. As a result, I was convinced that construction was in
> good shape and the quality of work was much higher than at other
> construction sites in the Urals, although there were a few expendi-
> tures that exceeded estimates.
> In the middle of February, Sergo called from Moscow and asked
> about conditions at the construction site and what crimes had been
> discovered. I replied that the factory was well built and was complete,
> although there were a few expenditures that exceeded estimates. But
> at present, construction has slowed down and the workers don't know
> what to do. . . . To Sergo's question: Had I been at other construction
> sites?—I answered that I had been, and in comparison with other
> sites, the one in Nizhnii Tagil had a number of advantages. Sergo
> asked me again if this were possible. I observed that I always tell
> everything as it is. If that's the case, said Sergo, find Pavlunovskii and
> quickly return to Moscow. Dictate a short note in the train car to the
> stenographer, in my name, about conditions at the Ural Coach Con-
> struction Factory, and upon arrival immediately drop by my place.[15]

At the February–March plenum, Molotov subjected Ginzburg and
Pavlunovskii to harsh criticism. The commission, in his words, "failed to
take into account the lessons of sabotage, and had adopted an all too
reassuring manner" in maintaining that "the activity of wreckers at the
construction site hadn't been widespread."[16]

According to the recently published memoirs of one of the NKTP
colleagues, Ziskind (as recounted by I.N. Kramov), Ordzhonikidze,

while preparing a report on sabotage in heavy industry, sent "eleven
of his deputies" to the factories "in order to check on the situation in
the provinces." Material prepared on the basis of the inspections, in
Ziskind's words, "was divided into two categories: testimony of the
defendants on trial addressing sabotage in heavy industry, and the reports of commissariat deputies who verified that testimony in the
provinces, as well as reports concerning meetings at Sergo's place by
leaders of several large metallurgical, chemical, and aviation factories. All these accounts proved that the defendants on trial had lied."[17]
At the February–March plenum, however, Molotov maintained that
there were only three commissions: the Ginzburg-Pavlunovskii one,
the Osipov-Shmidt one, and the Galperin commission. Considering
that the commission materials were not well known (it is possible
that some of them were stashed away in archives that remain closed),
it is impossible to check on the accuracy of any one source.

It is worth noting, however, that in the previously mentioned
speech of February 5, Ordzhonikidze reported that he had sent his
deputies to the provinces and demanded that the heads of the Central Directorate "lock up their directorates, and send all who are
appropriate and capable of doing anything to the factories. . . . It's
necessary to leave for the factories, since no one needs your reports
here. . . . Try to give me better reports from there in the future. . . ."[18]
"Sergo got prepared for his comprehensive and crucial report. He
sent many of his aides to the factories and mines in order to closely
examine them and verify data. The aides who returned from the provinces reported to the commissar in detail on the materials collected.
Attentively evaluating the reports, Sergo drew some conclusions and
shared his thoughts," wrote Ordzho-nikidze's deputy, O.P. Osipov-
Shmidt, in Pravda on February 21, 1937.[19] This confirms Ziskind's assertions concerning numerous commissions. But it is impossible to
exclude the possibility that Ordzhonikidze himself might have informed the Politburo about only the three reports of the most authori-
tative commissions. There were grounds for hiding the true scale of the
investigation conducted by the NKTP, even from Molotov.

Irrespective of the number of NKTP commissions, however, we can
say with assurance that Ordzhonikidze seriously prepared for the ple-

num and gathered facts refuting the secret police's assertions. Organizing an independent verification concerning "sabotage" was the strongest move Ordzhonikidze could undertake in these circumstances. The gathered evidence constituted the basis of an important argument in his quarrel with Stalin.

Taking into account that one of the central issues of the previous plenum was the case of Bukharin and Rykov, there were grounds for also examining Ordzhonikidze's relations with leaders of the "Right Deviation."

Being Control Commission chairman, Ordzhonikidze, as already mentioned, played a major role in Stalin's victory over the Bukharin group. Moreover, passions in this struggle became so heated that opponents often forgot about rival political programs and made personal attacks, not sparing scathing words and nasty epithets. Such an exchange occurred, for example, between Bukharin and Ordzhonikidze at the April 1929 plenum of the Central Committee and the Central Control Commission, at which the Stalinist majority succeeded in decisively crushing the "right":

> *Ordzhonikidze:* Is it [the so-called theory of the "peaceful transition of the kulaks to socialism," in a proclamation that accused Bukharin—O.Kh.] correct or incorrect?
>
> *Bukharin:* Just a minute! I'll speak as I wish! I think the Central Control Commission chairman is obliged to demonstrate *maximum patience* in spite of his southern temperament! (laughter)
>
> *Ordzhonikidze:* I think the general secretary of the Comintern can be questioned, even if he is politically bankrupt.
>
> *Bukharin:* Submit questions in writing, and I'll answer later if they let me.
>
> *Ordzhonikidze:* Up until now, we thought we could ask questions orally.
>
> *Bukharin:* You simply keep me from speaking, interrupting my speech, as do your friends—neighbors! . . . Why do you interrupt me? You laugh at me and interrupt!
>
> *Ordzhonikidze:* Well then, is laughter forbidden? The law does not forbid this.
>
> *Bukharin:* I know that nobody forbade you to beat your chauffeurs in the face. What in fact is going on here?[20]

In principle, similar "discussions" could fully ruin, and in many instances actually spoiled, personal relations between political opponents. In the case of Ordzhonikidze and Bukharin, however, it appears that this did not happen. Their relations remained friendly enough. This became even easier when their political disagreements soon disappeared: Rykov, Bukharin, and Tomskii, having lost the battle, acknowledged the correctness of the Stalinist majority.

It is also worth noting that for Ordzhonikidze and other members of the Politburo who supported Stalin, Bukharin's group was not the same as the previous oppositionists, such as Trotsky and Zinoviev. Bukharin, Rykov, and Tomskii, even in the period of greatest confrontation, remained more "theirs" than, for example, Trotsky, Zinoviev, and Kamenev. The "right" spoke less bitterly, tried to maneuver within the confines of an extremely narrow party legality, did not make categorical demands to replace individuals in the Politburo, and thus earned the label of a "deviation" and not an "opposition." They acknowledged the very power of the Stalinist Politburo after their defeat and constantly repented. While not fully absolved, they received secondary leadership positions. Bukharin was the most solidly "rehabilitated." Alternating between periods of confrontation and neutrality in his relationship to Stalin, Bukharin finally adopted the leader's position.

Joint work improved relations between Bukharin and Ordzhonikidze. During 1929–34, Bukharin was a member of the VSNKh Presidium and a colleague of the People's Commissariat of Heavy Industry, as he headed a center for scientific research in Ordzhonikdize's department. Only a few documents have been preserved that throw light on their relationship. Judging from them, Bukharin viewed his boss as a potential guardian from numerous unpleasantries, and possibly even as a patron. To what extent was Ordzhonikidze prepared to play this role? Undoubtedly, he regarded Bukharin with sympathy. But he could translate this sympathy into concrete action only so far as it did not contradict Stalin's intentions. Ordzhonikidze did not plan to clash with the "boss" on Bukharin's behalf, especially "over trivialities."

The history of Bukharin's purge in November 1933 proves this point. According to the established rules for Central Committee members that were in place when Bukharin joined the party, members could be purged only in the event that one or more party gatherings or a group of party members submitted justification. It is clear that in 1933 such an initiative could no longer come from below. If it did, as everyone well knew, it was inspired by the party leadership. This was a signal of disfavor, a harbinger of new remonstrations. The news that they intended to purge Bukharin was just so perceived in November 1933.

On November 5, the party collective of the NKTP's Scientific Research (NIS) and Technical Propaganda Sector (Tekhprop), headed by Bukharin, resolved:

> It is especially necessary in our collective during the upcoming purge, on the basis of Bolshevik self-criticism, to check the work of the party collective and each party member individually to determine the extent to which each member maintained the party's general line. The party collective bureau therefore raises before the commission involved in purging the commissariat's party cells the question of the removal of the former leader of the right deviation, Comrade Bukharin, head of the NIS and Tekhprop and a member of our collective.[21]

Naturally, Bukharin took this "initiative" of his subordinates very painfully. He learned of the impending purge and rushed to Ordzhonikidze that day. But Bukharin was told that Ordzhonikidze was asleep. He went to the apartment of Molotov, who said that no decision about a purge had yet been made, but even if one took place, there was nothing to get terribly worried about as it was nothing unusual. Not having met with Ordzhonikidze, Bukharin wrote him a short, emotional letter:

> Today there was universal commotion and gossip about me in the apparatus office; everybody speaks about my forthcoming purge. Everyone was convinced until today that I would be spared this bitter cup. . . . Meanwhile, it is *precisely* because people thought until today that there wouldn't be a purge, that the leadership's mistrust toward me took a turn for the worse. This realistically means that the acts of semi-sabotage aimed against me will only intensify. . . . I can't grasp *what* this is all about. If it's necessary not to elect me to the Central Committee at the next congress [the upcoming Seventeenth Party Congress at the beginning of 1934—O.Kh.], then so be it. In general, a purge makes sense only to verify whether a person is qualified to be

a party member, or whether it's necessary to expel him. All of *you* who have known me for decades could make such an evaluation much better than any commission. Everyone knows that I don't work like a bureaucrat. What did I do to have my party membership placed in doubt *now?* If this isn't the case, then *what's* the point of torturing me and complicating all my affairs? I *earnestly* entreat you—if you can do something—to do it. They've already done enough to me without this. And after the purge—I won't be able to live. Greetings and apologies. Your Bukharin.[22]

Whether Ordzhonikidze tried to help Bukharin is not known. He probably felt, like Molotov, that the problem did not merit his intervention. In fact, the decision had already been made, and Bukharin understood this. But while trying somehow to improve his situation, he turned to Ordzhonikidze with a new request:

Dear Sergo, excuse me for God's sake for pestering you. I have one request if they purge me . . . come to the hearing so that it will be done in *your presence.* People don't understand things. After all, I don't have a whole commissariat, but only a handful of Communists who are forced to turn in statements against me. I have to work with them the next day. . . . It's a hellish situation. . . . I'm already forty-five years old. I must define a future path for my life so that some good will come of this. Help me, Sergo. I'm very grateful to you for your kindness. I'm sure that if they hadn't set Koba on me, he would have seen everything differently. I understand all too well that things are difficult for him, and that he doesn't want to complicate the situation on my behalf, especially as the state of affairs is terribly complex and will become even more so. But perhaps you could forbid them from tripping me up, and stop the game begun five years ago, *for old times' sake,* and do all that's possible to give me the opportunity to work now. Once more, forgive me. Your Nikolai.[23]

This time, however, Ordzhonikidze did not respond to Bukharin's request, and did not come to his purge hearing. The purge followed all the rules. Bukharin had to drink from the cup of humiliation in full measure, to confess, and to speak of Stalin's greatness, while denouncing his own mistakes.[24]

In spite of the purge, Bukharin, one of the former oppositionists, was heard at the Seventeenth Party Congress without pejorative cries and reprimands. He was selected a candidate member of the Central Committee, and soon appointed to the post of editor of *Izvestia*. For a former member of the Politburo and one of the country's leaders, this was of course not much. But it gave hope to a disgraced oppositionist who had repeatedly been branded and hunted.

Aleksei I. Rykov was also chosen a candidate member of the Central Committee at the Seventeenth Congress. Stalin clearly regarded him as worse than Bukharin, and this predetermined the ill will of other Politburo members. In this case, however, Ordzhonikidze kept to his own opinion. A telltale fact is cited in the reminiscences of Rykov's daughter, Natalia Alekseevna:

> Late in the spring of 1935, there was a play in honor of K.E. Voroshilov in a school club of VTsIK [the All-Russian Executive Committee—Ed.]. In one row, alongside us, sat Iagoda with his wife. Both pretended not to see us, and didn't greet us. Father noticed this. When Politburo members entered the half-lit hall and took up their places in the first row, Ordzhonikidze left the group, separated from us by seven or eight rows, approached us and embraced us, shook my parents' hands, and asked about their health and affairs. This was even somewhat demonstrative for the time.[25]

One and a half years after this, however, Ordzhonikidze had to take more courageous measures to support Bukharin and Rykov than appearing at a purge hearing or shaking hands in a crowded hall. In August 1936, newspapers published the confessions of Kamenev and Zinoviev made at the show trial in Moscow. Among other things, they "acknowledged" their connections with former leaders of the "right." On August 21, 1936, the procurator of the USSR, Andrei Ia. Vyshinskii, stated in court: "I consider it necessary to report to the court that yesterday I ordered an investigation of these statements regarding Tomskii, Rykov, Bukharin, Nikolai A. Uglanov (1886–1940), Radek, and Piatakov. Depending upon the results of the investigation, the procurator will start legal proceedings for this case." Tomskii understood all that was happening and committed suicide the next day. In a letter to Stalin written before his death, Tomskii categorically denied his guilt and accused Zinoviev of slander. Soon after this, the NKVD received a confession from the arrested Grigorii Ia. Sokolnikov (1888–1939). He was also forced "to acknowledge" that the "right" had formed a bloc with the underground "Unified Trotskyist-Zinovievite Center."

On September 8, Kaganovich, Ezhov, and Vyshinskii confronted Sokolnikov, Bukharin, and Rykov in the Central Committee. Sokolnikov stood by his confession, but stated that he did not have any direct evidence. The accusations increased, and Stalin made the next maneuver with his assistants: On September 10, the newspapers published the procurator's statement that evidence existed for instituting judicial proceedings against Bukharin and Rykov.[26]

This respite was temporary. Stalin demonstrated "objectivity" and demanded that the NKVD work with redoubled energy and obtain new, more damaging confessions against the "right" than the Chekists had. Bukharin and Rykov undoubtedly understood that the case would not be closed with the statement from September 10. Bukharin once again turned to Ordzhonikidze for help and support. In particular, in one of his preserved letters from October 19, 1936, he wrote:

My dear, kind, warmly beloved Sergo! I just now sent a letter to Comrade A.A. Andreev requesting that I be relieved from my responsibilities as editor of the journal *Socialist Reconstruction and the Sciences.* I put forward these reasons: (1) You now need a scientific-technical journal for the commissariat and I have not worked for you in a long time; (2) I presently don't have the nerve to defend myself from a new wave of attack that began in the press against the journal (that is, against me).

The small thread that connected me with your commissariat, where I once worked, has been broken. I'm telling you this because I want you to know about it.

Don't be surprised if my article doesn't appear for your birthday. [He had in mind the article for Ordzhonikidze's fiftieth birthday, forthcoming on October 28, 1936, in the newspaper *Izvestia.*—O.Kh.] Although I'm editor in chief, I was intentionally not asked to write about you, as if I had just come to work for the paper. I'm writing not to complain, but so that you don't draw the wrong conclusions. The slanderers tried to eat me alive. Even now there are those who harass and torment me.

I want only to convey to you my most sincere and heartfelt congratulations, upon which my deep love for you is based. My heart aches as I write you this letter. Stay healthy, strong, and happy.[27]

The tragic premonitions with which Bukharin's letter was filled were soon confirmed. In the fall of 1936, the NKVD tried its best to collect compromising material on the "right." Using various means and methods, they beat confessions out of the arrested former oppositionists about the underground counterrevolutionary activities of Bukharin, Rykov, and Tomskii. They took supporters of Bukharin sentenced earlier from jail, brought new charges against them, and demanded they acknowledge the terrorist activities of the "counterrevolutionary organization of the right." Stalin obtained new evidence this way, and decided to submit the question of Bukharin and Rykov to a Central Committee plenum for review.

Nothing was known about this plenum, which lasted from December 4 to December 7, 1936, until very recently. Reference to it was forbidden by Stalin's order at the plenum itself. Such secrecy was not accidental. The main point on the plenum's agenda was discussion of Ezhov's report, "On Anti-Soviet, Trotskyist, and Right Oppositionists," which presented "fresh facts" obtained through coercion by the NKVD after attempts to compromise Bukharin and Rykov on the confessions of Zinoviev, Kamenev, and Sokolnikov had been set aside. This time Ezhov prepared much more carefully. It was clear nonetheless that the NKVD did not have enough evidence. Bukharin and Rykov were equally active at the plenum. They picked up on the contradictions of their accusers, and proved that from the very beginning the affair was conducted without their participation, that they had been denied a face-to-face confrontation, that Zinoviev and Kamenev had been shot beforehand, and that the procuracy on September 10 had already admitted the lack of facts for instituting judicial proceedings against the "right." "There isn't a word of truth in anything that was said against me here. I had my only face-to-face confrontation with Sokolnikov. . . . At the end, I asked that it be recorded that he didn't have any political conversations with me, that he was passing on what Tomskii had said, but Tomskii was no longer alive," said Bukharin. "I maintain that all charges against me from beginning to end are lies. . . . Kamenev stated at the trial that he met with me every year, right up to 1936. I asked Ezhov to find out where and when I met with Kamenev so that I could somehow refute this lie. They told me that Kamenev wasn't asked about this, and now it's impossible to ask him." "They shot him," Rykov repeated.[28]

It is also worth noting that only a relatively small group of Central Committee members participated in the attack on Rykov and Bukharin. Apart from the report of Ezhov and Stalin, mention of which was deleted from the stenogram, Beria, Kaganovich, Molotov, Eikhe, Kosior, Sarkisov, and several other supporters of the measure came down upon the "right" both from their seats and in their speeches. The majority of Central Committee members, in spite of the clear invitation to back the position of the party leadership, remained silent. Ordzhonikidze's behavior, in particular, was very revealing. His "speech" was recorded in the stenogram only once, under the following circumstances:

> *Bukharin:* Sergo asked me at his apartment, Tell me, please, what is your opinion of Piatakov? I literally told him that he struck me as a man who's so tactful that he doesn't know that he is telling the truth or acting out of tactical considerations.
> *Ordzhonikidze:* That's correct.
> *Bukharin:* There, Sergo agrees. So I had to recommend my accomplice and leader?
> *Beria:* You could also have done this out of tactical considerations.

It is not difficult to see that Ordzhonikidze's rejoinder looked more like support for Bukharin. Ordzhonikidze did not say another word at the plenum. Afterward, like other Central Committee members who had spoken, he received the stenogram with a standard accompanying note from Aleksandr N. Poskrebyshev (1891–1965):* "Please verify your enclosed remarks at the plenum and return them today if possible." Ordzhonikidze's reaction to this request was revealing. The papers were returned to the Central Committee together with Poskrebyshev's cover letter, upon which one of Ordzhonikidze's assistants had written: "Comrade Sergo won't correct them."[29]

It cannot be excluded that the relative restraint of the plenum forced Stalin to retreat temporarily. At his prompting, conference dele-

---

*Aleksandr N. Poskrebyshev. Communist Party member who in 1928 was appointed to head Stalin's chancery within the Secret Department, the "Special Sector" (*Osobyi sektor*). In this capacity Poskrebyshev served as Stalin's chief assistant, for the Special Sector was the true seat of power. Poskrebyshev remained at this post for twenty-eight years, that is, until Stalin's death in 1953.

gates adjourned ahead of schedule and agreed to return to the matter after further investigation.

At the very end of 1936 and the beginning of 1937, new arrests ensued in which the NKVD quickly fabricated fresh evidence against Bukharin and Rykov. Not long before their arrests, Ordzhonikidze gave a hopeful sign. "Approaching the house," remembered Bukharin's wife Anna Mikhailovna,

> I saw Ordzhonikidze coming out of the entrance next to ours, the one closer to Troitsky Gates. As he headed for his car, he noticed me and stopped. But what could I say to him at that moment? We stood silent for several seconds. Sergo looked at me with eyes so full of grief it is impossible for me to forget that gaze to the present day. Then he squeezed my hand and said two words: "Stand firm." He got in his car and left.[30]

While this squeeze and appeal to stand firm did not promise too much, Bukharin nonetheless perceived it as a good sign. He learned about the meeting with Ordzhonikidze from his wife and immediately sat down to write him a letter. He asked Ordzhonikidze to believe in his innocence, and to take care of his family if he were arrested.

Rykov's family also counted on Ordzhonikidze's help. "On February 18," recalled his daughter,

> The newspapers came out quite late. Upon her arrival, the maid told us that funeral flags hung at the House of Unions and that they weren't allowing traffic through Hunter's Row. Apparently, a government leader had died. My parents were surprised, because no one, it seemed, was seriously ill. Finally, newspapers turned up in the mailbox. I saw that Sergo Ordzhonikidze had passed away. Mother grabbed the paper and cried out: "Our last hope . . . ," and fell to the floor unconscious. She didn't get up for several months.[31]

In general, Ordzhonikdize most likely did not believe the assertions of Stalin and Ezhov about the existence of an underground organization of the "right," although this of course did not mean that he was prepared to defend Bukharin and Rykov decisively at the upcoming plenum.

Chapter 12

The Last Days

The tension caused by the arguments and conflicts between Stalin and Ordzhonikidze over many months peaked just before the opening of the February Central Committee plenum. On February 15 and 16, Ordzhonikidze worked on materials for the plenum and on official duties at the commissariat. He soon finished the draft resolution ordered by the Politburo concerning sabotage in industry, and readied a report—"outlining theses on little sheets and in a notebook," as Zinaida G. Ordzhonikidze recalled two years later.[1] Okudzhava's fate was decided in Moscow at this time. This circumstance, together with thoughts about the impending plenum, was apparently the impetus for Ordzhonikidze's questioning of Ginzburg, after Ordzhonikidze pressed him to return to Moscow to prepare the report.

We can learn a great deal about Ordzhonikidze's work habits on February 17 from information compiled by his secretary, as well as from the testimony and reminiscences of eyewitnesses.[2]

Ordzhonikidze arrived at the commissariat from his home that day at 12:10 P.M., although he usually appeared at ten in the morning, according to A.P. Zaveniagin (who at this time worked in the commissariat's central apparatus in Moscow).[3] Any number of things, of course, could have delayed Ordzhonikidze. But it indirectly confirms an account, apparently from Ordzhonikidze's wife, cited in a book by I. Dubovskii-Mukhadze, that on the morning of the seventeenth, Sergo had a private conversation with Stalin that lasted for several hours.[4]

We will never find out the exact nature of this talk. But several assumptions about Ordzhonikidze's final arguments with Stalin can be made by drawing on well-known facts. Taking into account that Stalin prepared thoroughly for the Central Committee plenum, and that a Politburo meeting dedicated to the discussion of documents from the plenum was scheduled for 3:00 P.M. that very day, it is logical to assume they discussed those same issues. It is possible that Ordzhonikidze spoke about arrests in the NKTP and Bukharin's fate. The next day, February 18, Ordzhonikidze and Gvakharia, the director of the Makeevsk Metallurgical Factory who enjoyed the special patronage of Ordzhonikidze, were supposed to meet. Gvakharia had recently been accused of having Trotskyist connections and he most likely came to Moscow to seek Ordzhonikidze's help.[5] Ordzhonikidze could well have spoken with Stalin about Gvakharia's fate. (Gvakharia was arrested soon after Ordzhonikidze's death.) It cannot be dismissed that Sergo mentioned Papulia Ordzhonikidze and Okudzhava, whose fate he was concerned with at the time. The discussion probably touched upon the results of Ginzburg's inspection and those of other NKTP commissions. (Ginzburg had returned to Moscow early on the morning of February 18, whereupon Poskrebyshev reported to him by telephone that "I.V. Stalin asked that you send a note about the state of affairs at Ural Coach Construction, which Sergo had told him about.")[6]

In prevailing upon Stalin, Ordzhonikidze could quite likely have utilized letters of managers concerning the difficult situation in the provinces. He must have transmitted one of these letters from the director of the Dnepropetrovsk Metallurgical Factory, S.P. Birman, to either Stalin or Molotov, because it was cited in Molotov's speech at the February–March plenum.[7] Birman wrote (the original is lost, but the letter is cited here as it was read by Molotov to the participants of the February–March plenum):

> The situation, especially of late here in Dnepropetrovsk, compels me to appeal to you, as to an old comrade and Politburo member, for instructions and assistance. I think that the directive of the higher party organs about the full development of criticism and self-criticism here in Dnepropetrovsk has been misunderstood in several ways. The foreign word "criticism" here is often confused with the Russian word "to blather" (*trepat'sia*). It seems to me that the party directive is aimed at uncovering real enemies and disclosing real shortcomings,

by means of conscientious criticism. But many here understand it as meaning that it's necessary at any cost to sling mud at each other, especially at a certain category of leading workers.

Above all it is the managers and directors of large factories who make up this certain category of leading workers, as if by waving a secret magic wand they became the primary target in this round of self-criticism. It has been determined that the attack on party work by the party organizations was one of the key reasons for everything that happened. Instead of turning into real self-criticism, however, many speeches by party workers during the recent three-day meeting of regional party members blamed all misfortune on the managers.[8]

But whatever Stalin and Ordzhonikidze spoke about on the morning of February 17, the conversation had to have ended relatively peacefully. On the eve of the Politburo meeting, Stalin would not have brought affairs to a head, but would rather have tried to instill some hope in Ordzhonikidze. Indeed, Ordzhonikidze's workday on February 17 followed his usual routine, without any sign of excessive edginess or apprehension.

Ordzhonikidze stayed a little more than two hours at the commissariat, then left at 2:30 P.M. to see Molotov in the Kremlin. He apparently intended to resolve some problems with the Sovnarkom chairman on the way to the Politburo meeting. The session began at 3:00 P.M. in the Kremlin and was well attended. Apart from all the Politburo members—Andreev, Voroshilov, Kaganovich, Kalinin, Mikoyan, Molotov, Ordzhonikidze, Stalin, and Chubar—candidate members Zhdanov and Petrovskii were present, as well as a large group of Central Committee members—Antipov, Bauman, Bubnov, Vareikis, Gamarnik, Ezhov, Krupskaia, Litvinov, Mezhlauk, Piatnitskii, Khrushchev, Shvernik, and others; Central Committee candidate members; members of the Party Control Commission bureau, members of the Soviet Control Commission bureau (including Zemliachka and Ulianova); and leaders of groups from within the Party Control Commission. They considered one question—the draft decrees of the impending plenum. Following discussion, the draft resolutions of Zhdanov's report on upcoming elections, Stalin's on the shortcomings in party work, and Ezhov's on the "lessons of sabotage, diversion, and spying" were on the whole affirmed. But the draft resolutions on the reports of Ordzhonikidze and

Kaganovich were approved with reservations, and they were ordered to draft a final text on the basis of adopted Politburo amendments and addenda.[9]

At first glance, this fact in some measure corroborates rumors Ziskind repeated to I. Kramov: "Then I found out that Ordzhonikidze had said at the Politburo meeting that there's no sabotage in heavy industry. Stalin interrupted him: 'You don't understand anything, or pretend that you don't understand anything. Get out of here.' Ordzhonikidze left without finishing his report."[10]

Of course, Ordzhonikidze might have made some innuendos at the meeting comprehensible only to Stalin but nobody else. In any event, none of the numerous participants of this Politburo meeting (including Khrushchev, who, as will be shown later, knew nothing of the conflict between Stalin and Ordzhonikidze for many years) recalled anything special that caught their attention or seemed unusual. This is understandable. In the presence of others, Ordzhonikidze and Stalin acted with restraint, and most likely to assure this restraint, Stalin met with Sergo the previous evening.

An hour and a half later, at 4:30 P.M., Ordzhonikidze went with Kaganovich to Poskrebyshev's, where they spent two and a half hours. Judging from the time, they probably worked on the draft of the resolutions agreed to, and included in the text criticisms raised by the Politburo.

At 7:00 P.M., Ordzhonikidze and Kaganovich left Poskrebyshev's, walked around the Kremlin, said goodbye when they reached Ordzhonikidze's apartment, and went home. Sergo came in at 7:15 P.M. He likely ate dinner ("He ate dinner at various times, sometimes at six or seven o'clock in the evening, but occasionally at two in the morning," later recalled Ordzhonikidze's wife about the last months of his life.)[11] At 9:30 P.M. he left for the commissariat.

The Kremlin was very close to the commissariat building on Nogin Square, and Ordzhonikidze received Professor Galperin in his office at 10:00 P.M. Galperin had returned only that afternoon from the inspection trip to Kemerovo. Judging from the haste with which this meeting was organized, the commissar was keenly interested in facts gathered by the commission. According to Galperin's memoirs, Ordzhonikidze listened to his findings, asked questions concerning construction work and the state of equipment, and requested that he compose a written report and prepare all orders that were to be given in connection with the inspection that had taken place in the commissar's name. Ordzhonikidze scheduled a new meeting with Galperin at 10:00 A.M. on February 19.[12] Taking into account that the head of Main Nitrogen, E. Brodov, was slated to report to Ordzhonikidze that very hour, a chemical industry conference must have taken place on the morning of February 19.[13]

In and of itself, the time frame for these meetings is quite revealing. The other concerns that Ordzhonikidze dealt with in the commissariat the night of February 17 were ordinary, and did not suggest anything unusual. As always, he signed a large number of papers, and listened to some reports. Ordzhonikidze's last three orders were dated February 17 (granted, it is not known which ones he reviewed in the morning, and which in the evening). They concerned fulfilling the demands of the Commissariat of Defense for portable funicular railways; cadre appointments (a new administrator of the Coke Chemical Installation, the main engineer of Rostov Agricultural Machinery and the Donsod Factory, the director of the Novo-Tulskii Metallurgical Combine, etc.); and the important order "On Measures to Ensure the Introduction of New Capacities in 1937 by the Regional Electric Power Stations of Main Energy."[14]

Around midnight, Ordzhonikidze met and conversed with his deputy who managed the chemical industry, O.P. Osipov-Shmidt.[15] Osipov-Shmidt, as mentioned, several days before this headed a commission Sergo had sent to the Donbass Coke Enterprise. Their conversation probably was about that very trip. Not long before he left the commissariat, Ordzhonikidze signed a telegram: "Stalino (Donbass). Riazanov. Shipment of the pipe procurement in January–February was unsatisfactory. Guarantee the rolling and shipment of the pipe procurement in full, without delays. Henceforth, roll and ship the pipe procurement in the first half of each month. Report fulfillment. Ordzhonikidze."[16] This telegram was dispatched from the commissariat at one in the morning, not long before which, at 12:20 A.M., Ordzhonikidze had left his office for home.

All of the events that took place up to this time testify that Ordzhonikidze's work followed a normal routine, and that nothing presaged a tragic outcome. In any case, would a man who had decided to commit suicide send a telegram about pipe procurements and schedule meetings the next day with his associates? Undoubtedly, some key events occurred after Ordzhonikidze's return home. Unfortunately, however, our knowledge about the last hours of Ordzhonikidze's life is extremely limited.

According to Dubinskii-Mukhadze, Ordzhonikidze spoke by telephone with Stalin after returning to his apartment. A quarrel erupted with mutual insults and cursing both in Russian and in Georgian.[17] S.Z. Ginzburg asserts that Ordzhonikidze's wife told him the following: Not long before Ordzhonikidze's arrival, NKVD agents searched his apartment. Ordzhonikidze returned and immediately phoned Stalin, who calmly told him, "Sergo, why are you upset? This body can at any moment conduct a search at my place as well."[18] Ordzhonikidze allegedly answered, "Does this mean that the state security apparatus stands over the government and Politburo, and rules us?" (We can observe in passing that if such a conversation took place, Ordzhonikidze would not have used the word "state security," which is of a later provenance.) Stalin invited Ordzhonikidze to his place to talk. Sergo rushed into the street without his coat, and Zinaida Gavrilovna hurried after him with her husband's overcoat and Caucasian fur cap. She waited outside Stalin's home for nearly one and a half hours. "Sergo sprang out of Stalin's place in a very agitated state, didn't put on his coat or hat, and ran home."[19]

Regardless of how this evidence is viewed, something actually did take place on the night of February 17. The whole course of previous and subsequent events suggests this. Most likely, Stalin, after calming Ordzhonikidze on the eve of what was to be a well-attended Politburo meeting, made some provocation that evening (such as the search), in order to put Sergo "in his place" and intimidate him just in case. This was fully consonant with Stalin's behavior. And the conversation that took place in connection with this hastened the outcome.

There is of course no documentary evidence concerning the details of the last quarrel, whether by telephone or in private, between Stalin and Ordzhonikidze.

It is possible that the conversation resembled that portrayed in Aleksandr Bek's novel, *The New Appointment*:

Sergo spoke loudly and without restraint. His conversation partner answered softly even perhaps, in a deliberately slow pace. . . . The discussion was in Georgian. . . . Sergo continued to speak heatedly, almost shouting. His pale face turned an unhealthy shade of crimson. He waved both hands, prevailing upon Stalin and reproaching him. But the latter stood in his customary soldier's uniform, with his arms folded in front of him.[20]

The hot-tempered and unrestrained Ordzhonikidze became agitated in tense moments. According to the memoirs of the well-known contemporary journalist S.R. Gershberg, Ordzhonikidze "would go into a frenzy, leap around, gesticulate, speak incoherently, and hiss and become tongue-tied. It seemed as if he might suffer a stroke."[21] We can only guess how he spoke with Stalin. Ordzhonikidze likely did not stay at Stalin's for long. Underneath his outer composure, which much of the time was simply for show, he was a man of extreme harshness and crudeness.

Further events, at which quite a few witnesses were present, are depicted almost identically in all the sources. On the morning of February 18, Ordzhonikidze did not get out of bed and have breakfast as usual. He asked that no one disturb him, and did some writing while remaining in his bedroom. Gvakharia showed up in the afternoon, but Ordzhonikidze did not let him in. At dusk, Zinaida Gavrilovna heard a shot in the bedroom, rushed in, and saw her dead husband on the bed. A short time later, Stalin and other Politburo members arrived. Stalin rudely cut off Zinaida Gavrilovna's lamentations: "Shut up, you fool!" and stated that Sergo died from a heart attack. No one dared contradict the leader, and this account was released as the official one.

According to some evidence, the sister of Ordzhonikidze's wife ran into the room and took some sheets of paper from the table. Stalin seized them from her. Whether this was a suicide note is not known. Roy Medvedev, who heard this story from Ordzhonikidze's relatives, reported only that the sheets were written in "Sergo's minute handwriting."[22] But in fact, Ordzhonikidze wrote in a large, bold hand. Of course, this does not mean that there were no papers. Moreover, like all typical suicides, Ordzhonikidze simply must have left a suicide note. While one may be disclosed someday, until then it will be difficult to hope for conclusive proof to resolve the controversy that continues up to the present. Was Ordzhonikidze killed or did he commit suicide?

Chapter 13

Murder or Suicide?

On February 19, 1937, Soviet newspapers reported on Ordzhonikidze's death. The official version had it that the commissar of heavy industry died suddenly from a heart attack on February 18 at 5:30 P.M. during his daily rest at his apartment.

The majority of the country's population, accustomed to believe the most incredible reports, likely harbored no doubts. But rumors circulated, as usual. They were circulated only among trusted friends, and arose not from facts that contradicted those published in newspapers, but more from the growing premonition of the Great Terror, which led everyone to suspect the worst.

Moreover, Ordzhonikidze's death was cause for such suspicions. After all, the fifty-year-old commissar, a middle-aged man, had died suddenly. Wide-scale arrests were conducted in his department just prior to this, and several leading comrades, including his first deputy, Piatakov, had been sentenced to be shot. The entire country read the trial proceedings in newspapers in January 1937. Insofar as reliable information was unavailable, the rumors were quite varied and contradictory.

"Flags of mourning unexpectedly caught our eyes," recalled the wife of a famous Georgian poet, Titian Tabidze (1895–1937), who was visiting Moscow with her husband at this time.

Pilniak* stopped the first policeman he met and asked the reasons for the official period of mourning. The policeman replied: "Sergo died." In photographs published in the newspapers, Ordzhonikidze's widow and Stalin's political entourage surrounded the coffin—Stalin himself, Ezhov, Molotov, Zhdanov, Kaganovich, Mikoyan, and Voroshilov. Sinister rumors spread throughout Moscow that Ordzhonikidze had been driven to suicide. People spoke about this in a whisper at Peredelkino.[1]

The Menshevik journal in Paris, *Socialist Herald*, painstakingly collected information from the USSR and responded immediately to Ordzhonikidze's death with the following "Letter from Moscow":

> The sudden death of Ordzhonikidze has sparked a barrage of rumors here. These rumors were so persistent that the authorities had to indirectly refute them in official reports. Read attentively the "government reports" from February 19, and all other official statements and reports from the 20th, 21st, etc., and you will see how insistent they are that Ordzhonikidze died *in his own apartment*, and that for a long time he had suffered from heart ailments, etc. The problem is that after the trial [against Piatakov and other "Trotskyists" in January 1937—O.Kh.], the status of Kaganovich and Ordzhonikidze was seriously compromised. Extremely harsh attacks were inflicted upon the latter in connection with the upcoming trial in the Caucasus. Almost all the Old Georgian Bolsheviks were arrested there. . . . Others were also arrested—his relatives (a male cousin), old friends, and acquaintances. Ordzhonikidze thus found himself in a tough bind. A Politburo member was not supposed to have so many intimate friends and relatives among those subjected to prosecution and execution for "Trotskyism." On the other hand, Ordzhonikidze apparently could

---

*Boris Pilniak. A writer who never accepted the revolution or the party's controls over literature. Most accounts suggest that Stalin had a bone to pick with Pilniak. Back in 1925, the author published his "Tale of the Unextinguished Moon," about an army commander who was forced by "No. One" to undergo unnecessary surgery, as a result of which the commander died. That very year Mikhail Frunze, who headed the Red Army, had died on the operating table and was replaced by a Stalin protégé, Klim Voroshilov, during the height of the conflict between Stalin and the Zinoviev-Kamenev faction. Dismissed from the Union of Writers in 1929, Pilniak later disappeared into the Stalinist purges after he was declared an enemy of the people during the Great Terror.—Ed.

not reconcile himself to his friends' massacre. In any event—as a reliable source tells us—either he died *at the very meeting* of the Politburo on February 18, the day of his death, or he collapsed at the meeting and this proved fatal.[2]

Trotsky, in his book *Stalin*, offers yet another account of this event: "They said that Ordzhonikidze might have died from poisoning, as did Maxim Gorky. Both had defended Old Bolsheviks from extermination."[3]

The overwhelming majority of the population of the USSR, however, undoubtedly did not draw such conclusions. The powerful grip of state terror and widespread denunciations could easily cut off any rumors and conversations unfavorable to the authorities. In any event, what could a Soviet citizen have done if he or she had heard something about Ordzhonikidze's suicide? In the best case, he would have tried to forget about it in order not to let the cat out of the bag accidentally somewhere. In the worst case, he would hurry to inform on the source of his information so as to avoid being denounced himself. For its part, the government did everything possible to bolster the official version of Ordzhonikidze's death. He was increasingly depicted as a faithful supporter of Stalin, the anniversaries of his death were solemnly observed, and numerous eyewitness memoirs about the commissar's last days were published, from which one could only draw a single conclusion: that his death was sudden and natural. Sergo had been in a great mood, full of plans and ideas. Any information that cast the smallest doubt on this version was categorically denied.

A bizarre conflict erupted over this subject between two of Stalin's closest associates, Beria and Lev Z. Mekhlis (1889–1953), in regard to the publication of Ordzhonikidze's selected articles and speeches in 1938. The book had already been typeset and was about to be published under the editorship of A.I. Mikoyan, L.Z. Mekhlis, L.P. Beria, and Z.G. Ordzhonikidze, when an argument flared up over the introduction written by Mekhlis. Many years later, Ordzhonikidze's widow wrote about what troubled Beria, in particular, Mekhlis's concluding passage:

> As is well known from the medical diagnosis, Sergo suffered from "serious sclerosis of the heart muscles and vessels." But, as the party and working class knew, the contemptible Piatakov and other Trotsky-

ists finished him off. Working in the People's Commissariat of Heavy Industry, Piatakov and his gang played a vicious double game, betraying this highly idealistic Bolshevik and great proletarian revolutionary. . . . The betrayal, which Sergo didn't expect, affected his health terribly and aggravated his poor condition.

The despicable and thrice-damned Trotskyist gang of double-dealers, traitors, spies, and heinous restorers of capitalism are responsible for the premature death of our beloved Sergo, favorite of the entire party and the working class. Piatakov and Bukharin—all these agents of fascist intelligence prepared to murder Sergo. They did not succeed, and the band of criminals was caught. But all the wrecking, vile, double-dealing, traitorous work of Piatakov and his despicable company wore on Ordzhonikidze's health. They shattered his nerves, and irreparably damaged his heart. This hastened the fateful denouement.

At first glance, there is nothing in this text that sets it apart from a number of verbose publications that uncovered "enemies" and "spies." But it was no accident that Beria demanded it be deleted. Undoubtedly, he judged it inappropriate and even dangerous to make any references connecting Ordzhonikidze's death with the repressions against his former colleagues and the shocks that the commissar of heavy industry lived through in the last days of his life. The less details about his death, the better. Beria was apparently not the only one to think this way. Publication of the book was delayed, and the "seditious" paragraphs removed. The recrafted introduction was matter-of-factly brief on Ordzhonikidze's death: "Sergo gave all his strength, all of himself to the party cause, to the working class cause. He worked feverishly. The revolutionary underground, tsarist hard labor and exile, and combat on various fronts of the Civil War, in which he did not spare himself—all of this stressful activity affected his health. Sergo died at his post as a great son of a great party."[4]

The veil of complete silence over the circumstances of Ordzhonikidze's death was not removed until Khrushchev's famous speech at the Twentieth Party Congress,* in which he all but openly stated that

---

*Khrushchev's speech at the Twentieth Party Congress. Khrushchev stunned congress delegates by reading a detailed report on the crimes of the Stalin era. Although Khrushchev left many issues untouched, his speech promoted sweeping reexamination of the Stalin years both at home and abroad.—Ed.

the commissar of heavy industry committed suicide, because he could not endure Stalin's persecutions. Afterward, eyewitnesses spoke up. Many of them, including doctors who had signed official medical diagnoses, and Ordzhonikidze's closest associates, had been killed in the years of repression. Those still alive, above all Ordzhonikidze's wife Zinaida Gavrilovna and several other surviving relatives, left memoirs that became the foundation for the most widespread contemporary accounts of Ordzhonikidze's suicide.[5] From time to time, however, there are those who maintain that Ordzhonikidze had been murdered. Several Old Bolsheviks who survived the Great Terror, for example, insist on this and cite information that circulated in 1937. The recollections of one of these, Fedor N. Petrov (1876–1973), were written down by Iu. Semenov. Petrov tried to demonstrate that Ordzhonikidze was prepared to speak out against Stalin at the upcoming February plenum of the Central Committee, and might have been able to stop the terror.

> In a word, they said that Stalin ordered the security chief, Ezhov, to kill Sergo. Sergo was then shot in his own apartment. . . . The most trusted said that Sergo had committed suicide—that he had been too friendly with Bukharin, Rykov, and Piatakov. But the evidence after all could not be concealed: Those who were the first to enter Ordzhonikidze's apartment signed their own death sentences by compiling a document stating that there were seven cartridges in Sergo's Mauser (pistol), but no smell of powder in the chamber. . . . They shot these impertinent investigators—within a week! Do you understand?! And we learned the truth.[6]

Analogous evidence can be found in the well-known book by Aleksandr Orlov, *The Secret History of Stalin's Crimes*. One of the NKVD officials who arrived in Spain in the fall of 1937 allegedly told Orlov: "They even finished off Ordzhonikidze! . . . I know the details of this case. Ordzhonikidze also had Caucasian blood flowing in his veins—he thus quarreled with the boss. He met his match, all on account of Piatakov."[7]

Another piece of evidence has recently come to light. An engineer at the Cheliabinsk Tractor Factory, L.S. Komarov, recorded the account of a former high-level employee of the People's Commissariat of Heavy Industry, V.N. Sidorova, who in turn had heard it from Z.G. Ordzhonikidze. These memoirs were published verbatim, although thirdhand, by S.Z. Ginzburg:

During the day on February 18, 1937 (in the first half of the day), an unknown man arrived at Ordzhonikidze's apartment (in the Kremlin) who identified himself as a driver who needed to hand over a folder of documents from the Politburo to Grigorii Konstantinovich. Zinaida Gavrilovna asked: "But where is Sergo's personal chauffeur, Nikolai Ivanovich?" The man answered that Nikolai Ivanovich was off that day.

This person then went up to Sergo's office on the second floor. Within several minutes a shot rang out. The man emerged from the office, came downstairs, and asked Zinaida Gavrilovna: "Did you hear a shot?"

When Zinaida Gavrilovna entered the office, she saw Sergo slumped in an armchair with his right arm hanging over it, and a pistol lying on the floor to his right.

Before the man's arrival, Sergo had had a heated exchange in Georgian over the telephone (likely with Stalin).[8]

It seems that Sidorova's memoirs (or their recounting) were apparently used in the acclaimed novel *Fear* (sequel to *Children of the Arbat*) by Anatoly N. Rybakov, which undoubtedly spread the account that Ordzhonikidze had been murdered.[9]

None of this evidence can be verified, and some of it gives rise to questions (for example, how could the NKVD employees have made such a crude mistake with Ordzhonikidze's pistol, and would NKVD officials have allowed an investigation to be conducted in this case) that contradict other information. Further, the Old Bolshevik E.P. Frolov, whose notes Roy Medvedev used, also thought that Ordzhonikidze was murdered, but he put forth an argument that directly refutes Petrov's version of the inquiry: "No investigation into the circumstances of Ordzhonikidze's death took place, and there was not even an examination of the bullet hole."[10] This is also the case with Z.G. Ordzhonikidze's recollections, which play a key role in this instance. According to accounts taken down by V.N. Sidorova (which we must use cautiously as she was far removed from the actual events), Zinaida Gavrilovna felt that Sergo had been murdered. (We are speaking here of the question of a two-story apartment in which Ordzhonikidze's wife and his assassin might have easily missed each other). Ordzhonikidze's widow told historian Roy Medvedev a completely different version:

It was dark. Zinaida Gavrilovna decided to check in on her husband in the bedroom once more, and turned on the light while passing through the living room. At that moment, a shot rang out in the bedroom. She rushed there and saw her husband on the bed. He was already dead. According to Zinaida Gavrilovna, in addition to the back door to the apartment that everyone used, there was also a front door. However, this was not only closed, but blocked by bookshelves. That entrance led into the living room, and could not have been used by the murderer since Ordzhonikidze's wife was in the room at the time of the shot.[11]

There are other, logical arguments apart from the various testimonies by advocates of the Ordzhonikidze-was-murdered account. Ordzhonikidze, they maintain, was not the type of man who would have committed suicide. He was prepared to challenge Stalin to the very end, and intended to give him a fight at the February–March plenum, thereby signing his own death sentence. Stalin was afraid of Ordzhonikidze, and secretly sent an assassin. "All who were close to Ordzhonikidze and knew him well, to whom his actions, intentions, and thoughts were known, in particular while he prepared for the impending Central Committee plenum those last days," wrote Ginzburg, "were unable to accept the idea of his suicide. This was a tenacious fighter of the Leninist type. He was thoroughly prepared to rebuff Stalin's exaggerated thesis that the class struggle would inevitably escalate as socialism succeeded, and to decisively speak out against the mass slaughter of party comrades and leaders of industry and construction."[12] While sharing this very viewpoint and greatly contributing to its currency, Rybakov included in his novel the following dialogue between Stalin and Ordzhonikidze:

> "Have you prepared the theses of your speech for the plenum?"
> "No! . . ."
> "When will they be ready?"
> "I don't know."
> "The plenum opens in two days, and you can't delay because all the other speakers have turned in their theses."
> "I'll submit them when they're ready, if I consider it necessary. I'm a member of the Politburo and have the right to decide what I'll speak about. I don't need Ezhov's approval."

Stalin fell silent, and then said:

"Yes, you're a member of the Politburo, and can voice your own opinion to it. But at a Central Committee plenum, you must present the viewpoint of the Politburo and the party leadership. Otherwise, you'll place yourself in opposition to the Politburo and the party leadership. You'll pit yourself against the party. Think about the consequences of such a decision. Remember what happened to those who tried to oppose the party earlier. Think about it! Go home, calm down, and think about it. Once you've calmed down, we'll talk.

Ordzhonikidze got up, noisily pushing his chair aside.

"We'll talk at the plenum."

He then left, slamming the door.[13]

Is Ordzhonikidze's determination to speak out against Stalin so evident? At first glance, the above facts about the numerous quarrels between Stalin and Ordzhonikidze support the suppositions of Ginzburg and Rybakov. Several arguments exist, however, that place them in doubt. Ordzhonikidze's political career clearly demonstrates that he was a Stalinist. Even if he wavered and was capable of independent acts and opinions (within strictly defined limits, of course), he remained a Stalinist. In order to challenge Stalin, he needed something more than just the hope of gaining support in the Politburo, or if worse came to worst, the Central Committee. Above all, he needed tremendous inner strength, a clear idea of how and against whom to act, and a sense of the prospects of such actions. Stalin did not agree with Ordzhonikidze. What came next? Removing Stalin? Inciting the Central Committee against Stalin and inducing a split that would inevitably end in the destruction of one of the opposing camps? Ordzhonikidze was not capable of either of these possibilities. He also understood all too well the real alignment of power in the party leadership, because he himself had a hand in the incredible consolidation of Stalin's authoritarian power that rested on the omnipotent NKVD. Finally, what could Ordzhonikidze say at the plenum? Express his lack of trust in the NKVD and Ezhov? From the mouth of Ordzhonikidze, whose closest colleagues and even relatives had been arrested one after another, this would only look like an attempt to justify himself, a step taken out of desperation.

Ordzhonikidze must have understood that he could not count on

support at the plenum for even the mildest, most inoffensive sugges-
tions and appeals. All his efforts before the plenum, viewed today as
preparation for an attack on Stalin, most likely were merely attempts on
the eve of the plenum to make Stalin change his mind again, by prov-
ing the innocence of the managers, and to renounce his intentions of
continuing the terror. Otherwise it is simply impossible to explain why
Ordzhonikidze, in preparing a strike, showed Stalin all his cards up
front by reporting on the commissions and their findings. Incidentally,
Ordzhonikidze turned in the theses of his report on time. Stalin reprimanded him, as already noted, and Ordzhonikidze took this to heart.

In general, Ordzhonikidze's actions before the plenum suggest that
he was only trying to make Stalin change his mind. The very possibility
of this, incidentally, was a logical and widespread illusion in a system
where almost everything was decided by one leader. All that those who
disagreed could do was to try to win over the leader.

In hypothesizing about Ordzhonikidze's mood and intentions on the
eve of the plenum, one must consider the important factor of the state
of his health. Getting embroiled in a struggle required great strength
and nerves of steel. At one time Ordzhonikidze had these. "He was
young and strong and seemed as if he had been born in his long
military overcoat and Red Army helmet. With his legs in high boots, he
treaded firmly, assuredly, but at the same time lightly on the wooden
floor of the train."[14] This is how E.M. Bogdateva recalled Ordzhonikidze in 1920. But the years had passed. Ordzhonikidze became
ill, endured a serious operation and lost one kidney, worked long
hours, and grew older. "Sergo Ordzhonikidze in those years was heavy,
and his bushy mustache and curly, thick head of hair were covered with
gray," as the famous pilot Georgii F. Baidukov described him in 1935.[15]

Ordzhonikidze often took ill in 1936. Because of his health, the
Politburo had resolved in January that "Comrade Ordzhonikidze must
leave for his dacha outside Moscow on the morning of January 9, and
thereafter see only a limited number of people (not more than one or
two people a day)." At the end of January, Ordzhonikidze returned to
work. But the Politburo arranged a mercifully light schedule for him:
three workdays every six, with a mandatory rest outside the city for the
remaining three days, and a sharp curtailment of his responsibilities.
On March 25, Ordzhonikidze once again was granted vacation leave

until May 1. Several participants of the People's Commissariat of Heavy Industry's council, which took place on June 20, remembered Ordzhonikidze's poor health: "He was unrecognizable, as if he suffered from a serious illness," recalled I.I. Gudov many decades later.[16] "As his speech came to a close, we observed with alarm how very tired he grew," related the director of the Dnepropetrovsk Metallurgical Factory, S. Birman.[17] At that very time, the end of June, it was decided to invite to Moscow from abroad the famous specialist, Professor Noorden, who examined Ordzhonikidze.[18]

The difficulties endured in connection with the arrests within the commissariat and of his brother also took their toll on his health. In November, Ordzhonikidze suffered a heart attack. In general, Ordzhonikidze's physical condition also suggests that he committed suicide.

Would suicide mean that Ordzhonikidze had resigned himself to Stalin's intentions and had given up? Judging from everything, it is precisely this circumstance that most disturbs those who contend that he was murdered. But in fact, such a conclusion does not at all follow from suicide.

Politically motivated suicides were a widespread phenomenon in the party. The wave of suicides among those hostile to the introduction of the NEP, for example, readily comes to mind. One of Trotsky's leading supporters, the diplomat Adolf A. Ioffe (1883–1927), consciously chose suicide in 1927 during an inner-party struggle. The increase of political terror in the 1930s was also accompanied by a rise in suicides. While condemned, suicide was typically viewed for a long time as proof of the victim's innocence, and a protest against injustice. This complicated implementation of the politics of terror, and by order from above another evaluation of suicide began to take hold: shooting oneself meant that one was guilty and had gotten entangled in criminal activities.

Not long before Ordzhonikidze's death, two well-broadcast suicides took place in Moscow. On August 22, 1936, following court testimony against Kamenev and Zinoviev concerning connections of the former "right" with the Trotskyist-Zinovievite Center, Mikhail P. Tomskii shot himself. This suicide was a protest, an attempt at the cost of his own life to prove his innocence. In a final letter to Stalin, Tomskii wrote: "I appeal to you not only as party leader, but also as an old comrade-in-arms, to respect my last request: Don't believe Zinoviev's impudent slander. I never joined any bloc, and did not take part in any conversations against the party."[19] This suicide did not enter into Stalin's calculations, and in order to prevent its undesirable effect and stop the rumors, the party leadership quickly offered an official account. On August 23, *Pravda* already published the following report: "The Central Committee reports that candidate member of the Central Committee, M.P. Tomskii, involved with the counterrevolutionary Trotskyist-Zinovievite terrorists, committed suicide at his dacha in Bolshevo on August 22."

But it was another similar event—the death of a well-known member of the Moscow City Party Committee, V.Ia. Furer—which shows that suicide continued "to disturb minds," and cast a shadow on the new turn in the "general line," generating sympathy for its victims even from hard-line Stalinists. Furer shot himself after the arrest of the deputy commissar of communications in the USSR, Livshits, whom he had befriended. This suicide was also an appeal, an attempt to convince the party leadership of the destructiveness of the adopted course. In a long letter to Stalin, Furer sought to demonstrate that the arrest of Livshits and other Communists was a mistake. The letter was full of praise for Stalin and other Politburo members. Stalin was not in Moscow and Furer's last letter fell into Khrushchev's hands, who brought it to Kaganovich. "Kaganovich read it aloud in my presence," Khrushchev recalled, "and he cried, simply sobbed, while reading. He finished and couldn't calm down for a long time." By Kaganovich's order, Khrushchev circulated a copy of the letter to Politburo members. Furer received an official funeral, in which the Moscow City Party Committee participated, asserting his innocence and praising him for his service. When Stalin returned in the fall, however, he gave the case a different interpretation. He summoned Khrushchev and told him: "Furer shot himself, that worthless man. . . . He took the liberty of characterizing Politburo members, and wrote all sorts of complimentary words about them. But he was really trying to disguise himself. He's a Trotskyist who shares Livshits's ideas. I summoned you in order to tell you this. He's a dishonest person, and there isn't any need to feel sorry for him."[20]

The fact that these suicides seriously alarmed Stalin is made clear by his speeches at the Central Committee plenum in December 1936. Ordzhonikidze and other Central Committee members listened to Stalin's reasoning on the meaning of the suicides. The deaths of Tomskii, Lominadze, and Furer, said Stalin, are attempts by enemies to evade responsibility and inflict a blow on the party. "Tomskii's suicide," Molotov stated at this plenum while developing Stalin's thought, "is a premeditated conspiracy, in which Tomskii arranged with not one, but several people to commit suicide and once again strike a blow at the Central Committee."[21]

After the December plenum, these assessments, despite their being classified, circulated within the party. Andrei A. Andreev, for example, who went to Rostov-on-Don to fire leaders of the party organization at the beginning of January 1937, repeated Stalin's interpretation of Furer's suicide at the plenum of the Azov–Black Sea party committee: "Furer, a member of the Moscow committee," he said, "shot himself and left a long letter of almost fifteen pages. This letter reads as if it's a cry from the soul of an innocent man. How did things actually turn out? It turned out that he was a member of the Ukrainian Center of terrorists. . . . See what these suicides cost. From now on we'll view them only as confirmation that an enemy shot himself."[22]

The party leadership's negative reaction to political suicides demonstrates that this problem seriously upset, if not frightened, the organizers of the Great Terror. But the public viewed suicide as a protest against arbitrariness and saw it as evidence of government injustice. Back then, suicide remained the only means for an individual citizen to fight against an all-powerful state. For just that reason, the wave of suicides did not taper off.[23]

Undoubtedly, Ordzhonikidze's suicide was also a protest. Having failed to change Stalin's mind, Ordzhonikidze decided on this desperate step, on the one hand, to escape new humiliations, not wishing to participate in organizing more repressions. On the other hand, in demonstrating his innocence, he may even have sought revenge against Stalin. Incidentally, this is how Ordzhonikidze's suicide was understood by those who were sworn to secrecy about the cause of his death:

> He found an easy way. He thought about himself. Some leader! You merely put Stalin in a very difficult position. And he was such

a devoted Stalinist who defended Stalin in everything. He had served time at hard labor, which also elevated his authority. . . . But this last step of his showed that he wavered. Against Stalin, of course. And against the party line, yes, against the line. It was a very bad step. It's impossible to interpret this otherwise.

This was Molotov's evaluation many years after Ordzhonikidze's suicide.[24] So thought Stalin as well. This became clear several days after Ordzhonikidze's death.

Chapter 14

After the Funeral

(Ordzhonikidze and Molotov)

Ordzhonikidze was given a funeral with "full state honors," just like those of top party and state leaders for many years. The coffin was placed on display in the Hall of Columns at the House of Unions, through which hundreds of thousands of people passed. With Stalin himself in the lead, Politburo members solemnly carried out the urn containing the ashes to Red Square. The memorial service took place at Lenin's mausoleum, after which the urn was set in the Kremlin wall.

Over the next several days, all the newspapers printed obituaries, condolences, touching reminiscences, and numerous photos of grieving comrades-in-arms—Stalin and Politburo members at Ordzhonikidze's apartment, in an honor guard by the bier, and at the mausoleum. The leaders' facial expressions captured in these photos reveal their reactions—sad but determined—befitting the events and their own status.

Many people attended the lengthy funeral service on Red Square, despite a bitter frost—the newspaper photographs show people bundled up, with upturned collars, while Stalin, as usual in such situations, lowered the "ears" of his fur cap. Government officials spoke, as well as workers and representatives of labor collectives. Molotov began the funeral proceedings. "Comrades," he intoned with "deep emotion," as the *Pravda* correspondent reported,

> we have lost one of the best leaders of the Bolshevik party and the
> Soviet state, one of the most ardent and fearless fighters for the Com-

munist cause, one of the brightest, most beloved, and sincerest comrades, Sergo Ordzhonikidze. . . . Under his leadership, our heavy industry turned into one of the world's mightiest and became the Bolsheviks' base for the technical reconstruction of the entire national economy. Under his leadership, not only the First, but the Second Five-Year Plan in heavy industry was triumphantly fulfilled in four years.

Several days later, however, at the Central Committee plenum, which the Politburo postponed from February 20 to February 23 at 6:00 P.M. because of Ordzhonikidze's death, the party leadership revealed its true attitude toward the dead commissar.[1]

Instead of Ordzhonikidze, Molotov reported at the plenum on sabotage in heavy industry. Quoting in detail from the confessions of arrested "wreckers," he assailed colleagues in the People's Commissariat of Heavy Industry with numerous charges of "self-complacency," "self-satisfaction," "political blindness," and defending "dangerous people." As already mentioned, Molotov sharply attacked the report of the commissariat commission, which on Ordzhonikidze's order had verified information concerning sabotage at Ural Coach Construction, in the Donbass, and at Kemerovo. Molotov promised to check on the commissions themselves, and condemned Birman's letter to Ordzhonikidze as the manifestation of a knee-jerk defense of his department. The irritable tone of Molotov's report and his harsh wording suggest the seriousness of his conflict with Ordzhonikidze. Attacks on Ordzhonikidze's department were published as well—Molotov's report, partially abridged and reworked, was one of the few materials from the plenum to appear in the press. The published text was sufficiently transparent to reveal the essence of the managers' position, and the reasons for their political failure: "Our managers didn't help to expose wrecking, and sometimes even hindered our efforts";[2] "now one often encounters claims that talk of sabotage is vastly exaggerated, and that if wrecking has been so widespread, then we would not have had the accomplishments of which we are so proud. They say the success of our industry demonstrates that [charges of] sabotage were inflated by someone," and so on.[3]

Molotov's harsh speech against the NKTP at the February–March plenum provided the basis for several studies that focus on the conflicts between Molotov and Ordzhonikidze, portraying them as representing two opposing political lines. J. Arch Getty has presented and developed this view most fully. One of the sections of his well-known book is entitled "Ordzhonikidze and Molotov, Radicals and Moderates." In Getty's opinion, Ordzhonikidze and Molotov headed two conflicting factions in the party leadership—the supporters of radical politics, and the "moderates," who supported, in particular, more balanced rates of industrialization. Maneuvering between these two camps, Stalin supported the radicals during the First Five-Year Plan, took the side of the moderates at the beginning of the second, and inclined even more toward radicalism in the middle of the 1930s. The rout of the economic cadres, Piatakov's arrest, and the circumstances that drove Ordzhonikidze to suicide, in Getty's opinion, were the result of the efforts of Molotov, who had allied himself with Ezhov. In the final analysis, they reflected the victory of the radical policy of high growth rates.[4]

Publications with similar hypotheses, however debatable they might be, undoubtedly have stimulated study of state power in the USSR, and have compelled scholars to seek new arguments to confirm traditional concepts and widen the parameters of discussion. But there are reasons to reexamine the relationship and conflicts between Molotov and Ordzhonikidze. Like Beria, Molotov took part in the tragic turn of events in Ordzhonikidze's fate; the degree of his participation is of prime importance for the topic under review.

As leader of a commissariat, Ordzhonikidze was subordinate to Molotov, who held the post of Sovnarkom chairman. Like the other commissariat leaders, Ordzhonikidze had to deal with Molotov through the appropriate channels on a variety of vital matters requiring resolution by Sovnarkom. Molotov's job was to unite numerous and often contradictory interests of the various departments, settle conflicts between them, and guard "common state interests." This happened especially often when ratifying production plans and distributing material and financial resources. Departmental chiefs literally bombarded Sovnarkom with requests concerning allocation of supplementary means and funding, itemized lists of the most important new construction sites, and amendments for lowering target plans. Molotov and his deputies, as a rule, were uncompromising, and in most cases refused the supplicants.

Molotov's colorful notes to the Commissar of Agriculture (USSR),

Iakov A. Iakovlev, are instructive in showing Molotov's style of relating to his commissars, and open a window on the Sovnarkom chairman in general. On December 26, 1932, Iakovlev appealed to Molotov to reexamine a resolution just adopted concerning the sharp reduction in financing his commissariat's scientific-research institutes. He received the following reply:

> I'm surprised at your manner of dealing with Sovnarkom. Despite the fact that you're aware of Sovnarkom's final decisions, reached only yesterday, December 25 (granted, you were absent, since your "being busy" prevented you from staying until the end of the conference), you have the guts to write a letter like this to Sovnarkom.
>
> Since I can't take such attitudes seriously, I'm returning this paper to you for *you* to decide what to do with it.[5]

Since Ordzhonikidze was a Politburo member, Molotov could not have reprimanded him in such a fashion. Arguments and clashes, however, between leaders of the NKTP and Sovnarkom, including those between Molotov and Ordzhonikidze, occurred quite frequently. The most serious of the well-known conflicts, examined by the Politburo, took place at the end of 1931. On December 23, the Politburo considered reorganizing the economic commissariats, in particular the Supreme Council of the National Economy. The adopted resolution (stamped "special file") reads:

> (a) Adopt the draft resolution proposed by Comrade Stalin on restructuring the work of the economic commissariats and transmit for final editing to the commission comprised of Comrades Stalin, Molotov, Ordzhonikidze, and Kaganovich.
>
> Convocation of the commission by Comrade Stalin.
>
> (b) Reject Comrade Ordzhonikidze's proposed resignation.
>
> (c) Schedule a special meeting of the Politburo to review Comrade Ordzhonikidze's statement concerning his relationship with Comrade Molotov.

Since the materials related to the Politburo protocols remain closed, it is difficult to say exactly why the conflict between Molotov and Ordzhonikidze occurred. On the basis of other documents, however, it is possible to make several suppositions about it.

The reorganization of industrial administration, examined at a Politburo meeting on December 23, envisaged the liquidation of VSNKh and its replacement by several commissariats: heavy, light, and timber industries. Such a decision was eventually adopted.[6] Ordzhonikidze, as already mentioned, headed the Commissariat of Heavy Industry, but initially opposed reorganizing VSNKh. The following note, written by Ordzhonikidze, is preserved in Valerian V. Kuibyshev's personal papers at RTsKhIDNI: "I heard about these conversations, but personally think they are wrong. The separate branches of industry are so tightly interconnected that their immediate inclusion into STO [Council of Labor and Defense—Ed.] would greatly hamper and complicate the situation. I'm categorically against it." Kuibyshev added a postscript on the first page: "Sergo's note from October 1 [apparently 1931—O.Kh.] regarding the liquidation of VSNKh."[7] Most likely, this was the cause of the conflict between Ordzhonikidze and Molotov, as well as Ordzhonikidze's proposal to resign. Whether the Politburo further discussed the relationship between Ordzhonikidze and Molotov is unknown.

Especially serious conflicts arose between the economic departments, on the one hand, and on the other, the Sovnarkom leadership, Gosplan, and the Commissariat of Finance, which distributed the resources, during preparation of the national economic plan (by quarter, year, or five-year period). Here we see one constant tendency: the commissars sought maximum capital investment and lower production targets. Gosplan and the Commissariat of Finance, while supporting the Sovnarkom leadership, tried to cut capital investment and demanded greater return from current funding levels. This happened yet again as the Second Five-Year Plan was being approved.

In carrying out the decision of the January 1933 Central Committee plenum to sharply lower the pace of economic growth in the Second Five-Year Plan, Gosplan prepared a draft five-year plan in the summer of 1933 that calculated an average annual increase in industrial production of 14 percent and 97 million rubles of capital investment for the five-year plan. As usual, the departments began to protest and demanded an increase in capital investment of up to 135 million rubles. Gosplan yielded and agreed to raise the level of capital investment to almost 113 million rubles. During the discussion of the draft five-year plan in the Politburo at the end of 1933, however, important changes

Ordzhonikidze addressing a Communist Party gathering in 1935.

were made in the document. To all appearances, the party leadership decided to accelerate the rate of industrial production and raise the level of capital investment along the lines of Stalin's proposal for a significant increase in the production of Group "B" industries.[8] As a result, a draft five-year plan was submitted to the Seventeenth Party Congress that envisaged an average annual growth of 18.9 percent in industrial production and the volume of capital work at 133.4 billion rubles for five years.

On February 3, 1934, congress delegates listened to reports by Molotov and Kuibyshev on the tasks of the Second Five-Year Plan, based on these figures. But already on the following day, Ordzhonikidze reported to the congress that in agreement with other Politburo members, he proposed a reduction in the annual growth of industrial production from 18.9 percent, as originally planned, to 16.5 percent. At the same time, it is worth noting that Ordzhonikidze emphasized that plans for capital investment during the five-year plan remained unchanged.[9]

This episode has attracted the attention of specialists for a long time, and allows them to advance various hypotheses. J. Arch Getty, for example, sees this as proof of the existence of a conflict between Molotov and Ordzhonikidze, heads of the radicals and moderates, respectively.[10] At first glance, this incident at the congress actually suggests such a conclusion. It is apparent that Ordzhonikidze publicized his proposals for lowering rates, while it follows from Molotov's concluding remarks that he was not very happy with this decision and instead proposed that the goals of the five-year plan be over-fulfilled.[11] So far, no documents have surfaced that allow us to elucidate why "Ordzhonikidze's amendment" appeared. But available evidence does not support the contention that the decision to decrease the pace was the result of a struggle between two political groups, a political confrontation between Molotov and Ordzhonikidze.

Drawing on the facts presented above concerning the drafting of the five-year plan, the incident that took place at the congress can be viewed only as the continuation of the interdepartmental struggle over the balance of production rates and capital investment. Broken by the dramatic increase of rates before the congress, the compromise between Gosplan and the economic commissars was reestablished. The commissariats received higher limits on capital investment, for which they had always fought, and lower targets for manufactured products. In other words, the departments could produce less while receiving the very same amount of money. It is difficult to say what played a greater role in undermining the intended shift to a more moderate economic policy: attempts to raise economic growth rates during higher levels of capital investment, which Sovnarkom and Gosplan advocated, or the approach of the departments that had triumphed—lowering growth rates while maintaining enormous capital investment. In any event, these competing viewpoints could not be attributed simply to either a moderate or a radical policy, let alone be given political significance.

Thus, documents available today corroborate only the existence of departmental conflicts between Ordzhonikidze and Molotov. Such clashes, which in one way or another were a feature of any state apparatus, occurred between Molotov and other commissariat leaders. They inevitably cropped up all the time and were a normal feature of economic administration. Speaking about his relations with Molotov, Kaganovich recalled many decades later:

When we worked in the Central Committee, we cooperated; but when he became Sovnarkom chairman, and I the minister of communications, we argued over business. I demanded more rails and more capital investment. Mezhlauk, the Gosplan chairman, didn't provide them, and Molotov supported him. Therefore, I quarreled with Molotov and Mezhlauk over this, and complained to Stalin. . . .

Ordzhonikidze had the same concerns as I—they say that he also argued and fought with Molotov. But Sergo quarreled with him as well on the basis of capital investment and attitude toward industry. He argued. We complained to Stalin. Molotov was offended that we complained about Sovnarkom. But we considered the Politburo the highest authority.[12]

Molotov, always faithful to Stalin, undoubtedly supported the mass repressions, including those in the NKTP. Facts that allow one to call Molotov the initiator of the rout of Ordzhonikidze's department, however, are hard to come by. The only such evidence to come to light concerning the conflict between the NKTP and the Sovnarkom leadership regarding the arraignment of a group of employees of the People's Commissariat of Heavy Industry actually shows that Molotov could help Ordzhonikidze.

The conflict under consideration that flared up at the end of November–December 1936—following the Kemerovo trial, which sparked repressions against managers after the arrests of Piatakov and Papulia Ordzhonikidze—clearly marked a confrontation between Ordzhonikidze and Stalin. In September–October 1936, the Soviet Control Commission proposed an examination, conducted jointly with the NKVD, of the activities of the Dzerzhinskii Construction trust, which revealed numerous financial violations—a rise in construction costs, salary fund overdrafts, and so on. Sovnarkom recommended that the NKTP adopt measures against the trust leader. On November 11, Ordzhonikidze's deputy, Rukhimovich, issued a corresponding order. Apparently taking into consideration that the violations with which the trust chief was charged were quite common, Rukhimovich limited himself to relatively mild sanctions: the trust head was given a severe reprimand with a warning, the main accountant of the trust was fired, and several other employees were fined. The leaders of the Soviet Control Commission, however, felt that this action was insufficient, all the more so because it was not published and circulated to other construction organizations, and complained to Sovnarkom. On November 25, on Molotov's instructions, Sovnarkom resolved that the NKTP prosecute the trust chief, Poznanskii, the main engineer, Raizer, and the head accountant, Gorbatsevich. Despite the fact that he was already under attack, Ordzhonikidze appealed to Molotov to repeal this decision. On November 27, he sent Molotov a new draft order from the NKTP with the following accompanying note: "I'm sending the draft of an order concerning Dzerzhinskii Construction, about which I spoke to you by telephone. I ask you to stop at this and refrain from prosecuting Comrades Poznanskii, Raizer, and others."[13]

While Ordzhonikidze's new order dismissed the one signed by Rukhimovich "as an insufficient" command, it differed from Rukhimovich's only in its stronger wording, and not in its essence. "Considering that Comrades Poznanskii and Raizer deserve the strictest condemnation and prosecution for similar behavior, but taking into account their previous work on the construction of Magnitogorsk Construction and the Dzerzhinskii Factory," the harshest reprimand that Ordzhonikidze proposed came "with a warning to Comrades Poznanskii and Raizer that in the event of the slightest repetition of such behavior, they'll be removed from their positions and prosecuted." Previous forms of punishment awaited other trust employees.

In spite of this, Molotov yielded to Ordzhonikidze. He made a minor correction to the draft order, and attached instructions: "To publish (with amendments)."[14] The order was published in such form on December 3 in the newspaper *For Industrialization.*

Molotov's highly critical address at the February–March plenum once again followed Stalin's lead. Setting the tone of the plenum, Stalin made several speeches and repeatedly heckled others from his chair. Molotov's accusations against the managers practically repeated Stalin's remarks at the plenum (there was undoubtedly agreement before the plenum). But only Stalin, and not Molotov, rained brutal and basically unexpected criticism on Ordzhonikidze himself.

"And take Comrade Ordzhonikidze," Stalin stated abruptly in his concluding remarks on March 5. "He was one of the first and best Politburo members among us, a top-notch economic leader, I would say. But he also suffered from becoming attached to others, from declaring people to be personally devoted to him and fussing over them, in spite of warnings from the party and the Central Committee." After making such a significant remark, Stalin, as already mentioned, told participants at the plenum about Ordzhonikidze's role in the Lominadze Affair and the dead commissar's defense of other arrested "enemies," illustrating with these examples the fallaciousness of spine-lessness and liberalism.

In preparing his speeches for publication, Stalin deleted all passages concerning Ordzhonikidze. Departing Central Committee members, however, did not receive any instructions regarding Stalin's speech and they informed party organizations in detail about everything that happened at the plenum, not sparing criticism for the dead commissar of heavy industry: "And then Comrade Stalin dwelled on one mistake of Comrade Sergo Ordzhonikidze," stated, for example, the first secretary of the Gorkii Regional Party Committee, E.K. Pramnek, at the plenum,

> Comrade Stalin criticized Comrade Sergo several times. Stalin often emphasized that Sergo was the best Politburo member and that he liked him as much as anyone. . . . Despite this, Comrade Stalin told the plenum about one of Comrade Sergo's mistakes, citing Comrade Sergo's relations with Lominadze. In 1926–27, Comrade Sergo knew about Lominadze's serious political mistakes, yet at that time still carried out a lengthy correspondence with him. Lominadze wrote Comrade Sergo letters of an anti-party nature, but because of his kindness, as Comrade Stalin said, Comrade Sergo didn't report them to us, and we didn't know about them. If we had known, we wouldn't have promoted Lominadze so readily. If we had known about Lominadze's waverings, we would have treated him differently and possibly could have warned him and set him straight. I told Sergo, "See, you made too much of a fuss over Lominadze and wouldn't do him in. If you don't correct small mistakes, you'll invite bigger ones— which can ruin you." Sergo, said Comrade Stalin, had an aristocratic attitude toward people. Sergo, who trained thousands of managers, had related improperly to many of them.[15]

Emphasizing the clashes he had had with Ordzhonikidze over Lominadze, Stalin averted potential rumors about the conflicts in 1936–37 that led to the tragic outcome. The impression was created that in the last years of his life, Ordzhonikidze in general supported Stalin's undertakings. It was conveyed at the plenum that Ordzhonikidze actively participated in the struggle with "wrecking." In the following days, these very ideas were repeated in the press.

As subsequent events revealed, however, Stalin's real attitude toward Ordzhonikidze was much worse than could have been surmised after hearing the relatively moderate criticism at the February–March plenum. Even before the plenum ended, a wave of repressions crashed down on the employees of the Commissariat of Heavy Industry. In a short time, almost all of Ordzhonikidze's comrades-in-arms, assistants, and managers whom the commissar had supported were destroyed. Papulia Ordzhonikidze was shot in November 1937; his wife was then arrested, and Ordzhonikidze's younger brother Konstantin wound up in the labor camps before the war.

In spite of the fact that Ordzhonikidze was dead, the NKVD understood Stalin's attitude toward him and continued to beat testimony out of people that compromised the dead man. On September 9, 1937, the arrested I.D. Orakhelashvili was forced to sign a statement with these words:

> I'm personally very much obliged to Sergo Ordzhonikidze, but my feeling of gratitude and devotion to him won't prevent me from throwing light on his actual role in events associated with the rise of factions and counterrevolutionary organizations hostile to the party and Soviet power. . . . In general, I must say that in the living room of Sergo Ordzhonikidze's apartment and on days off at his dacha (in Volynsk, and then in Sosnovka), our counterrevolutionary organizations met frequently and conducted the most candid counterrevolutionary discussions while awaiting Sergo Ordzhonikidze. They didn't abate in any way even after Ordzhonikidze showed up.[16]

For Stalin, Ordzhonikidze always remained if not an enemy then a troublesome annoyance. Stalin, of course, did not intend to speak about this openly—only the absolutely dedicated could know that one of the most respected politicians in the country had spoken out against the leader. But from time to time, Stalin's true attitude toward the dead man manifested itself. In his memoirs, Khrushchev wrote about a typical episode:

> One day (I think this was already after the war), I arrived from Ukraine. We were at Stalin's place, just shooting the breeze and kill-

ing time. I said: "Sergo—now there was a man! He died prematurely, while still young. What a pity to lose him." Beria then made an unfriendly retort about Sergo, and nobody said anything else. I felt that I'd said something amiss in this company. Dinner ended, and we left. Then Malenkov said to me, "Listen, why'd you talk so carelessly about Sergo?" "What do you mean, carelessly? Sergo was a respected political figure." "But after all, he shot himself. Don't you know about this?" I said, "No. I buried him, and back then they told us that Sergo (who apparently had kidney illness) died suddenly on his day off." "No, he shot himself. Didn't you notice how awkward it was after you said his name?" I said that I had noticed and was surprised.[17]

After the war, according to S.Z. Ginzburg, Stalin personally expunged Ordzhonikidze's name from a list of Soviet officials to whom monuments were to be raised in Moscow.

Conclusion

The facts presented in this book allow us to argue with confidence that serious conflicts existed between Stalin and Ordzhonikidze. Stalin had prepared the so-called Great Terror with singleminded determination. Although Ordzhonikidze never spoke out against the purges as such and took a hand in organizing many acts of state terror, he considered some of the repressions excessive and actively tried to defend his friends and comrades. Overall, Ordzhonikidze's position can be called one of "soft Stalinism," oriented toward the Stalinist general line, but rejecting extremes of terror, mainly in relation to "his own people." Was such a political line viable?

Many think not. Stalinists, after all, are those who believed that the policy of mass purges was the only option, owing to the growing threat of war and the existence of a potential "fifth column." Some anti-Stalinists view the mass repressions as an essential element of the system, as its very trademark, and believe that the only way to avoid them would have been to destroy the system itself. But another line of reasoning also exists: real Stalinism was "excessively" terroristic, and gave rise to extremes, superfluous even from the point of view of its own laws and strategies. An "underlying network of fear" fortified by terror was a fundamental and necessary feature of Stalinism. They went so far, however, that they often weakened despotic power. It follows from this that differences of opinion even within the framework of the strategy worked out by the Stalinist leadership at the end of the 1920s included less terroristic alternatives and more realistic policies.[1] In some ways, what took place immediately after Stalin's death supports this point of view: His successors, without encroaching upon the foundations of the system, quickly repudiated many of the extremes of state terror.

But this does not mean that the nation's development in the 1930s could have unfolded differently. The spectrum of possible options was limited by the existence of a rigid political regime, by the need to implement an industrialization long overdue, and by the social and cultural realities of a relatively backward country. Nevertheless, the so-called command-administrative policy clearly is not the same as Stalinism. Even in the 1930s, preconditions existed in society for the successful implementation of a more moderate, less arbitrary, and less terroristic command-administrative system. It is sufficient to note that the greatest successes of the 1930s were registered during periods of a relatively moderate and balanced economic policy and somewhat restrained repression.

But whenever we speak of historical alternatives, the question inevitably arises of whether there were forces, including those at the highest levels of power, capable of implementing them. The facts presented in this book, it would seem, allow one to maintain that Ordzhonikidze would have supported a "softer" strategy.

One of the bases for the relative "softening" of the general line might have been strengthening various party and state structures as well as the authority of their leaders. Only in this case might a weak but nevertheless real counterforce to the authoritarian power of the leader have emerged. As little Stalins in their own turfs, each of these leaders to some extent adhered to the general rules of the game and was prepared to compromise and submit to the ultimate arbiter—Stalin. But even Stalin, who saw himself as boss, had to reckon with the existence of "petty fiefdoms." This, despite the well-known costs and conflicts, might have held together a more balanced and less arbitrary system. The formation of such a balance of forces, destroyed after the defeat of the opposition at the end of the 1920s, took place gradually in the first half of the 1930s.

The Commissariat of Heavy Industry played no small role in this process. In the 1930s, it was transformed into one of the most powerful and influential agencies, capable of declaring and fighting for its interests. The claim commissariat employees made for a degree of indepen-

Ordzhonikidze in Stalin's shadow, 1935.

dence was one of the most important among these interests, as was their desire to protect themselves from the interference of party and state controllers and the punitive organs. Ordzhonikidze fully shared these intentions. Running his commissariat with a firm hand, he preferred to determine the fate of his subordinates himself. The NKTP leader's position, characteristic of that of leaders of other departments as well, in some sense stabilized the political situation and restrained the organization of mass repressions.

Stalin's attempts to upset the complex political balance that had taken shape and his designs to take away the remaining independence from his old colleagues aroused Ordzhonikidze's resistance. Unlike other Politburo members (who also merit special investigation), he took action. Ordzhonikidze's personal qualities and the fact that he could rely on the support of a sufficiently cohesive economic nomenklatura in operation for some time also played their role. To a certain extent, Ordzhonikidze expressed the interests of party members who had good reason to fear a new round of terror. In the provinces, economic and party leaders often presented a united front.

At the same time, it is unlikely that Ordzhonikidze was ready to get involved in a serious struggle with Stalin. He was too much a Stalinist and too dependent as a political figure. Compared to the poorly educated Ordzhonikidze (and also Kaganovich, Voroshilov, and others), Stalin appeared as a great theoretician and a prominent politician. Ordzhonikidze himself must have understood this. It is not surprising, therefore, that the available facts suggest that Ordzhonikidze only tried to make Stalin change his mind, although he did so insistently, and, it can be said, fearlessly.

After his death, Stalin's comrades-in-arms, many of whom, like Ordzhonikidze, were "soft Stalinists," partially dismantled the system and rejected the extremes of state terrorism. They opted for a variant that had germinated back in the 1930s and was in some measure connected with Ordzhonikidze.

Notes

Introduction

1. *Istochnik* (1993/0), 9–22.
2. See, for example, the repentant letter from Bukharin to Stalin before the former's death, extracted from the Kremlin Archive. Ibid., 23–25.
3. R.A. Medvedev, *Let History Judge: The Origins and Consequences of Stalinism* (New York, 1989); R. Conquest, *The Great Terror: A Reassessment* (New York, 1990); and R. Tucker, *Stalin in Power: The Revolution from Above, 1928–1941* (New York–London, 1992).
4. J.A. Getty, "The Politics of Repression Revisited," *Stalinist Terror: New Perspectives*, ed. J. Arch Getty and Roberta Manning (Cambridge, 1993), 55–56.

Chapter 1

1. V.S. Kirillov, A.Ia. Sverdlov, *Grigorii Konstantinovich Ordzhonikidze (Sergo): Biografiia* (Moscow, 1986), 24.
2. Ibid., 130–31.
3. Quoted in *O Sergo Ordzhonikidze: Vospominaniia, ocherki, stat'i sovremmenikov* (Moscow, 1981), 109–10.
4. V.V. Zhuravlev, A.P. Nenarokov, "V.I. Lenin: 'Vmeste i naravne' . . . ," *Urok daet istoriia* (Moscow, 1989), 112–34.
5. V.I. Lenin, *Polnoe sobranie sochinenii*, 5th ed. (Moscow, 1964), vol. 45: 358.
6. Ibid., vol. 54: 329.
7. Ibid., 330.
8. L.D. Trotskii, *Stalin*, vol. 2 (New York, 1985), 196–97.
9. *Izvestiia TsK KPSS*, no. 4 (1991), 198.

10. RTsKhIDNI, f. 17, op. 3, d. 246, vyp. IV, ll. 57–58.
11. Ibid., l. 90.

Chapter 2

1. RTsKhIDNI, f. 17, op. 2, d. 246, vyp. IV, l. 28.
2. Similarly, see V. Nadtocheev, " 'Triumvirat'ili 'semerka'?" *Trudnye voprosy istorii* (Moscow, 1991), 68–70.
3. RTsKhIDNI, f. 558, op. 1, d. 3259.
4. Ibid., f. 85, op. 26, d. 5.
5. *Izvestiia TsK KPSS*, no. 7 (1991), 130–31.
6. V.S. Kirillov, A.Ia. Sverdlov. *G.K. Ordzhonikidze (Sergo): Biografiia,* 199. (RTsKhIDNI, f. 17, op. 3, d. 586, ll. 4, 5.)
7. *Izvestiia TsK KPSS*, no. 7 (1991), 132–33.
8. RTsKhIDNI, f. 17, op. 2, d. 257, l. 10; *XV konferentsiia Vsesoiuznoi Kommunisticheskoi partii (b): Stenograficheskii otchet* (Moscow and Leningrad, 1927), 765–66.
9. RTsKhIDNI, f. 85, op. 1/c, d. 52, ll. 1–2.
10. M.V. Rosliakov, *Ubiistvo Kirova: Politicheskie i ugolovnye prestupleniia v 1930-x godakh* (Leningrad, 1991), 108.
11. RTsKhIDNI, f.17, op. 3, d. 768, l. 5.
12. Rosliakov, *Ubiistvo Kirova,* 109-10.
13. RTsKhIDNI, f. 17, op. 3a, d. 86, ll. 7–11.

Chapter 3

1. RTsKhIDNI, f. 85, op. 1/c, d. 59, l. 28.
2. S. Cohen, *Bukharin: Politicheskaia biografiia, 1888–1938* (Moscow, 1988), 515.
3. RTsKhIDNI, f. 558, op. 1, d. 2891, l. 12.
4. Ibid., f. 17, op. 3, d. 750, ll. 2, 5; d. 752, l. 3; d. 753, l. 4.
5. Ibid., f. 85, op. 1/c, d. 115, ll. 6-10.
6. Ibid., ll. 1–5.
7. *Kommunist,* no. 13 (1991), 56-57. (RTsKhIDNI, f. 17, op. 2, d. 607, ll. 267–69.)
8. See I.P. Ikonnikova, A.P. Ugrovatov, "Stalinskaia repetitsiia—nastupleniia na krest'ianstvo," *Voprosy istorii KPSS,* no. 1 (1991), 68–81.
9. R.W. Davies, "The Syrtsov-Lominadze Affair," *Soviet Studies,* vol. 33 (January 1981); B.A. Starkov, "Pravo-levye fraktsionery," *Oni ne molchali* (Moscow, 1991); S.A. Kislitsyn, *Variant Syrtsova (Iz istorii formirovaniia anti-stalinskogo soprotivleniia v sovetskom obshchestve v 20–30-e gg.)* (Rostov-on-the-Don, 1992).
10. RTsKhIDNI, f. 589, op. 3, d. 9251, ll. 187–202, 310–14.
11. Ibid., ll. 246-59.
12. Ibid., f. 17, op. 2, d. 607, ll. 270–71.

13. S.A. Kislitsyn, "Pravo-'levatskii' blok Syrtsova-Lominadze," *Kentavr*, no. 1 (1993), 119.
14. RTsKhIDNI, f. 17, op. 162, d. 9, l. 57
15. *Pravda*, 2 December, 1930.

Chapter 4

1. For further details, see R.W. Davies, *The Soviet Economy in Turmoil, 1929-1930* (London, 1989).
2. See "Pis'ma Stalina Molotovu," *Kommunist*, no. 11 (1990), 95–106.
3. R.W. Davies, "Some Soviet Economic Controllers—III. Kuibyshev," *Soviet Studies*, vol. 12, no. 1 (July 1960), 32.
4. E.A. Rees, *State Control in Soviet Russia* (London, 1987), 170.
5. R.W. Davies, "Some Soviet Economic Controllers—III. Ordzhonikidze," *Soviet Studies*, vol. XII (1960); A.F. Khavin, *Kratkii ocherk istorii industrializatsii SSSR* (Moscow, 1962) and *U rulia industrii: Dokumental'nye ocherki* (Moscow, 1968); V.S. Lel'chuk, *Industrializatsiia SSSR: Istoriia, opyt, problemy* (Moscow, 1984); Sheila Fitzpatrick, "Ordzhonikidze's Takeover of VESENKHA: A Case Study in Soviet Bureaucratic Politics," *Soviet Studies*, vol. 37, no. 2 (April 1985).
6. RTsKhIDNI. Zapis' besedy s A.S. Tochinskim (newly declassified documents).
7. *Voprosy istorii*, no. 2 (1990), 107.
8. RTsKhIDNI, f. 85, op. 29, d. 442, ll. 1–2.
9. Ibid., d. 445, ll. 1-2. For the causes of still another of Ordzhonikidze's clashes with Molotov's apparatus, see d. 444, ll. 1–4.
10. For several episodes in the struggle of Ordzhonikidze's department to distribute capital investment, see R.W. Davies and D. Khlevniuk, "Vtoraia piatiletka: Mekhanizm smeny ekonomicheskoi politiki," *Otechestrennaia Istoriia*, no. 3 (1994), 95–97.
11. For further details, see R.W. Davies, "Sovetskaia ekonomika v period krizisa, 1930–1933 gody," *Istoriia SSSR*, no. 4 (1991), 202–3.
12. Hiroaki Kuromiya, *Stalin's Industrial Revolution: Politics and Workers, 1928-1932* (Cambridge, 1988), 28–35, 272–76.
13. G.K. Ordzhonikidze, *Stat'i i rechi*, vol. 2 (Moscow, 1957), 268–69, 277–81.
14. Kendall E. Bailes, *Technology and Society Under Lenin and Stalin: Origins of the Technical Intelligentsia, 1917–1941* (Princeton, 1978), 144–51; Fitzpatrick, "Ordzhonikidze's Takeover," 164.
15. RTsKhIDNI, f. 558, op. 1, d. 5243, l. 4.
16. Ibid., l. 1.
17. Ibid., f. 17, op. 3, d. 811, l. 9.
18. Ibid., f. 558, op. 1, d. 2960, ll. 7, 9, 23.
19. Ibid., f. 17, op. 3, d. 816, l. 10, and d. 824, l. 9.
20. Ibid., f. 17, op. 3, d. 826, l. 2.

21. Ibid., d. 828, ll. 32–33.
22. Ibid., f. 85, op. 28, d. 7, l. 8.
23. Ibid., l. 38. This fact from Rumiantsev's speech is inaccurately depicted in the literature. Scholarly convention is wrong to hold that half of all engineers and technicians in the Donbass were arrested by 1931. Arrest and sentencing to hard labor are not analogous.
24. Ibid., f. 85, op. 28, d. 8, ll. 160, 192.
25. Ibid., f. 17, op. 3, d. 835, l. 25.
26. Ibid., f. 17, op. 114, d. 285, ll. 28–35.
27. Ibid., ll. 1–2.
28. *Spravochnik partiinogo rabotnika*, vyp. 8 (Moscow, 1934), 475.
29. RTsKhIDNI, f. 17, op. 114, d. 332, ll. 150–51.
30. Ibid., ll. 4, 20.
31. Ibid., d. 353, l. 37; d. 351, l. 14.
32. GARF, f. 5446, op. 82, d. 26, ll. 34–36.
33. Ibid., l. 37.
34. Ibid., ll. 18–20.
35. Ibid., ll. 21–22.
36. *Pravda*, 23 August, 1933.
37. RTsKhIDNI, f. 17, op. 3, d. 929, l. 21.
38. *Kommunist*, no. 11 (1990), 105.
39. Ibid., 105–6.
40. RTsKhIDINI, f. 17, op. 3, d. 930, l. 13. See also, R.W. Davies, "Rancorous Luminaries," *London Review of Books*, vol. 16, no. 8 (April 20, 1994), 7.
41. *Sovetskaia iustitsiia*, no. 15 (1934), 18.
42. RTsKhIDNI, f. 17, op. 3, d. 935, ll. 24, 26.
43. *Sovetskaia iustitsiia*, no. 23 (1934), 2.
44. RGAE, f. 7297, op. 38, d. 113, ll. 3–4.
45. RTsKhIDNI, newly declassified materials.
46. GARF, f. 5446, op. 22, d. 81, ll. 108-11.
47. Ibid., f. 5446, op. 24/13, d. 3, ll. 269–70.
48. Ibid., l. 262.
49. RTsKhIDNI, f. 17, op. 3, d. 935, l. 29.
50. Ibid., f. 17, op. 114, d. 391, l. 27.

Chapter 5

1. R.A. Medvedev, *O Stalin i stalinizme* (Moscow, 1990), 294–96; A.V. Antonov-Oveseenko, "Stalin i ego vremia," *Voprosy istorii*, no. 4 (1989), 93–94; "Memuary N.S. Khrushcheva," *Voprosy istorii*, no. 9 (1990), 77-78.
2. A.N. Iakovlev, "O dekabr'skoi tragedii 1934 goda," *Pravda*, 28 January, 1991, 1.
3. Krasnikov, St., *Sergei Mironovich Kirov. Zhizn' i deiatel'nost'* (Moscow, 1964), 198.
4. For example, in the memoirs of one of Ordzhonikidze's closest col-

leagues published recently in a scholarly journal, Ginzburg maintains: "On the eve of Kirov's departure for his last trip to Moscow, Ordzhonikidze, as if foreseeing tragedy, detained Kirov for a long time, and entreated him to be careful." See S.Z. Ginzburg, "O gibeli Sergo Ordzhonikidze," *Voprosy istorii KPSS*, no. 3 (1991), 89. This fact clearly shows how doubtful the testimony of contemporaries is who did not witness the events themselves.

5. RTsKhIDNI, f. 85, op. 1, d. 164, l. 32 ob.
6. See the notes of Z.G. Ordzhonikidze on the manuscript of the memoirs of the Tbilisi doctor, I.S. Frangulian, compiled on January 15, 1958 (RTsKhIDNI, newly declassified materials).
7. RGAE, f. 6884, op. 1, d. 130, l. 158.
8. RTsKhIDNI, f. 85, op. 1, d. 164, l. 32 ob.
9. RGAE, f. 6884, op. 1, d. 130, l. 138.
10. *Kommunist*, no. 13 (1991), 55 (RTsKhIDNI, newly declassified documents). For the Politburo decision "On Comrade Ordzhonikidze," see RTsKhIDNI, f. 17, op. 3, d. 955.
11. Ibid.
12. *Izvestiia*, 18 February 1939, 4.
13. Ginzburg, "O gibeli Sergo Ordzhonikidze," 89.
14. Ginzburg, *O proshlom—dlia budushchego* (Moscow, 1984), 192.
15. Ginzburg, "O gibeli Sergo Ordzhonikidze," 89.
16. I. Kramov, "Iz rasskazov Ziskinda," *Kontinent*, no. 2 (1992), 228–29.
17. Ibid.

Chapter 6

1. *Voprosy istorii*, no. 4 (1990), 80.
2. J. Scott, *Za Uralom: Amerikanskii rabochii v russkom gorode stali* (Moscow, Sverdlovsk, 1991), 102.
3. *XVII s"ezd VKP(b). Stenograficheskii otchet* (Moscow, 1934), 118–20.
4. RTsKhIDNI, f. 85, op. 1/c, d. 162, ll. 30–34.
5. Ibid., ll. 22–23.
6. Ibid., l. 28.
7. Ibid., ll. 8–15.
8. Ibid., f. 17, op. 3, d. 947, ll. 2, 41–44; f. 85, op. 1/c, d. 162, ll. 7–7 ob.
9. Ibid., f. 85, op. 29, d. 454.
10. *Izvestiia TsK KPSS*, no. 7 (1989), 65–85; no. 1 (1990), 36–58.
11. RTsKhIDNI, f. 589, op. 3, d. 9251, l. 35.
12. *Kommunist*, no. 13 (1991), 58 (RTsKhIDNI, newly declassified materials).
13. RTsKhIDNI, f. 589, op. 3, d. 9251, l. 333.
14. Ibid., l. 343.

Chapter 7

1. For a detailed review of the literature and a more complete summary of the history of the Stakhanovite movement, see L.H. Siegelbaum,

Stakhanovism and the Politics of Productivity in the USSR, 1935–1941 (Cambridge, 1988).

2. RGAE, f. 7297, op. 38, d. 177, ll. 46–47.

3. RTsKhIDNI, f. 85, op. 29, l. 119, l. 114.

4. Ibid., d. 460, ll. 2–3.

5. *Pravda*, 11 October, 1935.

6. *Pravda*, 13 October, 1935

7. For more details, see Siegelbaum, *Stakhanovism*, 82–84.

8. V.I. Stalin, *Voprosy Leninizma* (Moscow, 1952), 535.

9. *KPSS v rezoliutsiiakh*, vol. 6: 286.

10. RTsKhIDNI, f. 73, op. 1, d. 141, ll. 201–50.

11. A.A. Andreev, *Stakhanovskoe dvizhenie i nashi zadachi* (Moscow, 1935), 28.

12. Stalin, *Voprosy Leninizma*, 542.

13. Francesco Benvenuti, "Stakhanovism and Stalinism, 1934–1938" (Centre for Russian and East European Studies, University of Birmingham [CREES], Discussion Papers, 1989), 42–45.

14. *Sovet pri narodnom komissare tiazheloi promyshlennosti SSSR, 25–29 iiunia 1936 g.: Stenograficheskii otchet* (Moscow, 1936), 37–38.

15. Ibid., 81–82.

16. Ibid., 89.

17. Ibid., 92–93.

18. Ibid., 399.

19. Ibid., 390.

20. Ibid., 390, 395.

21. E.A. Rees, *Stalinism and Soviet Rail Transport, 1928–41* (London, 1995), pp. 147–48.

22. RTsKhIDNI, f. 85, op. 29, d. 722, l. 1.

23. Ibid., f. 17, op. 3, d. 980, l. 79.

24. Ibid., l. 75.

25. Ibid., newly declassified materials.

26. Ibid.

27. V.S. Popov and V.T. Oppokov. "Berievshchina (po materialam sledstviia)," *Beriia: Konets kar'ery* (Moscow, 1991), 378.

28. D. Volkogonov, *Triumf i tragediia: Politicheskii portret I.V. Stalina*, bk. 1, pt. 2, 48; *Istochnik*, no. 2 (1993), 16.

29. *Istochnik*, no. 2 (1993), 16.

Chapter 8

1. Lenin, *Polnoe sobranie sochinenii*, vol. 45: 345.

2. For interesting observations on Piatakov's formative years and the evolution of his views in connection with the development of the Russian Revolution, see A. Graziosi, "G.L. Piatakov (1890–1937): A Mirror of Soviet History," *Harvard Ukrainian Studies*, vol. 16, no. 1/2 (1992), 102–66.

3. "Deiateli SSSR i revoliutsionnogo dvizheniia Rossii," *Entsiklopedicheskii slovar' Granat* (Moscow, 1989), 593.
4. RTsKhIDNI, f. 85, op. 1/c, d. 136, l. 46.
5. Ibid., l. 47.
6. Ibid., l. 48.
7. *Izvestiia TsK KPSS*, no. 9 (1989), 37.
8. RTsKhIDNI, f. 17, op. 120, d. 189, ll. 39–40.
9. Ibid., f. 85, op. 1/c, d. 136, ll. 59–65.
10. J. Arch Getty, "The Politics of Repression Revisited," *Stalinist Terror*, 55 (RTsKhIDNI, f. 17, op. 2, d. 573, l. 33).
11. Ibid., f. 17, op. 3, d. 981, l. 26.
12. *Izvestiia TsK KPSS*, no. 9 (1989), 40.
13. RTsKhIDNI, f. 85, op. 1/c, d. 186.
14. Ibid., l. 16.
15. Ibid., l. 18.
16. Ibid., f. 85, op. 29, d. 150, l. 53.
17. Ibid., f. 17, op. 2, d. 576, l. 61.
18. A.M. Larina (Bukharina), *Nezabyvaemoe* (Moscow, 1989), 327–28.
19. RTsKhIDNI, f. 85, op. 29, d. 422, l. 2.
20. A. Orlov, *Tainaia istoriia stalinskikh prestuplenii* (New York–Jerusalem–Paris, 1983), 179–81.

Chapter 9

1. RTsKhIDNI, f. 17, op. 3, d. 981, l. 7.
2. Ibid., f. 85, op. 29, d. 710, l. 1.
3. For Ordzhonikidze's business correspondence in this period, see RGAE, f. 6884, op. 1, d. 38, 130.
4. *Izvestiia TsK KPSS*, no. 9 (1989), 39.
5. RTsKhIDNI, f. 85, op. 27, d. 93, l. 22.
6. Ibid., ll. 12–13.
7. Ibid., op. 29, d. 435, l. 11.
8. RGAE, f. 6884, op. 1, d. 38, ll. 68–69, 160–160 ob.
9. *Izvestiia TsK KPSS*, no. 2 (1991), 150, 175, 183.
10. Popov and Oppokov, "Berievshchina," 267–81.
11. Amy Knight, *Beria: Stalin's First Lieutenant* (Princeton, 1993), 51.
12. Ibid., 38–40, 51.
13. Popov and Oppokov, "Berievshchina," 368.
14. A. Antonov-Ovseenko, "Put' naverkh," *Beria: Konets kar'ery*, 42.
15. Ordzhonikidze's doctor, Levin, reported to him on his favorable impressions of Noorden in a letter from October 17 (RTsKhIDNI, newly declassified materials).
16. RTsKhIDNI, f. 85, op. 1, d. 144, l. 51.
17. *Kommunist*, no. 13 (1991), 62–63 (RTsKhIDNI, newly declassified materials).

18. RTsKhIDNI, f. 558, op 3, d. 317, l. 21.

19. Ibid., ll. 25–27, 33–36, 38–46, 65, 70, 74, etc.

20. Ibid., 33, 34. (For the meaning of Stalin's typical method of placing leading associates in opposition to the "collective leadership," the Central Committee, see L. Maksimenkov, "Kul't. Zametki o slovakh-simvolakh v sovetskoi politicheskoi kul'ture," *Svobodnaia mysl'*, no. 10 [1993], 27–28.)

21. Ibid., 109.

22. *XVI s"ezd VKP(b): Stenograficheskii otchet,* (Moscow, 1935), vol. 1: 578.

Chapter 10

1. *Pravda,* 23 November, 1936.

2. RTsKhIDNI, newly declassified materials.

3. Ibid.

4. Ibid.

5. See *Sovetskoe gosudarstvo i pravo,* no. 3 (1965), 24.

6. RTsKhIDNI, newly declassified materials.

7. Ibid.

8. Ibid., f. 85, op. 1/c, d. 152, l. 1.

9. Ibid., f. 17, op. 71, d. 43, l. 1.

10. Ibid., ll. 50–58.

11. Ibid., newly declassified materials.

12. *Za industrializatsiiu,* 22 February, 1937, 8.

13. *Pravda,* 8 March, 1937, 2.

14. *1937-i na Urale* (Sverdlovsk, 1990), 185.

15. Ibid., 187.

16. RTsKhIDNI, f. 17, op. 21, d. 3952, l. 58.

17. Ibid., d. 3951, l. 390.

18. RTsKhIDNI, d. 3952, l. 121.

19. *Pravda,* 25 January, 1937, 2.

20. Ibid., 28 January, 1937, 3.

21. Quoted from *1937-i na Urale,* 191.

22. RTsKhIDNI, f. 17, op. 21, d. 3981, l. 40 ob.

23. *Bolshevik,* no. 8 (1937), 31.

24. *Kommunist,* no. 13 (1991), 56.

Chapter 11

1. RTsKhIDNI, f. 17, op. 3, d. 983, l. 51.

2. Ibid., l. 54.

3. Ibid., f. 558, op. 1, d. 3350, l. 1.

4. Ibid., l. 16.

5. Ibid., f. 17, op. 3, d. 983, l. 64.

6. *Kommunist,* no. 13 (1991), 60 (RTsKhIDNI, f. 558, op. 1, d. 3350).

7. RTsKhIDNI, f. 85, op. 29, d. 156, l. 6.

8. Ibid., ll. 9–10.
9. Ibid., l. 12.
10. Ibid., ll. 5–6.
11. Ibid., l. 14.
12. *Za industrializatsiiu*, 21 February, 1937, 8. Galperin's frank reminiscences, written "hot on the heels" of events, must be considered fortunate for the historian. The material managed "to slip" into print during a narrow opening in a period of relative uncertainty from the time of Ordzhonikidze's death to the devastating appraisal of NKTP activities, including those of Galperin himself, at the February–March plenum.
13. *Voprosy istorii*, no. 8 (1993), 18.
14. Ibid.
15. Ginzburg, *O gibeli Sergo Ordzhonikidze*, 91–92.
16. *Kommunist*, no. 13 (1991), 61 (RTsKhIDNI, f. 17, op. 2, d. 591, ll. 53–54).
17. I. Kramov, "Iz rasskazov Ziskinda," *Kontinent*, no. 2 (1992), 229.
18. RTsKhIDNI, f. 85, op. 29, d. 156, ll. 2, 14.
19. *Vospominania, ocherki, stat'i sovremmenikov* (Moscow, 1981), 277. *O Sergo Ordzhonikidze*, 277.
20. N.I. Bukharin, *Problemy teorii i praktiki sotsializma* (Moscow, 1989), 271, 278.
21. *Voprosy istorii KPSS*, no. 1 (1991), 83.
22. *Voprosy istorii KPSS*, no. 11 (1988), 47–48.
23. Ibid., 48–49.
24. For the record of Bukharin's speech at the purge hearing, see ibid., nos. 1 and 3 [sic] (1991).
25. Quoted in D. Shelestov, *Vremia Alekseia Rykova* (Moscow, 1990), 285.
26. For more detail about these events, see *Izvestiia TsK KPSS*, no. 5 (1989), 70–72.
27. *Voprosy istorii KPSS*, no. 11 (1988), 49.
28. *Izvestiia TsK KPSS*, no. 5 (1989), 75.
29. RTsKhIDNI, f. 17, op. 2, d. 576, l. 61.
30. A.M. Larina (Bukharina), *Nezabyvaemoe* (Moscow, 1989), 333.
31. Quoted in Shelestov, *Vremia Alekseia Rykova*, 288.

Chapter 12. The Last Days

1. (Z.G.) Ordzhonikidze, *O Sergo Ordzhonikidze*, 275.
2. RTsKhIDNI, f. 85, op. 1, d. 143, l. 1.
3. *Za industrializatsiiu*, 21 February, 1937, 6.
4. I. Dubinskii-Mukhadze, *Ordzhonikidze* (Moscow, 1963), 6.
5. Francesco Benvenuti, "Industry and Purge in the Donbass, 1936–37," *Europe-Asia Studies*, vol. 45, no. 1 (1993), 61–63.
6. S.Z. Ginzburg, *O proshlom—dlia budushchego* (Moscow, 1984), 195.
7. F. Benvenuti thinks that this letter might have been discovered in

the papers of Ordzhonikidze by the commission created after his death to establish a personal archive of the deceased (such commissions, by the way, were created after the death of all Politburo members). See F. Benvenuti, *Stakhanovism and Stalinism,* 72. It is unlikely, however, that Molotov (and thus Stalin) would have attached such great significance to an ordinary letter from a factory director if Ordzhonikidze himself had not used it as an argument in his quarrels with Stalin.

8. *Bolshevik,* no. 8 (1937), 38–39.
9. RTsKhIDNI, f. 17, op. 3, d. 983, l. 1.
10. *Kontinent,* no. 2 (1992), 229.
11. (Z.G.) Ordzhonikidze, *O Sergo Ordzhonikidze,* 274.
12. *Za industrializatsiiu,* 21 February, 1937, 8.
13. Ibid., 20 February, 1937, 7.
14. RGAE, f. 7297, d. 211, ll. 147–57
15. (Z.G.) Ordzhonikidze, *O Sergo Ordzhonikidze,* 278–79.
16. *Za industrializatsiiu,* 21 February, 1937, 6.
17. Dubinskii-Mukhadze, *Ordzhonikidze,* 6.
18. Roy Medvedev provides similar evidence in his book. See Roy Medvedev, *O Staline i stalinizme* (Moscow, 1990), 357.
19. Ginzburg, *O gibeli Sergo Ordzhonikidze,* 92–93.
20. A. Bek, *Novoe naznachenie* (Moscow, 1988), 35.
21. (Z.G.) Ordzhonikidze, *O Sergo Ordzhonikidze,* 181.
22. Medvedev, *O Staline i stalinizme,* 358.

Chapter 13

1. Quoted in B. Pil'niak, *Rasplesnutoe vremia* (Moscow, 1990), 582.
2. *Sotsialisticheskii vestnik,* no. 5 (1937), 16.
3. L.D. Trotsky, *Stalin,* vol. 2: 252.
4. For Z.G. Ordzhonikidze's note concerning the circumstances of preparing the selected articles and speeches of G.K. Ordzhonikidze for publication, and galley-proofs of the various introductions, see RTsKhIDNI, newly declassified materials.
5. See Dubinskii-Mukhadze, *Ordzhonikidze,* 6; Medvedev, *O Staline i stalinizme,* 356–60.
6. Iu. Semenov, *Nenapisannye romany* (Moscow, 1989), 23, 26.
7. A. Orlov, *Tainaia istoriia stalinskikh prestuplenii* (New York, 1983), 180–81, 187–89.
8. Ginzburg, *O gibeli Sergo Ordzhonikidze,* 96–97.
9. A.N. Rybakov, *Strakh,* bk. 2 (Moscow, 1990), 116.
10. Medvedev, *O Staline i stalinizme,* 357.
11. Ibid., 358.
12. Ginzburg, *O gibeli Ordzhonikidze,* 96.
13. Rybakov, *Strakh,* 113–14.
14. (Z.G.) Ordzhonikidze, *O Sergo Ordzhonikidze,* 68.

15. Ibid., 194.

16. Ibid., 259.

17. *Za industrializatsiiu*, 20 February, 1937, 5.

18. RTsKhIDNI, f. 17, op. 3, d. 978, l. 75.

19. *Izvestiia TsK KPSS*, no. 5 (1989), 71.

20. *Voprosy istorii*, no. 5 (1990), 54.

21. RTsKhIDNI, f. 17, op. 3, d. 575, l. 122.

22. Ibid., f. 17, op. 21, d. 2196, l. 33.

23. For more information, see O. Khlevniuk, *1937-i: Stalin, NKVD i sovetskoe obshchestvo* (Moscow, 1992), 196–206.

24. *Sto sorok besed s Molotovym: Iz dnevnika F. Chueva* (Moscow, 1991), 191–92.

Chapter 14

1. RTsKhIDNI, f. 17, op. 3, d. 984, l. 4.

2. *Bolshevik*, no. 8 (1937), 29.

3. Ibid., 23.

4. J.A. Getty, *Origins of the Great Purges: The Soviet Communist Party Reconsidered, 1933–1938* (Cambridge, 1985), 128–35.

5. GARF, f. 5446, op. 27, d. 4, ll. 135–36.

6. RTsKhIDNI, f. 17, op. 3, d. 867, ll. 11–12.

7. Ibid., f. 79, op. 1, d. 570, ll. 1–2.

8. RGAE, f. 4372, op. 92, d. 17, 18; GARF, f. 5446, op. 22, d. 27, ll. 230–34. For more detail, see O. Khlevniuk and R.W. Davies, "The Role of Gosplan in Economic Decision-Making in the 1930s," Centre for Russian and East European Studies, University of Birmingham [CREES], Discussion Papers, 1993, 33–43.

9. *XVII s"ezd VKP(b): Stenograficheskii otchet* (Moscow, 1934), 435.

10. Getty, *Origins of the Great Purges*, 16–17.

11. *XVII s"ezd VKP(b)*, 523.

12. F. Chuev, *Tak govoril Kaganovich* (Moscow, 1992), 61.

13. GARF, f. 5446, op. 18, d. 90, l. 6.

14. Ibid., l. 7.

15. RTsKhIDNI, f. 17, op. 21, d. 878, ll. 93, 94-ob.

16. *Beriia: konets kar'ery*, 377–78.

17. *Voprosy istorii*, no. 4 (1990), 81.

Conclusion

1. Alec Nove was one of the first to propose and substantiate this point of view. For more detail, see his latest work, the introduction to the anthology, *The Stalin Phenomenon*, ed. Alec Nove (New York, 1993), 24–29.

Index

Oleg V. Khlevniuk, born in 1959 and educated at the Institute of Russian History of the Russian Academy of Sciences, is an editor of the public affairs journal *Svobodnaia mysl'* (Free Thought), which superseded *Kommunist* (Communist), the theoretical journal of the Communist Party. Khlevniuk is well known outside Russia for his book *The Year 1937: Stalin, the NKVD, and Soviet Society,* published in 1992. The author is currently revising this work for publication in The New Russian History Series, incorporating newly declassified documents made available since its first appearance. The present volume is based on his study *Stalin and Ordzhonikidze: Conflicts in the Politburo in the 1930s,* published in Moscow in 1993. Khlevniuk is also co-editor (with Oleg V. Naumov and Lars T. Lih) of the second volume in Yale's Annals of Communism series, *Stalin's Letters to Molotov, 1925–1936* (New Haven, 1995).

Translator **David Nordlander** is a Ph.D. candidate at the University of North Carolina, Chapel Hill, where he is writing a dissertation, "Stalinism in the Soviet Far East: A History of Magadan and the Gulag, 1929–1941." His articles have appeared in the *Russian Review* and *Pacific Historical Review.*

Series editor **Donald J. Raleigh** is professor of history at the University of North Carolina, Chapel Hill. He is the author of *Revolution on the Volga: 1917 in Saratov,* and is now at work on a sequel, "The Experience of Civil War: Politics, Society, and Revolutionary Culture in Saratov, 1918–1922." Professor Raleigh is also editor of *Soviet Historians and Perestroika: The First Phase,* editor and translator of *A Russian Civil War Diary: Alexis V. Babine in Saratov,* and translator and editor of E.N. Burdzhalov's *Russia's Second Revolution: The February 1917 Uprising in Petrograd.*

Editorial assistant **Kathy S. Transchel** is a visiting lecturer at East Carolina University. She is completing her Ph.D. dissertation at the University of North Carolina, Chapel Hill, a study entitled "Under the Influence: Drinking, Temperance, and Cultural Revolution in Russia, 1900–1932."